A Global Monetary Plague

A Global Monetary Plague

Asset Price Inflation and Federal Reserve Quantitative Easing

Brendan Brown

First published 2015 by
PALGRAVE MACMILLAN

Palgrave Macmillan in the UK is an imprint of Macmillan Publishers Limited, registered in England, company number 785998, of Houndmills, Basingstoke, Hampshire RG21 6XS.

Palgrave Macmillan in the US is a division of St Martin's Press LLC, 175 Fifth Avenue, New York, NY 10010.

Palgrave Macmillan is the global academic imprint of the above companies and has companies and representatives throughout the world.

Palgrave® and Macmillan® are registered trademarks in the United States, the United Kingdom, Europe and other countries.

ISBN: 978–1–137–47884–9

This book is printed on paper suitable for recycling and made from fully managed and sustained forest sources. Logging, pulping and manufacturing processes are expected to conform to the environmental regulations of the country of origin.

A catalogue record for this book is available from the British Library.

A catalog record for this book is available from the Library of Congress.

To the memory of Irene Brown

Contents

Foreword

What is the most financially dangerous institution in the world? Brendan Brown shows us that it is the Federal Reserve.

Nothing else can or does create as much systemic financial risk as the Fed does by its monetary manipulations. Since the dollar is the dominant international currency, the risk is created not only for Americans, but for people all over the world. The scale of the current manipulation, or in Dr. Brown's phrase, the "Great Monetary Experiment", which the Fed is imposing on everyone, is unprecedented. But there is nothing new in the Fed's creating systemic risk and blundering while it's at it. As the book relates in detail, this has been going on for nearly a century. For example, the "powerful global asset price inflation" of the mid-1920s was "fuelled by the monetary disequilibrium created by the Benjamin Strong Fed".

The Ben Bernanke/Janet Yellen Fed of our day has explicitly sought to inflate bond, stock and real estate prices. Other central banks, especially the European Central Bank and the Bank of Japan, have joined in, and a vast asset price inflation has indeed been achieved. As one financial market observer has said, bonds internationally have surpassed "any known previous high of any recorded era", and "every department of the credit markets is making all-time lows in yield". Brown reasonably characterizes this as yet another cycle of irrationality in asset prices stoked by monetary expansion – or more rhetorically, as a viral global disease infecting financial markets. What the final outcome of the Great Monetary Experiment will be is uncertain, but it certainly risks being ugly.

One of the most remarkable religious developments of modern times is the widely held faith in the Federal Reserve. This odd faith results in many otherwise intelligent people, especially professional economists, ardently maintaining that the Fed should be an "independent" or virtually sovereign fiefdom, free to carry out, without supervision from the Congress or anybody else, whatever monetary experiments it wants. But no part of a democratic government should be such an independent power.

The promoters of Fed independence, including of course the Fed itself, share a common, unspoken assumption: that the Fed is competent to have the unchecked power of manipulating money or in a more grandiose version of "managing the economy". It is assumed that the Fed knows what it is doing with its experiment of monetizing $1.7 trillion in real estate mortgages and $2.5 trillion in long-term government bonds and blowing its balance sheet up to $4.5 trillion. Brown maintains to the contrary that the Fed does not know what it is doing, that it is flying by the seat of the pants, and he works through a hundred years of financial history to show that it was ever thus.

Indeed, there is no evidence at all that the Fed has the special economic knowledge to make it competent to be entrusted with its enormous power and a lot of evidence to show that it does not. Believers in the Fed's special competence are operating purely on a credo: "I believe in the Fed; I believe in a committee of economists manipulating money according to unreliable forecasts and debatable and changing theories from time to time in fashion".

The Fed has no credentials to merit faith. But the Fed is excellent, as Brown shows, at causing financial instability while claiming to be promoting stability. It is also excellent at allocating resources to big government spending.

An essential part of the Fed's current theory, which has become a central banking fashion, is that central banks should create a perpetual inflation in goods and services prices. Prices must increase forever, at a rate of 2% per year. This means they will quintuple in a normal lifetime. Under this theory, which Brown calls "deflation phobia", average prices must never, never be allowed to decline, even if a period of marked innovation and accelerating productivity would lead them naturally to decline in a free market, thereby increasing real wages. "No!" says the current Fed, "prices must be forced up to our 2% inflation target". Brown addresses at length how this doctrine of permanent inflation is perverse.

"Tell me one more time why we think 2% inflation is good", as one financial writer recently demanded. "When you lose 20% of your buying power in just 10 years, which span has included two deflationary recessions, the 2% inflation premise begins to look a little suspect". Indeed, it does – and more than a little.

As part of the permanent inflation doctrine, the Fed has twisted the term "stable prices", which the Congress has in statute instructed it to pursue. The term has a clear and obvious meaning: prices that are stable. As Brown points out, prices that are stable in the long run, sometimes go up and sometimes go down in the interim. If they never go down, they cannot be stable in the long term. Stuck with a Congressional assignment, but insisting that average prices can never go down, the Fed has a dilemma. So, it constantly claims that "stable prices" really means prices that always go up at 2% per year.

How did the Fed talk itself into that? Consider the transcript of an informative meeting of its Open Market Committee in July, 1996, now publicly released, in which the committee discussed the issue of "long-term inflation goals". "The most important argument" for perpetual inflation was that it allows "adjustments in relative pay in a world where individuals deeply dislike nominal pay cuts". In other words, its big advantage is that it fosters reductions in real wages. This is the classic Keynesian argument for inflation sometimes, which the Fed has turned into inflation always. The argument depends entirely on Money Illusion, which it was further argued, is "a very deep-rooted property of the human psyche" – a dubious proposition. One lonely non-economist suggested the committee should consider what Congress meant by stable prices, but no one else took him up on that! As the committee was meeting, the first of two great coming American bubbles was developing, but no one at all raised the question of asset price inflation.

Can monetary stability ever be achieved with such a Fed in charge? Brown concludes that it is not only unlikely, but impossible: "It is not possible for monetary stability to emerge under a regime where the Federal Reserve is manipulating interest rates based on its ever changing views about the state of the economy and its supposed special knowledge". Without fundamental monetary reform, which means reform of the systemic risk-creating Federal Reserve, we have only "the bleak prospects of continuing instability".

This book should be healthy intellectual therapy for Fed believers. I hope it will prove so.

Alex J. Pollock[1]

Note

1. Alex J. Pollock is a resident fellow at the American Enterprise Institute in Washington, DC. He was President and CEO of the Federal Home Loan Bank of Chicago 1991–2004 and is the author of *Boom and Bust* (2011).

Acknowledgements

In writing this book, I have gained immensely from conversations and continuing dialogues with several economists in the US, Japan and Europe who share a deep hope for a better monetary future and strive towards that end.

In particular, Alex J. Pollock (American Enterprise Institute) has been a non-tiring source of insight and encouragement.

I have also received much stimulus from Joseph Salerno (Mises Institute).

I appreciate deeply the supportive interest of the Hudson Institute in allowing me to promote the ideas here.

Professor Keiichiro Kobayashi invited me to present the initial research for this book at a seminar in November 2013 at the Canon Institute for Global Studies in Tokyo under the title of "Asset Price Inflation – a global economic virus which has its origins always in the Federal Reserve".

Over many years, I have enjoyed the friendship and stimulus of meetings with Professor Kazuo Ueda, and he has given me the opportunity of imparting these ideas to his classes of graduate students.

Robert Pringle read a preliminary text of the manifesto for US monetary reform in Chapter 4 and made invaluable comments along with a host of editing suggestions. The origins of this chapter stemmed in large part from discussing and authoring a joint paper during the spring and summer of 2010. He also reviewed the present project in embryonic form and helped steer the subsequent design.

In my writing about global credit bubbles and busts and the intimately related subjects of global capital flows and monetary disequilibrium, I have been influenced profoundly by my lifelong teacher Professor Robert Z. Aliber of the University of Chicago.

Elizabeth V. Smith, an economist and Master's graduate of University College London, provided great help in the toil of reading the manuscript at its various stages of preparation.

Introduction

When are global asset markets and ultimately the global economy most vulnerable to the forces of irrationality?

There is a loud and clear answer in this book. The greatest danger is when the US is leading the world in a monetary experiment which distorts the key capital market signals guiding the invisible hand.

The "Great Monetary Experiment" (GME) launched under the Obama Administration by its chosen Federal Reserve Chief Ben Bernanke was not the first in contemporary history. Indeed, since the Federal Reserve opened its doors, there has been a perpetual rolling out of monetary experiments, albeit the main officials in charge would never have agreed with that description. At most, they would have conceded that circumstances had forced them into monetary innovation, but this had not been their choice.

Those responsible for designing and implementing the GME had no such reticence. As we shall see in this volume, they were ready to gamble US and global prosperity on a set of theoretical propositions and innovatory tools as pioneered under their own chosen brand of neo-Keynesian economics. The justification for doing so was the darkness of the economic landscape in the immediate aftermath of the Great Panic (Autumn 2008) and their promise of an early dawn.

The big new idea in the Great Experiment was to "drive up asset prices" whilst simultaneously striving to prevent any whiff of price deflation appearing. "Quantitative Easing" was brandished as the magical tool. In fact, the experiment and the tool were not so new, and any transitory apparent effectiveness depended on a real life replay of the Emperor's New Clothes fable. As the real world theatre performance continued, many practical business decision makers remained anxious.

Intuitively, they realized the presence of asset price inflation, even though general knowledge about this disease remained scarce. A general foreboding that the end phase of the disease could be devastating – including possibly another crash and great recession – made many businesses and their shareholders cautious about entering into long-run high-risk ventures. In other cases, the trio of excess leverage, overinvestment and mal-investment, a hallmark of the disease, became apparent with the passage of time.

The plunge in energy prices during late 2014 and the extent of revealed overinvestment and mal-investment in the energy extraction industries suggested that energy might be the equivalent of US housing in the previous episode of asset price inflation disease or telecommunications in the one before that. An overpricing of high-risk debt issued by these lead sectors was a common feature in all three experiences.

In particular, the interest income famine under the GME led to a wide range of risky debt selling at prices which could not be justified on sober-rational calculation. These securities had been prominent in financing the shale oil and gas boom. They were also the key source of fuel to private equity which after suffering a near-death experience in 2008 entered an even bigger boom under the Great Monetary Experiment.

The investors buying the high-yield debt at inflated prices are in many cases aware of the irrational forces at work. Maybe they are confident in their ability to exit the inflated markets before they deflate. Alternatively, they may come to believe that "there is simply nowhere else to go" in their flight from the interest income famine in the safe bond markets. Or they may put an unjustifiably high probability on a miracle turning up which would underpin assets at their present inflated prices. Or they may have repeat to themselves that weary phrase "it is vain to fight the Fed".

The investors and commentators who steadfastly prevent their minds becoming enfeebled by such mantra face a challenge. They realize the danger of becoming the permanent pessimist who forecasts the next crash five years in advance and miss all the opportunities meanwhile. Ideally, they should read up on everything available about the disease of asset price inflation and develop skill and talent in its diagnosis and prognosis. Even so, they cannot predict the course of the disease exactly or time its end with precision. Nor can they be 100% certain of their provisional diagnosis.

This book is about the disease of asset price inflation, and one of the aims here has been to heighten our powers of diagnosis and prognosis. No two episodes of the disease are identical, but there are common elements. As Balzac wrote, the challenge for the author is to individualize types and typify individuals. The same challenge faces the analyst of business cycles and the would-be experts in asset price inflation.

There is also a bigger aim. How can the US and the world rid itself of this disease – asset price inflation? It is not enough just to say "End the Fed". First, a keen and widespread awareness must emerge that the Fed has indeed been responsible for spreading a deadly plague of market irrationality which has undermined economic prosperity and become a danger to economic and political freedoms.

A key step in creating awareness about this plague should be the exposure of deflation phobia as prevalent amongst leading monetary officials. Asset price inflation in modern times has originated always in a context where the Fed is fighting against an "incipient danger of deflation" – trying to stabilize prices or even push them up by 2% p.a. when the natural rhythm would have been downward for some time. Yet in today's world of information technology, this phobia of deflation becomes harder and harder to comprehend.

In this latest period of monetary experimentation led by the Federal Reserve, the central bankers have sought to terrify their audiences about widespread price falls and so justify their quantitative easing policies and use of other non-conventional tools, including negative interest rates. They are the Don Quixote of the monetary theatre, but unlike the fictional anti-hero, they have the real power to destroy and impoverish.

Beyond the cure of deflation phobia, there is the challenge of creating a new stable monetary order in the US. Is this possible without a return of the US dollar to a gold standard? The approach taken in this volume is to examine how the automatic mechanisms operating under the gold standard brought about monetary stability in general terms and then to examine whether these could be recreated without the dollar being convertible into gold.

The functioning of the automatic mechanisms depended on a tightly constrained growth in supply of monetary base in which there was nonetheless some flexibility in line with evolving cyclical and secular economic conditions, a strong demand for monetary base and no direct or indirect official interventions in the setting of long-term (or short-term) rates. In principle, a monetary system in the US could be reproduced with these qualities.

Without gold convertibility (meaning the widespread use of gold coins with these obtainable on demand against dollars at a fixed parity), though, there would have to be a vigorously defended monetary constitution beyond the reach of political interference. That aim of monetary stability enshrined in constitutional law would require for its fulfilment a general rolling back of financial regulation, deposit insurance and implicit promises of bailouts for "too big to fail" financial institutions.

To many, this may seem like an unrealistic agenda. But revolutions always seem impossible long in advance. And in the meantime, there is much work to be done both in the understanding of how irrational forces in asset markets become empowered by US monetary instability and in mobilizing opinion behind a US monetary reform agenda.

1
The Monetary Origins of Market Irrationality

There is a deeply held belief that order emerges out of chaos. If so, the Obama Administration's Great Monetary Experiment, designed and implemented by its appointed Federal Reserve chief, will have ultimately a happy ending. Social and economic turmoil resulting from years of vast monetary disorder would bring about a swing of the political pendulum, which could sweep away the Federal Reserve. In its place a new monetary order would be constructed. This would include constitutionally protected rules to guide the US along the path of monetary stability.

The Obama Federal Reserve (Fed) would stand accused of having designed and carried out a wild and highly controversial monetary experiment without any serious regard to known side effects .These emanate from its unleashing of irrational forces in global financial markets. The accusers would charge the Fed and ultimate puppet masters in the White House and Congress with having squandered long-run prosperity in the failed bet that the experiment would result in a fast pace of recovery from a great recession which stemmedfrom deeply flawed monetary policies through the previous two business cycles (1992–2007). In fact the economic upturn since the cyclical trough of Spring 2009 has been the weakest ever to follow a Great Recession.

A precondition for such a revolution to occur is a popular revulsion against all those responsible for the monetary misconduct – the senior Federal Reserve officials, the presidents who had nominated them for high office and the Congresses which had approved their policies and passed legislation mandating continued instability. The cause of that revulsion would not just be the cumulative economic damage but also the trauma delivered by the Federal Reserve to the delicate fabric of free society. Results of this trauma include the crony capitalism, monopoly power and intense regulation, which have been features of the US financial experience since the Great Panic.

The purpose of the Great Monetary Experiment

The best introduction to the purpose of the Great Monetary Experiment (GME) is a response that then Fed Chief Ben Bernanke gave at his first press conference (April 27, 2011). The question posed was about his view on the main thesis in Reinhart and Rogoff's book (2011) that economic upturns following recessions which feature financial panic are always slow and difficult.

Professor Bernanke responded at first with a joke: "I've known him (Rogoff) for a long time; I even played chess against him, which was a big mistake". Then the serious answer followed.

Yes, Professor Rogoff was right (in Bernanke's opinion). All such recoveries have indeed been slow. But this is not an immutable law. In particular, following such recessions in the past, economic policy had not been sufficiently vigorous. With unusual passion, Bernanke promised boldly that the path-breaking monetary policy tools, which the Federal Reserve was now pursuing under his leadership, would prove the pessimism expressed by Rogoff and Reinhart wrong on this occasion.

Bernanke, in agreeing with Reinhart and Rogoff that all recessions following financial panic have been slow and difficult, was not on firm ground. There has been a growing critique since their book's publication that US recoveries from such recessions had been strong – except for the particular recovery in question in the aftermath of the 2008 panic (see Taylor and John, 2012, Blog 17/10; Siems and Thomas, 2013; and Bordo and Haubrich, 2014). And then there is the time-honoured Zarnowitz rule, that the deeper the recession, the stronger the subsequent recovery. That rule was based on 150 years observation of US business cycle history (Zarnowitz and Victor, 1992).

Aside from the actual historical evidence conflicting with the Rogoff and Reinhart thesis, there is a body of theory – found in the economic writing of both the neoclassical school (Hoover, 2008) and Austrian school (Mises, 1971) – suggesting that the invisible hand of market forces in the context of monetary stability can indeed bring about a powerful long-term recovery from a great recession (and incidentally there would not have been a great recession in 2008–09 if there had been monetary stability in the preceding years) so long as government does not get in the way. As a new Keynesian economist, Bernanke like Rogoff and Reinhart had either rejected or ignored such theory, stressing instead all the various frictions which would enfeeble or paralyze benign market forces.

In particular, Bernanke had elsewhere (see Bernanke and Frank, 2014) made much of the argument that the invisible hand (of Adam Smith fame) would cease to function when interest rates fall to the "zero rate boundary" (as nominal interest rates cannot fall substantially below zero without triggering huge withdrawals of cash from the banking system). Yet under the conditions of heightened risk aversion and enlarged savings surplus which typify the aftermath of financial panics, the neutral level of short-term and even medium-term interest rates could indeed be negative. In the same vein, Bernanke has stressed the economic frictions which typify "balance sheet recessions" in the aftermath of a boom and bust. These handicap the invisible hand. In particular, high indebtedness weighs on new investment by the business sector and consumption by households.

Counterarguments to Bernanke-ite pessimism

What are the main counterarguments to Bernanke-ite pessimism? Top of the list is denying its premise of price inflexibility. If prices are flexible (both downwards and upwards) and confidence exists in a firm anchor to prices in the long run (as under the gold standard regime), then a procyclical pattern of prices would make the zero rate boundary discussion redundant (see Brown, 2013).

When business conditions are recessionary, many prices and wages would fall to a somewhat below normal level. Yet there would be expectations of higher prices into the eventual expansion phase. (Under the gold standard, the cyclical fall in prices including some nominal wage rates together with the fixed nominal price of gold would generate increased gold production as profits from mining increase – meaning a boost to monetary base growth). And so even with nominal interest rates somewhat positive, interest rates would be negative in real terms. The benign operation of the invisible hand does not depend on piercing the zero rate boundary.

As regards the pessimism about balance sheet recessions, the counterargument focuses on how excessive debt ratios can fall swiftly via the injection of equity and how a climate of enhanced profit prospects and entrepreneurship could indeed ignite a vibrant process of Schumpeterian creative destruction. Specifically, companies finding themselves with a hangover (from the boom-time) of high leverage, due to their total market value (debt and equity combined) having fallen sharply, can nonetheless respond positively to new investment opportunity by issuing equity. They might also conclude in some instances debt-equity swaps with existing debt holders (limiting the latter's windfall gains from new equity issuance which come at the expense of present equity holders).

Moreover, in the context of much economic destruction of capital stock during the recession (as mal-investment during the prior boom becomes apparent) and of abundant labour supply rates of profit should rise. This means that the set of investment opportunities would expand (so long as government supported banks are not keeping zombie companies alive and thereby sustaining excess capacity). And higher savings should go along with a lower cost of equity capital (as long as government and monetary policymakers are not adding powerfully to overall uncertainty) helping toward a recovery of investment (which might remain well below its previous boom high attained in the midst of much irrational exuberance) and its eventual blossoming.

Some of that investment might take the form of increasing capital intensity of existing production (more input of machinery, IT, knowledge) in specific sectors (not those which are heavy users of labour with little human capital – after taking account of economic obsolescence – now substantially cheaper than under the preceding bubble-economy conditions). Also in this situation, there could well be a flourishing of entrepreneurship based on finding new ways in which capital and now many types of cheaper labour (cheapness could be in absolute wage rate terms or when assessed relative to marginal productivity) can be combined profitably, often satisfying new types of demand for goods and services not apparent before.

President Obama chooses his designer for the "Great Monetary Experiment"

When Bernanke affirmed that he agreed with Rogoff and Reinhart about the weakness of recoveries following financial panic, the reporter had no chance to ask a follow-up question. This might have been why he (Bernanke) disagreed with all the critics and counterarguments as detailed here. It would have been an extraordinary press conference if such an interchange had taken place!

Yet in terms of practical monetary policymaking, it is unimportant why Bernanke disagreed or whether he was even fully aware of such alternative viewpoints. After all, President Obama had nominated Bernanke for a second term at the head of the Federal Reserve in Summer 2009 knowing full well his views, however well founded or not, on the understanding that he would pursue the GME and incidentally, also give his powerful backing to the omnibus Frank-Dodd financial market regulation bill making its way then through Congress. The advisers around the president, including, crucially, the director of his national economic council, Professor Larry Summers, and less importantly, his chair of the council of economic advisors, Professor Christina Romer, who would have influenced his choice, knew exactly what the renomination of Bernanke meant for the conduct of US monetary policy.

A core component of the GME has been what is widely described as "quantitative easing", or more popularly "QE". This has been allied to an earlier key shift in the US monetary framework toward targeting a "steady low inflation rate", which the Greenspan Federal Reserve put into effect surreptitiously in the mid-1990s. At a special FOMC meeting (July 1996) (only revealed in a Fed transcript published many years later), then Fed Governor Professor Janet Yellen persuaded Chairman Alan Greenspan that the aim of price level stability should be adapted to mean a steady state of 2% p.a. inflation. Bernanke was a keen advocate of inflation targeting and had set out ten principles to guide monetary policy under such a framework (see Brown, 2013).

Quantitative easing as practised by the Federal Reserve since 2009 has involved blowing up the size of its balance sheet for the declared purposes of pursuing recovery in the labour market, combatting "deflation danger" and sustaining inflation expectations (and inflation) around the 2% p.a. level.

How has the Fed expanded its balance sheet with monetary base as share of GDP rising from around 7% in 2007 to 23% in 2014?

This has occurred by the Fed Reserve issuing en masse a special category of liability (bank reserves) which pays a small positive interest rate (to the member bank) – above the prevailing zero rate in the market for short-maturity T-bills. These liabilities (bank reserves) are created when the Fed purchases assets including prominently long-maturity US T-bonds and mortgage-backed agency bonds (issued by housing corporations presently administered by the federal government). In effect, the Fed pays for these assets by creating high powered money (in this case, deposits at the Federal Reserve) to use in the settlement of the transaction.

QE is not money printing in the classical sense

Quantitative easing (QE) is not money printing in the classical sense of the central bank (in this case, the Federal Reserve) issuing non-interest bearing reserves or banknotes at a time when market short-term interest rates and the neutral level of interest rates (say short and medium-term) are substantially positive. In that context, the new reserves or currency are like hot potatoes which everyone tries to pass on as quickly as possible (either via lending or purchasing goods). Market interest rates fall sharply and bank lending climbs rapidly. Instead, we could describe the QE operations effected under the Obama Administration during the years 2009–14 as "quasi money printing".

The accumulation of long-maturity bonds by the Federal Reserve via the proceeds of quasi money printing together with an open-mouth policy about future prospects for short-term rate pegging and for the continuation of zero rate policy in particular are meant (according to the designers of the monetary experiment) to press down long-term interest rates to well below the so-called neutral level. Conceptually at any point of time, there is a set of short, medium and long-term interest rates across different maturities such that the given economy, here the US, follows a path of monetary stability characterized by first, goods and services prices on average following a flat trend over the very long run but fluctuating both up and down over the medium or short run and second, no asset price inflation. These are the so-called natural interest rates – in fact, distinct for each maturity. Where there are expectations of persistent steady state inflation over the long run, we can define the neutral rate as the natural rate plus that inflation rate. We will see later in this chapter how the Fed's "success" in manipulating downward long-term interest rate depends on its tools (including QE, zero rate policy, forward guidance) unleashing powerful forces of irrationality in the marketplace. These can foster, for example, extreme judgements about the likelihood of secular stagnation (in turn, influenced by positive feedback loops from capital gains on bonds) amidst a "reach for yield" (investors desperate for income pile into long-maturity bonds whilst convincing themselves that the risks involved are only small).

The same investor who has convinced himself or herself about the secular stagnation hypothesis as grounds to reach for yield in the long-maturity US Treasury bond market is not likely to be simultaneously optimistic about economic robustness when assessing equity investment, although in the world of the irrational, such schizophrenia is sometimes encountered! Some investors may not be convinced by the hypothesis of secular stagnation (technically they attach a very low probability to it proving to be correct) but are ready to speculate on how irrational belief in this will evolve. For example they may accumulate aggressive long positions in the 10-year US government bond market on the basis that the secular stagnation hypothesis will gain popularity for some time (meaning that many investors put large probabilities on its forecast outcome becoming reality). When this belief fades suddenly say in two to three years time the average maturity of the once aggressive bond portfolio would have shrunk to say 7 years and so be less vulnerable to price fall. (There is no corresponding fall in the average maturity of equities as the respective businesses in aggregate are continuously making new long-life investments). And in any case the investors might hope to make their exit before that point.

Heterogeneity of opinion and speculation in the form described can allow the equity market and bond markets to go their own ways to some extent, with the optimists on economic robustness crowding into equities and eschewing bonds. In the big picture, though, this degree of freedom is limited given the great mass of investors who are heavily entrenched in both markets. The neutral level of interest rates which reflects this shrunken confidence and also the damage to the longer-term economic outlook by monetary uncertainty (see p. 24) may be in real terms significantly below where it would be in an economic environment free of such handicap. In principle, when these handicaps are eventually removed – meaning the return to "monetary normality" – the neutral level in real terms would jump as the secular stagnation hypothesis lost plausibility amongst investors no longer suffering from income famine and as the dissipating of monetary uncertainty bolstered opportunity for business spenders; but first, there would be the final stage of the asset price inflation disease as described below in which speculative temperatures plunge and a business recession occurs.

Though the monetary experiment depresses the neutral level of rates as described it lowers market rates to an even greater extent, at least as regards long-maturity rates. Below neutral long-term market rates in the context of first, general concern about possible high inflation in the distant future (well in excess of the 2% inflation target) as provoked by the GME and second, desperation amongst investors suffering in the famine of income from risk-free assets (such as short-maturity T-bonds) fuel the process of asset price inflation as defined below. This should, according to the advocates of the Obama monetary experiment, buoy present consumer and investment spending. The hypothesis is dubious both in principle and in practice.

Asset price inflation – a disease of monetary origin

Asset price inflation is a disease of monetary origin which corrupts the "software" behind the determination of prices in the capital markets which guide the invisible hand. In this disease, irrational forces play havoc to an unknown and erratic extent across an array of markets. These forces do not operate with equal strength in all markets continuously but build in those where there are good speculative stories (see Brown, 2014 and below). Under conditions of asset price inflation, many investors make unrealistically high estimates of these stories being the truth.

The chief architect of the GME, Professor Ben Bernanke, has never admitted its key aspect of unleashing irrational forces. Indeed, asset price inflation is not a concept found in the neo-Keynesian economics which he espouses.

According to the neo-Keynesian view, the GME would help rebuild "animal spirits" (a Keynesian term) which had become enfeebled during the great recession. And if the experiment were successful in terms of lifting the US economy on to a long-term flight path of high employment and business spending growth, then the high asset prices induced early in the process could be sustained. Asset prices could climb still further. Hopefully technological progress and a related surge in productivity growth could give a helping hand as had occurred in say the 1920s and 1990s when strong re-bounds in the equity market at first prompted in part by monetary stimulus had subsequently been more than ratified by economic miracle (see chapter 7). Yet despite the chief architect's silence on the matter, as the great experiment continued, there has been more and more talk about asset price inflation, whether amongst market practitioners, commentators, economists or the policymakers themselves. The term, however, is barely ever defined in this growing discussion.

If we go back in the economics literature, we can find the term used in the older Austrian school literature (in say the 1920s). There it referred to the excessive rise in the relative price of capital goods (compared to consumer goods) under conditions where interest rates are being held below the neutral level. In turn, an overproduction of capital goods relative to consumer goods led on to overinvestment, falling profits and ultimately recession. That was the original version of Austrian business cycle theory (see Mises).

In modern times, asset price inflation has been linked to an increasing extent with such concepts as mal-investment (see Lachman, 1977) resulting from prices in a wide and varying range of key asset markets having been distorted by monetary disequilibrium. In this volume, a key aspect of that distortion is demonstrated as the strengthening of irrational forces in the marketplace. Sometimes these cause a state of "irrational exuberance" to form. Investors avidly pursue a sequence of highly speculative tales about which they would normally be sceptical.

Irrational exuberance and flaws in market judgement

Irrational exuberance is a term imported from the behavioural finance literature and applies to a market environment of excessive optimism. However, no discussion takes place there about the monetary origins of the phenomenon. Robert Shiller (2000) describes irrational exuberance as "not that crazy – more like the kind of bad judgement which we all remember having made at some points in our lives when our enthusiasm got the better of us". Separately, Shiller refers to various specific types of irrationality well known to psychologists and then describes those in the context of markets.

These forms include "magical thinking" (attribution of causal relationships between actions and events which cannot be justified by reason and observation), " mental compartmentalization" (an unconscious psychological defence mechanism used to avoid cognitive dissonance or the mental discomfort and anxiety caused by a person having conflict emotions, beliefs within themselves), "positive feedback loops" (a process in which a change from the normal range of function elicits a response that amplifies or enhances that change) and "the anchoring effect" (a cognitive bias that describes the common human tendency to rely too heavily on the first piece of information offered) .

How does central bank manipulation of market interest rates below their neutral level aggravate these disorders which are more general than the special case of irrational exuberance? Below are some examples.

Take *magical thinking*. The first time the FOMC pointed to a probable early use of non-conventional monetary policy tools, the equity market jumped and the long-term US T-bond yields slumped. Many analysts and investors given time to contemplate the issues might question whether those early reactions were sensible, and so a subsequent news item about an additional use of such tools could in principle bring a different market result. After all, stable monetary conditions are surely better for long-run economic prosperity than a highly unstable course. Equity prices may well get on to a higher long-run path if the invisible hands are allowed to function freely in a stable monetary environment than one where participants must worry about the potential end-stage of the asset price inflation disease characterized by bubble-bursting and recession at some uncertain point in the future, not to mention the long-term erosion of risk appetites. And could it not be that long-term bond prices should reflect the grown likelihood of high inflation in the long run in consequence of the pursuance of non-conventional monetary policy? Yet in the context of much magical thinking, the fact that the prices of bonds and equities rose on the first announcement would mean that there would be much speculation on a similar market reaction to the second announcement.

Another example of magical thinking is the following of almanacs. For example, investment almanacs tell investors that in the year following a mid-term Congressional election in a US president's second term where the opposition party emerges with control of both the House and the Senate, the stock market usually booms. Illustrations include the first half of 1987, the first half of 1999 and the first half of 2007. Yet the real story in all these cases had little to do with the outcome of the election but much more to do with the progress of an asset price inflation disease which the Fed had been generating for some considerable time before the polling date (the Volcker asset price inflation of 1985–87 stimulated by a monetary policy aimed at devaluing the dollar in line with the Plaza Accord; in 1996–2000, the Greenspan Fed aiming at a 2% inflation rate despite an economic miracle in the form of the IT revolution creating a bulge in productivity; in 2003–07, the great asset price inflation stimulated by the "anti-deflation" policies pioneered by Ben Bernanke and authorized ultimately by Alan Greenspan in the last years of his chairmanship of the Fed). And so when President Obama became a lame duck president in November 2014, it was magical thinking to project another lap of stock market boom without careful consideration of the fundamental monetary forces at work.

Take *mental compartmentalization*. Investors might think of interest or dividend income and how they spend out of it as distinct from capital gain. And so, as a first example, during the interest income famine of growing severity created by the Bernanke Fed in the aftermath of the panic of 2008, there was an endless sales pitch by the security houses that investors should favour "dividend-paying stocks" of "good quality companies" and high-yield bonds. Yet no rational investor would focus just on one subdivision of overall income rather than considering this jointly with the probability distribution of possible capital gains or losses on these same assets. The rational investor would not be fooled by the prospect of high dividends paid at the expense of capital gains. A second example has been the "reach for yield" in long-maturity government bond markets. It seems that many investors have been willing to assume large risk positions far out in the term structure of interest rates so that they can secure a pattern of modest (rather than zero) interest coupon income. Potential capital losses from the risk-positions are perhaps irrationally underestimated in the process. The same comment applies to the accumulation of high-risk credit paper in the effort to secure income flow in the present whilst underestimating potential loss from default. Take *positive feedback loops*. News of price increases spurs investor enthusiasm, which spreads by psychological contagion from person to person, in the process amplifying "speculative stories" that might justify the price increase. These bring in a larger and larger class of investors who, despite doubts about the real value of the investment, are drawn to it partly through envy and partly through a gambler's excitement.

And finally, take *anchoring*. An example would be the irrational tendency for investors to formulate their views about the outlook for interest rates many years from now based on where they are today and on where the Federal Reserve says it will steer them over the next two years. In principle, the rational investor should form their expectation of far-off rate levels on the basis of views about inflation and the neutral level under a whole range of scenarios which could be very different from the present. Yet investors desperate for yield in the context of income famine might have a particular vulnerability to irrational forces, willing to seize advantage from an apparent yield pickup in the long-maturity bond markets. And they might comfort themselves in doing so by listening to a good speculative story, even circulated by senior Fed officials, about how in "the new normal" the neutral level of rates will remain much lower than in the past. That story sometimes includes some version of the secular stagnation hypothesis (productivity growth and investment opportunity more meagre than in the past). This jars, though, with the irrational exuberance which the GME (Obama's Great Monetary Experiment) is designed to foster in the equity market.

A debate about the monetary diagnosis of market irrationality

The view that the GME has stimulated asset price inflation in some of the ways described in this volume has been challenged. For example, University of Chicago Professor John Cochrane has commented (2013):

> Consider the idea that low interest rates spark asset price "bubbles". Standard economics denies this connection: the level of interest rates and risk premiums are separate phenomena. Historically, risk premiums have been high in recessions, when interest rates have been

low. One needs to imagine a litany of "frictions" induced by institutional imperfections or current regulations to connect the two. Fed Governor Jeremy Stein gave a thoughtful speech in February (2013) about how such frictions might work, but admitting our lack of real knowledge deeper than academic cocktail party speculation.

There is a problem with Cochrane's scepticism about low rates of interest stimulating asset price inflation. He fails to make the key distinction between the situation where market interest rates (especially long-term) are low and the level of neutral interest rate is equally low, on the one hand, from the situation where the market interest rate is low and the level of neutral interest rate considerably higher on the other hand.

Even low rates in absolute terms may, under some circumstances (not considered by Cochrane) without any positive differential in favour of the neutral level, encourage a desperation for yield. This could be the case where for many years deflation phobic central banks have stood in the way of any periodic decline in prices (consistent with stable prices in the very low run). These bonuses consisting of a supplement to the real value of principal which accrue in the severe stage of a business recession make savers somewhat calmer and continually rational in the context of a long period of sustained negative real rates such as might typify the subsequent recovery phase following the business cycle trough.

The absence of these bonuses means the lid on irrationality in the marketplace can start to crack under the pressure of continued low interest rates even when these are at neutral level . Investors become more prone in income famished state to display the various forms of irrationality as detailed above. (Irrational exuberance is an important type, but there are also other forms, including, for example, the desperation for yield which emerges in the long-maturity US Treasury bond market). Also, stimulating irrationality despite low nominal rates being in line with neutral level could be concern about a possible eruption of inflation in the long run which would underpin now some rush into real assets.

The mid-19th century British financial commentator Walter Bagehot thought that John Bull would not tolerate below-2% interest rates – meaning that he (or she) would engage in irrational activity – even under the stable monetary regime of the gold standard under which prices indeed fluctuated both downward and upward. And indeed, as we shall discuss (see p. 144–5), short-term rates in Britain never fell below that level during the heyday of the gold standard in which the Bank of England was the "leader of the orchestra". Perhaps Bagehot was underestimating John Bull's rationality in the face of a transitory cyclical dip of short-term rates toward zero. Or perhaps we should indeed build into economic models an arbitrary numerical catalyst (here sub-2% nominal interest rate) to irrational behaviour (yield-seeking in this case). That is an empirical matter – and whatever the provisional finding, this should not be regarded as permanently fixed in the context of human ability to learn.

Turning to the most powerful driver of asset price inflation – market rates below neutral – we have already noted (see p. 10) that there is a whole span of neutral levels from short to long maturities. If there is a firm anchor to prices over the long run with periods of inflation and deflation offsetting each other, the neutral level of the long-run rate contains no inflation premium, and this is the same as the natural interest rate referred to in the economic literature (see Laubach and Williams, 2001).

No one knows the path of the neutral rate level. Many people make estimates of the path with varying degrees of confidence. Where central bankers are not pretending to know these, and interest rates are determined without any rate pegging for short maturities or stimulation of irrationality regarding long maturities, then market rates and neutral level are held together (not tightly) by a process of continuous experimentation and by the input of final user demand (households and businesses deciding whether or not to save more and spend less at the prevailing medium or long-term rate of interest). If speculative froth forms in various asset markets or visible goods and service inflation emerges, then the invisible hand guides market interest rates higher into line with a new revised estimation (in the marketplace) of the neutral levels.

Note that the key divergence between market interest rates and neutral level with respect to generating irrational exuberance is at long maturities, as these are important for market valuations, especially in equities and real estate. (By contrast, the divergence at short or medium maturities could be relatively more important for near-term economic activity and goods inflation). When the long-term forward-forward rates are well below neutral level then positive feedback loops form. Capital gains emerging in asset classes where there are good speculative stories then become market justification of these. Investors become more (falsely) confident of the stories' veracity. In a sober-rational mood, they would have remained sceptical. If these investors feel severely income famished – as they may do if there has not been any earlier period of real income bonus from a phase of deflation and if the absolute level of market interest rates has been feeble in real terms for a considerable period of time – then they are even more prone to irrational behaviour including being drawn into positive feedback loops.

This generation of irrational behaviour is potentially the most important influence running from low manipulated long-term interest rates to the equity market. Arithmetical valuation effects are more questionable. After all, the pattern of corporate cash flows, which the equity investor buys into, tends to be weighted heavily into the long run, even 20 or 30 years in the case of long-gestation projects. (Note that re-invested corporate profits are equivalent to new injections of equity capital by the shareholder out of funds which have been distributed only notionally). The equity market is many times larger than markets in such long-maturity government debt, especially in the inflation-protected form (which is the most relevant to valuation). And so in principle, it is these long-term bond markets which should take their valuation cue from the equity market rather than conversely. There are many obstacles in the way of risk arbitrage between long-term debt markets and equity markets. One important obstacle is the lack of reliable estimates regarding the size of the risk premium, especially taking account of expectations regarding trend growth in earnings.

Examples of speculative stories driving irrational markets

One speculative story is that the GME will be successful, where this is measured in terms of the chief architect's aims – to bring about an exception to the Rogoff and Reinhart pessimism about recoveries following a great recession. In principle, investors could chase this story even though they were unconvinced or not altogether sure about the mechanisms of the experiment or about the rationale for the experiment. The investors could "in the middle of the night" worry about the number of years that the experiment had already been running with such poor results so far. They would be like the courtiers in the fable of the emperor's new clothes.

It is not obvious that this story (of eventual success for the GME) has caught on in a big way, although it may well have been a factor in generating US equity market froth at various points in time especially during periodic episodes of stronger US economic data. As we shall see (p. 19), there has been an alternative narrative of probable eventual failure of the GME which has also influenced market prices and dulled the power of equity markets even when apparently buoyant (and the emperor's new clothes story playing in the daily market shows) to lift business spending. Federal Reserve officials implementing the GME must surely hope that investors in the equity market are not listening to the music of the secular stagnation theme which they are simultaneously pumping into the long-term interest rate market. It is not clear that these hopes have been fulfilled.

There is another speculative story which surfaced late in the equity market boom accompanying GME through its first six years. According to this, real wage rates in the US economy were lagging behind productivity growth due to grown competition for unskilled labour in particular from the emerging market countries (as an alternative possible locus of production whether for goods or services). As a counterpart, profits rates were growing. These trends should be expected to continue for a long time according to the storytellers. Meanwhile, interest rates remained depressed at low levels because the growing inequality of incomes meant there was a permanent tendency toward over-saving (under-consumption). (see Davies, 2014). This narrative was full of holes.

Firstly, it is not clear to what extent real wage rates were lagging behind productivity or whether emerging market competition was the main source behind declines in pay. There was the big issue of human capital becoming obsolescent as intelligent machines replaced once skilled workers performing routine tasks. And as workers who had now lost human capital crowded into non-skilled segments of the labour market, real wage rates fell there and so did productivity, as businesses would substitute cheap labour for capital.

Secondly, in principle, the higher profit rates (very likely reported rates exaggerated the underlying reality due to widespread financial engineering and other froth which accompanies the asset price inflation) should have stimulated business spending and productivity would have risen in consequence. Weak consumer spending would have been balanced by robust investment and the neutral level of interest rates would have risen in step. The failure of this wave of investment and productivity growth to occur was due to the huge monetary uncertainty, whereby business decision makers feared the next stage of the asset price inflation disease likely to feature stock market slump and recession (see p. 24).

The biggest speculative story in the years following the launch of the GME was about the growing shortage of energy as cheap sources of fuel would become growingly exhausted whilst demand in the ever-booming emerging market economies would grow exponentially. Overinvestment and mal-investment occurred on the back of this story and was stimulated by the availability of cheap high-risk debt capital and private equity alongside irrational exuberance of investors in innovatory commodity funds as marketed by Wall Street firms. The boom in the energy extraction industries was the most prominent amongst many examples of economic distortion by asset price inflation in this US cycle, just as US housing construction had been in the preceding episode of asset price inflation disease in the 2000s, or telecommunications and IT in the episode before that in the mid-late 1990s.

Yes, the massive investments in energy extraction and energy conservation did bring cheaper energy in the end for consumers, but if sober-rational calculation had prevailed, the pace of the global economy journeying down this path would have been slower. A larger share of scarce savings would have found their way under the guidance of an invisible hand, not distorted by monetary disequilibrium, into areas which would have brought greater economic prosperity in the short and medium term.

Is irrational exuberance greater in credit than equity markets?

In general, the asset price inflation disease with its origin in Fed quantitative easing has been more virulent in certain subsectors of say the US equity market than in the market as a whole (where there has been some concern and arguably partial pricing in of eventual danger at least with respect to far distant earnings). Along the way, this has included momentum stocks in social media or biotech or equity in shale oil and gas. The same could be said about the various hot spots in the global real estate markets. We can observe similarly hot subsectors in the credit markets, where speculative temperatures have risen to high levels – for example, emerging market paper, European periphery bonds, high-yield bonds (many related to private equity) – each with their own story. In the credit markets considered as a whole, rational scepticism limiting the power of an overall speculative story based on the GME has been arguably less visible than in the equity markets. And so spreads have been compressed throughout with not much sign of lenders (investors) pricing in the possibility of an eventual Day of Reckoning.

A differing vulnerability of the credit market than of the equity markets at an aggregate level to irrational forces would be consistent with ex-Fed Governor Stein's observations as referred to by Professor Cochrane in his *Wall Street Journal* piece (see above). Specifically, in his speech (2013), Stein contemplates how we might get variations in the pricing of credit risk over time. He is talking about what others might describe as periods of irrational exuberance in the credit markets, although he does not describe it so. He gives two views about what he describes as the "over-heating mechanism":

> According to the primitive view, changes in the pricing of credit over time reflect fluctuations in the preferences and beliefs of end investors such as households, where these beliefs may or may not be entirely rational. Perhaps credit is cheap when household risk toler-ance is high – say, because of a recent run-up in wealth. Or maybe credit is cheap when households extrapolate current good times into the future and neglect low-probability risks.

> But I am sceptical that one can say much about time variation in the pricing of credit – as opposed to the pricing of equities – without focusing on a second view, the roles of institutions and incentives. The premise here is that since credit decisions are almost always dele-gated to agents inside banks, mutual funds, insurance companies, pension funds, hedge funds, and so forth, any effort to analyse the pricing of credit has to take into account not only household prefer-ences and beliefs, but also the incentives facing the agents actually making the decisions. And these incentives are in turn shaped by the rules of the game, which include regulations, accounting standards, and a range of performance-measurement, governance and compen-sation structures.

> To be more specific a fundamental challenge in delegated invest-ment management is that many quantitative rules are vulnerable to agents who act to boost measured returns by selling insurance against unlikely events – that is, by writing deep out-of-the-money puts. Since credit risk by its nature involves an element of put-writing, it is always going to be challenging in an agency context, especially to the extent that the risks associated with the put-writing can be structured to partially evade the relevant measurement scheme.

> Let me suggest three factors that can contribute to overheating. The first is financial innovation (new ways for agents to write puts that are not captured by existing rules). The second related factor is regu-lation. New regulation will tend to spur further innovation as market participants attempt to minimize the private costs created by new rules. And it may also open up new loopholes, some of which may be exploited by variants on already existing instruments. The third factor is a change in the economic environment that alters the risk-taking incentives of agents making credit decisions. For example, a prolonged period of low interest rates, of the sort we are experiencing

today, can create incentives for agents to take on greater duration or credit risk, or to employ additional financial leverage, in an effort to "reach for yield".

Even so, the distinction that Stein makes between the irrationality which might sometimes grip retail investors in the equity market (and he does not discuss at all the monetary origins of this phenomenon) and the factors in the reach for yield by institutional (agent) investors in the credit markets (rational for the agent but irrational from the perspective of the ultimate investor) might be overblown.

First, risk arbitrage is possible between credit and equity markets, so if the reward for bearing unit risk as rationally appraised were to become thinner in credit than equities, then some investors would switch from credit to equities. Companies would leverage themselves up (so earning arbitrage profit for their shareholders) and private equity groups take advantage of just such a situation (making highly leveraged acquisitions).

Second, there are many retail investors chasing various speculative stories in the high-yield credit markets and also more generally in the carry trades, which flourish in the feverish conditions generated by the asset price inflation disease. These speculative stories are often the theme music for irrational exuberance and sometimes – as in the case of carry trades in long-maturity Treasury bonds – irrational depression. Even the agents are drawn by the stories.

There are three forms of carry trade – from low-rate into high-rate currencies (the trader ignoring or downplaying exchange risk as he or she is enticed by a story as to why the high-yield currency might continue to appreciate), from low-yield safe credits into high-yield safe credits (influenced by a story consistent with equity market strength in the case of corporate credits or by a story about sovereign risks in the case of government or public sector high-yield credits) or from short-maturity default-free government bonds (for example US Treasury bonds) into long-maturity government bonds (perhaps influenced by a story such as US and Europe are entering a Japan-style lost decade of secular stagnation).

The equity investors in the financial institutions or non-financial institutions now making good recorded profits from participating heavily in those carry trades may also be impressed by the stories, hence putting up no barrier to their agents pursuing their own self-interest (as regards bonuses or other forms of remuneration) by acting in this way. If these equity investors became disillusioned with the stories then the agents in these institutions could be constrained by the invisible hand (especially in the market for corporate control) to desist from their pursuit of the irrational.

Stein admits the likelihood that continuously low interest rates might stimulate irrational yield-seeking behaviour in credit markets; but like Cochrane, he fails to make the distinction between low interest rates in line with neutral and those which are far below neutral. Nor does he distinguish divergence (between market rates and related neutral level) at short maturities and long maturities.

In general terms, when the divergence is concentrated at long maturities, there may be no visible emergence of monetary inflation in goods and services markets (although this could be occurring below the surface in the form of a downward swing in prices explained by real non-monetary influences which did not take place). As we have already seen (see p. 17) that might depend much more on divergence between market and neutral level at short and medium maturities than at long maturities.

Furthermore, the neutral levels are determined in the context of a global economy where the dollar is the dominant currency. And so in an early post-recessionary environment in the US, the neutral level of dollar interest rates at far-off maturities may already be significantly above the low long-maturity market rates which the Federal Reserve may be nurturing, and so asset price inflation disease could already become virulent in asset classes outside the US.

Why asset price inflation with its source in quantitative easing lowers potential economic growth

Fed officials, when they designed their QE policies, had a vision of bearing down on long-term rates in a way which would stimulate economic expansion via pumping up equity markets and some other asset markets. In doing this, they were following in the footsteps of Keynes who had argued back in the 1930s that long-term interest rates should indeed be used as a policy tool. Keynes had criticized the "rigidities" in markets, which meant that long-term rates remained north of 2% during the Great Depression even when short-term rates were pinned down at zero (see Turner 2013).

There are strong counter-considerations to using long-term rates in this way (as a policy tool). These include (not in order necessarily of importance) first, the potential damage under conditions of violent price swings in the long-term bond market to the mechanisms which tie interest rates there to the unknown neutral level This interference with the price signalling function impedes the invisible hand from performing its benign task.

Second, the deliberate engineering of divergence between long-maturity market interest rates and their neutral level creates the asset price inflation virus, and in the case of the US, this becomes a global disease. Yes, sometimes there is a happy ending if an economic miracle arrives to justify the high asset prices, but this cannot be counted upon. Usually asset price inflation has a sad ending and inflicts long-term costs in the form of shrunken equity risk appetites and much mal-investment.

Third, manipulating downward long-term market interest rates favours big public spending and lending which is sponsored by government agencies (for example, in the case of the US, housing).

Fourth, the asset price inflation, especially in the equity market which is generated by long-term rate manipulation might be especially ineffective in stimulating business spending.

Let's take this last point in greater detail. Holding long-term rates below neutral may indeed be successful in driving up speculative temperature in the equity market to some degree. Future corporate earnings – especially those expected in the near-term and which are viewed as comparatively safe – could be discounted at a lower rate. A pattern of capital gains might generate some irrational exuberance with respect to particular equity market sectors where there are passing good stories to follow (momentum stocks, shale oil, technology). And there is the story that the GME will be successful (see above). In addition, reported corporate earnings might be swollen to an extent not realized fully by investors wearing rose-coloured spectacles under the influence of the asset price inflation. For example, many corporations may be engaged in leveraged financial strategies so as to take advantage of cheap long-term finance. One such strategy could be to build up "liquid assets", in effect pursuing the carry trade in its various forms possibly via foreign subsidiaries. Hence, non-financial companies may be heavily engaged in what the Japanese described as "Zai-tech" operations during the bubble of the late 1980s. Another example is financial engineering designed to boost present and expected earnings per share growth, including aggressive programs of equity buy-backs.

Yet many investors remain somewhat cautious toward equities, realizing that earnings in the long run could suffer in consequence of the GME eventually failing and that present earnings could be swollen in various ways. And as we have seen, these investors may have at the back of their minds the same fear of "secular stagnation" which is rationalizing (falsely) their yield-seeking behaviour in the long-maturity Treasury bond market despite historically high prices there (see p. 10). The widely heard term "the most unloved bull market" during the GME catches that current of concern. For example, at some stage in the future, many of the carry trades around the globe which have been buoying economic activity especially in the emerging markets may blow up in a sequence of boom and bust even if interest rate manipulation by the Federal Reserve continues "successfully". Speculative temperatures could fall sharply in the high-yield credit markets causing a reversal of economic activity which had thrived in the heat. And so stock prices based on present earnings may seem normal (as investors put some probability on such shocks in the future), yet in overall terms taking account of all scenarios (including blow up) the market is expensive.

And so we have the juxtaposition of an equity market expensive in fundamental terms, taking account of the likely eventual blow-up scenario and the fact that asset price inflation may well be swelling current earnings to far above their long-run trend, and yet superficially within a normal range of valuation as assessed on the basis of present or near-term earnings projections (using the crude price-earnings ratio). In these circumstances, a corporation when it implicitly presents a prospectus of future cash flows from a new project to its shareholders (actual and potential) finds a value put on it which takes some negative account (arguably not enough in terms of the rational expectations yardstick) of the possible blow-out scenario and which exhibits less froth than the price put on safe near-term cash inflows. And so it is incentivized to find low-risk shorter-term projects which might skirt the years of suspected possible crisis or be resilient to such crisis. In the context of asset price inflation, the equity market does not fully discount those bad scenarios (of possible blow-out).

The business decision maker might well be more cautious than the contemporary equity market. Today's equity market prices might reflect a lot of momentum trading with investors speculating on a continuation of irrational exuberance (which may continue to grow) for some time. But the decision maker in a big corporation may earn a substantial element of his or her remuneration in the form of long-term options on corporate stock. So he or she has no interest in pursuing bold capital spending strategies based on a present rational bubble in equity. And it is the same for small or medium size business owners motivated by maximizing their proceeds for selling the business many years into the future. These business decision makers realize explicitly or intuitively what the authors Feroli, Ksyap, Schoenholz and Shin write in their paper on "Market Tantrums and Monetary Policy" (February 2014): "QE offers

a trade-off between more stimulus today at the expense of a more challenging and disruptive policy exit in the future. Stimulus now is not a
free lunch and it comes with a potential for macro-economic disruptions
when the policy is limited". They may in fact have deeper knowledge
than those authors in their scepticism about whether there can even be
much stimulus today, given the shadow of those future dangers.

A tidal boom in private equity stemming from Fed QE and crony capitalism

Yes, there are some areas of economic activity where irrationally priced
credit paper might indeed stimulate activity despite equity investors
being wide-eyed to the transitory influences of asset price inflation. In
some highly leveraged areas, the effective subsidy enjoyed by equity
investors issuing risky debt at insane prices might actually justify aggressive capital spending implementation even if many equity investors
and the business decision makers retain some scepticism. In some cases,
though, equity investors would be adverse to their companies becoming
so highly leveraged due to concern about the costs and wider consequences of bankruptcy. These concerns may not be so heavy in the
private equity field as elsewhere.

The private equity industry is where the GME and crony capitalism
have come together to produce an almighty tidal boom, for which it is
impossible to forecast the extent of eventual revealed mal-investment
and other economic costs but which are likely to be immense.

The speculative story of the private equity industry chased under the
diseased conditions of asset price inflation has been its talent in increasing
efficiency and in spotting opportunities for new business ventures. In
turn, the huge capital gains which are realized on (highly leveraged)
private equity when the US equity market is rising and high yield debt
in ever greater demand from investors suffering interest income famine
have seemed to justify the story. This speculative narrative provides the
basis of the private equity industry achieving still higher leverage ratios
as the buyers of its junk bonds become even more confident. Investors
beg to become limited partners of the private equity groups at ever
higher prices (meaning bigger profits for the original partners who incidentally include some well-known university endowment funds). The
low cost of new equity to the private equity groups (as measured on any
rational-sober basis, not from the viewpoint of the new investors wearing
rose-coloured spectacles) under these conditions of asset price inflation,
together with the overpricing of junk-bond issuance, can justify a more

hectic pursuit of opportunities. Under the Obama GME, these opportunities have been prominently new business ventures in shale oil and gas, aircraft leasing, new ship leasing, sub-prime auto-finance, rental apartments and rental housing and health care (responding to new demands for services created by ObamaCare).

The crony capitalist part of the story is lost in much of the tale-telling. The huge capital gains reflecting in considerable degree the rise of the stock market and high leverage possible at cheap cost include several sub-plots.

First, there is the privileged tax treatment of "carry income" and the huge benefits of tax deductibility of interest.

Second, there is the pile up of incoming funds from state and public sector pension funds with little transparency about fees.

Third, we should consider the particular investment opportunities which open up due to close links with bureaucracy. These facilitate navigation through complex regulations and toward the ultimate possible prizes – whether in the area of investment in rehabilitation centres gaining from ObamaCare or shale oil and gas projects where local permission is crucial or accumulation of apartment blocks to rent and related agreements with construction companies again all heavily dependent on a regulatory process or a boom in sub-prime lending for auto purchase where financial regulations could become a bugbear or a boom in aircraft leasing especially to airlines for example in Asia which are state-owned; or long leases for ships made in state-aided yards; or the purchase of equity stakes in regional banks disposed ultimately by the TARP (the government organ as established by the Bush Administration to inject equity in the banking system during the panic of 2008). No wonder we observe a strong two way flow – ex top officials in Washington taking up a second career in private equity or titans in the private equity industry entering politics.

And fourth, there is the economy of scale in crony capitalism. The private equity group can spread the costs of making its political and regulatory connections across all its businesses, whilst the costs for any one business on a stand-alone business relative size would be much greater.

During the QE years, possible indications of this aggressive uplift of capital spending in response to high speculative temperatures in the credit markets have been evident in the shale oil and gas areas (where appetite for high-yield paper driven by irrational exuberance was huge) and more broadly in those industrial sectors where private equity groups have thrived. For example, finance companies run by private equity groups applied their highly leverage structures (selling high-yield bonds at crazy prices) to rapidly build up their portfolio of sub-prime loans for automobile purchases. This has had a knock-on effect of bloating current sales and profits in the automobile sector which in turn has justified some boost to business spending there even from the viewpoint of equity investors fully aware of the likely bad outcome of QE.

Alternatively, real estate developers, particularly of apartment-to-rent blocks, might be able to secure such high leverage on ultra-cheap terms (taking account of credit risks) that they could justify aggressively pursuing opportunities in this sector. Private equity owners here, as in the automobile finance or aircraft leasing industries, might look bankruptcy dangers in the face and reckon that they could arrange a good equity-debt swap in such dire circumstances. This confidence may stem in part from the fact that in recent years private equity groups have included affiliates which specialize in buying junk bonds. In principle, these could include bonds issued by the highly leveraged corporate entities put together in buyouts by the same private equity group. Superficially, it does not make sense for the latter to buy such bonds whose sky-high price was the original rationale of the buyout. But perhaps nonsense becomes sense if we realize that the private equity group might be on both sides of an equity-debt swap in the event of a bankruptcy-related corporate reconstruction. In some fields, the equity investor is a state institution enjoying perhaps a quasi-government guarantee, which might not be concerned with equity wealth management in a conventional sense. For example, state-run airlines were avid users of attractively priced leases (where the pricing depended on the ease of the leasers issuing high-risk debt at high prices).

Irrational forces operating in the long-term interest rate market

The corporate sector has behaved during the GME as if the long-term interest rate market has been subject to irrational forces from which it can profit. How else to explain the ballooning of long-maturity corporate bond issuance? Some part of the explanation could be corporates taking advantage of a perceived misalignment between their equity price and the implicit price of equity risk in the market-pricing of their bond issues. (As illustration, the spread of the yield on their bonds over Treasuries of the same security may be smaller than what arbitrage models based on their equity risk premium would suggest). But if that were all, they would swap their bonds issued into floating rate debt which would allow them to lock in low credit spreads without backing the view that long-term rates are fundamentally cheap. In general, this has not occurred.

Instead, many large corporations of prime credit rating have taken the view that long-term (so-called risk-free) interest rates, as benchmarked in say the swap markets, are at cheap levels relative to where fundamentals would justify. And if indeed the corporate decision maker sees this distortion of long-term rates as one key factor in equity market froth, then he or she might hope to limit the exposure of his or her wealth (business value in the case of the owner manager, long–term options in the case of the employee) to a dispersal (of the froth) by issuing long-maturity debt and matching this with short-maturity financial assets. That is not a wholly reliable strategy, as froth dispersal might go along with a sharp decline in long-term fixed-rates (as safe haven demand increases and recession risks weigh heavily).

A subsector of market participants acting in defiance (or more precisely to take advantage) of irrational forces as unleashed by powerful monetary disorder do not neutralize them unless a huge following emerges. Under the GME, these irrational forces have been the key transmission mechanism of the policy – driving long-term rates at times to such low levels as to be inconsistent with any sober weighing up of alternative future scenarios for the path of interest rates over the long run.

You would not know that listening to some of the apologist researchers in the central banks. They would have us believe that all the experiment involves is a shrinking of term risk premiums via central bank balance sheet expansion, without any distortion of expectations (away from rationality) regarding interest rates in the future. But this does not make sense.

The forward interest rates which lie behind the term structure of interest rates usually (in the absence of massive central bank accumulation of long-maturity bonds) are at a positive premium (term risk premium) over the expected interest rate at the relevant future date. For example, if the 5-year US T-bond rate is 1.65%, the 10-year rate at 2.50%, this means the five-year forward 5-year rate is at around 3.35%. A positive term risk premium would mean that the expected 5-year rate in 5 years' time is significantly below 3.35, say 3.15%. That would translate to a term risk premium of 0.20pp. Yet there is no convincing reason in theory why this premium should be positive or fluctuate significantly.

After all, many investors operate within a long-term horizon, and so they are concerned to reduce the potential volatility of what their wealth will accumulate to many years into the future. Such investors have a preference for long-maturity bonds (unless there is so much inflation uncertainty that fixed nominal interest rates translate into highly unpredictable real interest rate equivalents). Some borrowers also have a preference for locking in their long-run cost of financing. But it is not obvious a priori which habitat preference (borrowers or lenders) dominates the term premium in a positive or negative direction. And moreover, very small changes in the premium could be very effective in restoring balance between supply and demand at different maturities.

Now, in principle, if an agency of the federal government, the Federal Reserve, enters the long-term interest rate market as a huge buyer, meaning that it would absorb a significant share of the outstanding stock (of long-term rate exposure), that would put some downward pressure on the term risk premium (either making it less positive or more negative). Yet there is no reason to think the effect would be large (more than a few basis points) if there are many investors who are not strongly attached to one particular preferred maturity (sometimes described as "habitat") in their overall portfolio construction. And even when the Fed completed its balance sheet expansion in late 2014, the central bank was estimated to hold less than 40% of the total stock of T-bonds with a maturity of eight years and more.

There is also a huge volume of long-term interest rate exposure not in the form of US government debt (for example, corporate bonds, dollar bonds issued by foreigners, swap contracts, etc.). Perhaps the whole exposure held by the Federal Reserve is only 20% or less of the total in all forms. The holders of the other 80–90% continuously judge whether in view of their estimation of neutral rate levels and inflation and taking account of their own "preferred habitat" it makes sense to continue holding fixed-rate exposure at the present average maturity they had previously selected. We should also consider the potential supply of long-term interest rate exposure as illustrated above for the corporate sector from corporations or households or institutional investors speculating that long-term rates are unsustainably low.

Some analysts have tried to make empirical estimations of the term risk premium and how this has shifted under the influence of the Great Monetary Experiment. But there are huge question marks concerning these. Estimates of term risk premium are based in part on models which generate expected future interest rates. But how dependable are those models, and do they in particular take account of how expectations about future rates might themselves be influenced by the experiment especially under the influence of irrational forces?

For example, one study found that term risk premiums became significantly negative, perhaps by –25bp in the early aftermath of the Fed's announcement of QE-3 (open-ended purchases of long-term government and mortgage-backed bonds, financed by expanding the Fed's balance sheet) (see Krishnamurthy and Vissing-Jorgenen, 2013). Yet this negative term risk premium estimate would be totally wrong if in fact the launch of QE went along with speculation that the Fed might eventually transition to a programme of stabilizing long-term government bond prices at a high price (pegging long-term rates at an artificially low level) regardless of the state of inflationary expectations or prevailing estimates of the neutral level. Then the term risk premium would still be positive. True, such a programme might be impossible in the long run without triggering hyperinflation, but it could still persist over a period of many years such as to seriously influence expectations of far-out nominal interest rates in the term structure.

Alternatively, the adoption of QE could be viewed in the marketplace as signifying that "the people at the Fed" are genuinely pessimistic about long-run economic stagnation, and many might take note of Fed opinion and lower their own views of neutral level of interest rates in the long run. In turn, there could be a feedback loop from capital gains on long-term bonds to reinforcing such pessimism about long-run economic stagnation. This spreading of pessimism by the Fed, however, could be counterproductive as we have seen in terms of its aim (under the great experiment) to stimulate asset price inflation in the equity market. And so the Fed communications team might choose to emphasize the effect of QE on term risk premiums.

The same study refers to empirical work demonstrating the power of QE to influence long-term rates by focusing on the big price reactions to news about its launching. The problem with such studies is that they may be picking up much front-running by speculators who do not necessarily understand or agree with the economic assumptions of the programme but who believe that many investors will come to do so at which point they can sell out. Specifically, the front-runners may be speculating on the influence of the QE programme just announced on the term risk premium before this could be substantiated in the marketplace by a huge body of non-speculative transactions. But the front-running might not be profitable, and the speculators involved (not necessarily the first or second layer, but the latecomers) might have misjudged the long-run consequences for term risk premiums, expectations of long-run interest rates and other financial market prices.

In effect, it is hard to distinguish the influence of QE on long-term interest rate determination from the influence of all the other elements which go into the GME. One part of this experiment is pegging short-term rates at near zero and encouraging the belief that these will stay there for a long time and then only rise slowly. One method toward this end would be circulating the hypothesis that we are in an age of secular stagnation or disinflation, although this might be inconsistent with stimulating asset price inflation in the equity market. Alternatively, that hypothesis (about secular stagnation) – otherwise described as speculative story – could emerge without the sponsorship of the Federal Reserve and catch on amongst investors suffering from interest income famine and seeking justification for ploughing into longer maturities than normal so as pick up yield. And so the story would stimulate the carry trade from short-maturity government bonds into long-term government bonds, and it would gain plausibility amongst the positive feedback effects from present capital gains (on long-term bonds).

Now, it is possible that at some point the Fed's power to manipulate (downwards) long-term rates as described might suddenly dwindle as many in the market come to fear a big sell-off in the long-term bond market. A trigger could be a run of strong economic data or a sequence of data suggesting that goods and services prices are rising. This could force the Fed into raising short-term rates so as to calm a disorderly market. After all, sometimes markets are more powerful than the Fed. Yet so long as the short and medium-term rates are under the spell of the Fed, this could stimulate irrational behaviour in the long-term bond markets based on an anchoring of rates there to the shorter-term rates. In principle, though, expectations of interest rates many years into the future should be formed without significant reference to where short or medium-term interest rates are in the present.

Indeed, this is a big flaw (from a free market perspective) in short-term rate pegging. It can give rise to irrational forces operating in the longer-term markets (and such irrationality across many asset classes tends to emerge in any case in an environment where rates are below neutral). The danger was not present under monetary regimes where short-term interest rates could fluctuate widely day-to-day, and the monetary system was effectively pivoted on a vast monetary base whose rate of expansion was tightly constrained as under the pre-1914 gold standard and later in the historically brief monetarist experiments in Germany and Switzerland through the 1970s and early 1980s (see p. 152). In the pre-1914 gold standard, day-to-day rates did indeed fluctuate violently, but long-term rates did not thereby suffer from irrational anchoring. By contrast, in the 1920s, when the Benjamin Strong Fed stabilized short-term rates at very low levels (below neutral) and in effect targeted a stable price level even in the short and medium term despite rapid productivity growth, this generated long-term rates which were well below neutral level, and this became a powerful source of asset price inflation.

The power of anchoring effects and direct manipulation of market expectations even without QE can be demonstrated by a comparison of US and European long-term interest rates through the period of the great experiment. For example, in late 2014 long-term interest rates in the core of EMU – the German government bond market – were at around 0.6% whilst US 10-year yields were at around 2.3%, despite the fact that the ECB had not yet embarked on QE in the form of vast accumulation of German and other core government bonds. (Merkel-Draghi QE was eventually unleashed in January 2015).

The dominant factor in these near zero long-term German rates seemed to be the ECB having cut money rates to slightly negative levels, undertaking to keep short-term rates there for a long time, and continually warning about the dangers of deflation in the context of euro-area inflation having fallen more than widely expected to around 0.5% p.a. (as against an inflation target of 2% p.a.). We could hypothesize that sub-zero rates are a powerful catalyst to irrationality in the context of interest income famine, stimulating the carry trade from short-term government bonds to long-term. Many of the traders underestimate risks and chase the speculative stories related to secular stagnation or its equivalent. The ECB's balance sheet had shrunk to around 12% of euro-area GDP, compared to the Federal Reserve's balance sheet at 25% of GDP.

In sum, it is not superficially obvious from the European facts just cited that vastly expanding the central bank balance sheet to accumulate long-maturity government debt is the strongest fundamental component of any central bank strategy to manipulate down long-term interest rates. Of course, we could rescue the importance of QE in lowering long-term rates by hypothesizing that markets were anticipating an early introduction of QE in EMU amidst much media comment to this effect. The official announcement in November 2014 of an expectation that the balance sheet would increase by 1 trillion euros (no firm time limit) added to such speculation. And indeed, it could be argued that in some sense, the ECB was outsourcing QE to the banks by lending them cheap money to buy government bonds. Yet this is implausibly the whole story given the remaining serious doubts about how big any QE programme would be given the strong opposition of the Bundesbank.

Alternatively, (or alongside) the neutral level of interest rates in the euro-area especially at long maturities could be well below that in the US (perhaps because the latter economy was more dynamic or long-run inflation expectations were higher there), even though US QE was nonetheless effective in reducing long-term market rates well below that (higher) neutral level. One element in the higher US inflation expectations could have been QE itself – in that the bloated Fed balance sheet reflecting that institution's huge holdings of long-maturity government debt would make an early return to normal monetary conditions more difficult.

Is Fed quantitative easing a modern version of the Emperor's New Clothes fable?

Indeed, some analysts have hypothesized that the "signalling effects" of a huge Fed balance sheet are more powerful in their influence on markets than the "stock effect" of absorbing supplies of government debt from the market (and thereby influencing term risk premiums). What are the prime signalling effects?

First, a huge holding of government debt in long-term fixed-rate form means that in effect a substantial share of total government liabilities (consolidating the federal government with the Federal Reserve) has been converted into floating rate form. And so any rise in short-term rates has a much bigger negative influence on the federal budget. This means that political factors will weigh more than otherwise on the Federal Reserve's interest rate decisions.

Second, so long as there are huge excess reserves in the banking system, the Federal Reserve cannot drive up money market rates by making marginal changes in the path of monetary base growth. Yes, it could apply the novel tool of raising the interest rate which it pays on excess reserves. But it could prove politically difficult for the Federal Reserve to do this as there could be an outcry against paying huge amounts of interest to the bankers. (Prior to a legal change in 2008, no interest was ever paid on reserves at the Federal Reserve). The Fed leadership could use that political opposition (as in the first signalling effect above) to pursue an unsung agenda of getting inflation for some time above the 2% p.a. mark consistent in its view with 2% p.a. inflation average over the long run (meaning there should be periods when inflation is above 2% as well as below).

Third, the blowing up of the Federal Reserve balance sheet together with the growing importance of the interest rate on reserves as a policy tool would remove the monetary base even further from a pivotal position in the US monetary system. As we shall see later in this book, monetary base must be non-interest bearing if it is to be an effective pivot. The prospect of any return to sound money based on monetary base control and a low expansion rate of this variable – and its corollary of no central bank intervention in the setting of interest rates, short or long – would be virtually unthinkable.

These signalling effects are serious even though markets may take some account of the scenario where the political pendulum swings in the direction of monetary reform – meaning the end of 2% inflation target and the dual mandate and its replacement by a new regime of monetary stability as to be outlined in Chapter 5. A new Fed Chief installed by a politically conservative administration could rapidly slim down the Fed balance sheet by swapping the long-term fixed-rate government bonds into floating rate bonds via an agreement with the Treasury (and do not say this is not legally possible, the law could be changed so as to remove any technical obstacle). The Treasury under an orthodox secretary could set up a long-term programme of raising the share of the debt in the form of long-maturity fixed-rate paper. And the jump in the size of the interest bill could be blamed on the previous administration.

The GME has in part been a modern version of the Emperor's New Clothes fable. The power of the new non-conventional tools to achieve the 2% inflation target under the prevailing conditions of huge monetary uncertainty and real forces downward on an array of prices has been greatly overblown by the architects of the experiment. The widespread acceptance of a rationale for the 2% inflation target in the first place has turned on expert storytelling to audiences, who would admit only in private that that they are unconvinced. Yet the experiment's unleashing of irrational forces on the global financial marketplace is only too real. There is much to fear about the potential long-run consequences as highlighted in the remaining chapters of this book.

A rebuttal of Ben Bernanke's 2015 defence of the Great Monetary Experiment

In March 2015, ex-Fed chief Bernanke published in a Brookings blog a defence of the GME which he had played a large role in designing and implementing (see Bernanke 2015). It got much publicity at the time, much of it sympathetic. Yet there are powerful counterarguments which undermine Bernanke's case. The author published a list of these in a Mises blog (see Brown 2015). The lead charges are that Bernanke does not admit failure of the GME in terms of its originally stated aims and then he weeps crocodile tears for the plight of the small saver refusing to admit that long-lasting interest income famine has been created by Federal Reserve policy not by Mother Nature.

Indeed, Bernanke claims that the GME has been successful despite the non-appearance of strong economic expansion. Small savers suffering income famine right now is not due to monetary policy failure, the ex-Fed chief maintains, but to the harshness of the economic environment which has turned out to be greater that what anyone could imagine (including himself when he boasted to that reporter at his first press conference about proving that "this time would be different"). Now in the midst of the slowest ever economic expansion following the Great Recession, Bernanke boasts that his particular skill was to resist the premature calls to raise short-term rates from near zero, thus preventing a relapse of the US economy.

Amazingly, Bernanke, the notorious advocate of using long-term rates as a policy instrument, now contends that the Fed's power to influence real rates of return, especially long-term real rates, is transitory and limited. The weakness of these instruments, Bernanke tells us, has little to do with the Fed and much to do with the "Wicksellian interest rate" (which he defines as the real interest rate consistent with full employment of labour and capital, perhaps after some period of adjustment).

Hence, the blame for retirees able to obtain only very low rates of return on their savings does not rest with the Fed. Bernanke rejects criticism that he threw seniors under the bus. Rather, he writes:

Indeed, if the goal was for retirees to enjoy sustainably higher real returns, then the Fed's raising interest rates prematurely would have been exactly the wrong thing to do. In the weak but recovering economy of the past few years, all the indications are that the equilibrium real interest rate has been exceptionally low, probably negative. A premature increase in interest rates engineered by the Fed would have likely led after a short time to an economic slowdown and consequently lower returns on capital investment. Ultimately the best way to improve the returns attainable by savers was to do what the Fed actually did: keep rates low (closer to the low equilibrium rate) so that the economy could recover and more quickly reach the point of producing healthier investment returns.

This view that the Fed is not responsible for interest income famine and that it has the small saver's plight at heart faces four main challenges.

First, if the Fed had abandoned its relentless plan to gain 2% inflation and instead allowed prices to fall to a transitorily lower than normal level during the recession and early recovery, savers would have made real gains on their savings even though nominal interest rates would have remained low. In turn, expectations of price recovery further ahead would have stimulated spending both by consumers and businesses. Nominal rates would have remained positive throughout the cycle. Cumulatively, small savers would have been ahead in real terms even though real short and medium maturity interest rates would have been negative during the early expansion phase.

But that didn't happen. Instead, the actual monetary policy of zero rates and inflaming inflation expectations strengthened irrational forces in the marketplace as investors frantic for yield pursued one speculative story after another. In particular, in the early years of the GME, they chased the story of emerging market miracles and most of all a China miracle. Linked to this were claims of an oil shortage and an insatiable demand for iron ore. Commodity extraction industries boomed. Carry trades into emerging market currencies ballooned and fed vast consumer credit and real estate booms across the emerging market world. And here we come to the second challenge to Bernanke's claim (that the Fed is not responsible for interest income famine).

The steep fall of speculative temperatures across those specific asset classes from 2013 onwards (starting with the so-called "Fed taper tantrums") and the related severe slowdown in emerging markets (including China) and the downturn in commodity extraction industries has been an important factor in the decline in Bernanke's "Wicksellian interest rate". And there is another big factor to explain the continuing low rates – the third challenge. This relates to the huge monetary uncertainty which the GME has created. We have already seen how this uncertainty – and in particular the eventual likely end-phase of asset price inflation when speculative temperatures plummet – enfeebles the investment activity in the economy (except in those highly leveraged areas where the cost savings on debt trump other concerns). The weak investment which according to Bernanke explains low real interest rates is actually a direct consequence of the GME.

Finally, many investors suffering from interest income famine have become firm believers in "the secular stagnation hypothesis" to justify their search for yield in the long-maturity US Treasury bond market.

Investors who have convinced themselves about secular stagnation in their bond market strategies are not inclined to embrace long-run economic optimism elsewhere. In fact, their intuitive sense of a "day of reckoning" ahead becomes sharper. This is the fourth challenge to Bernanke's defence and directly links the GME to weak economic outcomes, low interest rates and small-saver blight.

2

How Fed Quantitative Easing Spread Asset Price Inflation Globally

Superficially, when we look at the monetary history of the years following the Great Panic and Recession, it seems that many countries, not just the US, were conducting big monetary experiments, where these involved deployment of non-conventional monetary tools, sometimes including so-called quantitative easing (QE). In fact, some economists including central bank officials have done a cross-sectional analysis on these experiments so as to refine their judgements about the effectiveness of QE in particular (see Gambacorta, 2014). Yet in reality, the experiments have not been independent of each other. The Obama Great Monetary Experiment (GME) plays a dominant role in determining the course and outcomes of all the other experiments.

Fed QE dominates foreign monetary experiments

This dominance of the GME over all other contemporaneous monetary experiments stems from the number one position of the US dollar in the global economy, and on the huge size, in absolute and relative terms of the US economy and US markets. For example, there are many investors outside the US who use the dollar as their primary money. They make their spending and investment decisions based on calculations in which the US dollar is their reference money. And so, these investors are directly affected by US monetary manipulations as described in the previous chapter.

In particular, the huge growth in the Federal Reserve balance sheet, the targeting of 2% inflation, the stirring up of US inflation expectations to match, the attempts of the Federal Reserve to manipulate long-term US interest rates well below neutral level and the assault against mythical deflationary threats have all induced patterns of irrational behaviour amongst such non-US investors. In consequence the reach of the asset price inflation disease (otherwise described as the plague of market irrationality with its source in the GME) is worldwide. Patterns of irrational behaviour emerge in many disparate market-places with investors on the lookout for exciting speculative stories not just in the US and in dollar-denominated paper, but everywhere, including non-dollar paper. And in particular, in the carry trades (whether in currencies, credit or long-maturity interest rates), the weight of dollar-based investors is especially heavy given the overall importance of the US currency.

By contrast, a similar monetary experiment in a small or medium size economy such as the UK has much less powerful effects in stirring irrationality beyond the national frontier. There are not many global investors outside the UK who "dream in pounds". And yes, UK investors might be prompted into irrational pursuit of speculative stories in the outside world (as inside), but they are not of sufficient weight to have much overall market impact (although this could be possible in some small sector where UK investor "taste" was especially important). Of course, they could have considerable influence on real estate markets in the UK if there is a good story there, as they are likely to be of considerable weight there. Their relevance to pricing in the domestic equity market is much less substantial given the greater practical scope for international arbitrage. If it is only UK investors who are wearing those rose-coloured spectacles characteristic of asset price inflation, and they bid up the price of UK equities (if indeed there is a good story there), then non-UK investors in UK equities would liquidate their positions.

In principle, the pursuance of QE and other non-conventional monetary policies by a small or medium size economy might become a speculative story which global investors, especially those based in the dollar, choose to chase (the hypothesis that QE will indeed be a powerful stimulus for the given economy) under the influence of Fed QE. There is not much evidence to support that type of storytelling in the UK equity market though it may well have been a factor – in addition to several others – drawing global funds into the UK real estate markets.

It is certainly plausible that the non-conventional monetary story became one speculative theme attracting global capital into the Japanese equity market (from the launch of Abe economics in early 2013) or into the European equity and high-yield bond markets (from the publication of the ECB's OMT programme to the launch of negative interest rates and on to QE). In any case, the euro-area is the 2nd largest currency zone in the world, and Japan the 3rd largest economy, so it is likely that non-conventional policies in those areas could unleash irrational forces with substantial impact beyond the home jurisdiction, albeit that this extraterritorial influence would be less than for the US case.

How can small dynamic economies fight off Fed QE asset price inflation?

Small dynamic economies can become overwhelmed by the pressure of funds ready to flow in from US dollar-based investors or to a lesser extent from the euro-area or Japan if indeed they have a good speculative story "to tell". Take the example of Israel in the aftermath of the Great Recession. That country's economic concentration on high-tech with a stellar record for innovation and related start-ups became a magnet for investors based in monetary areas afflicted with income famine. In addition to the flow of foreign funds into its equity markets (both public and private), there was the attraction of its currency (yielding positive interest) and its real estate markets (where the speculative story included an influx of affluent immigrants from France and elsewhere). As the currency (the shekel) rose and the real estate market boomed, the notorious positive feedback loops from price action to degree of belief in shaky hypotheses formed.

In turn, exporters in those small countries complain about the oppressive climate of such an overvalued domestic currency. Toward meeting their criticism, the central bank and treasury officials of the small country become inclined (or find themselves coming under political orders) to steer interest rates to a lower level than appropriate to the boom conditions there. This in turn fuels further asset price inflation most of all in the domestic real estate market but also possibly in domestic markets for high-yield credit paper. The cost of this strategy includes the likelihood of asset price inflation eventually turning into its next stage of severe speculative temperature fall, at which point the extent of malinvestment and overinvestment becomes evident amidst much financial distress.

Is there a better alternative path which the small central bank could pursue under those circumstances? One possibility would be to rule out foreign exchange market intervention whilst also holding back from any attempt to manipulate interest rates, short or medium-term, downward by abandoning its normal monetary rule with the aim of depreciating the currency from spectacularly high levels. This is simpler said than done.

In a small open economy, it is not evident that a stable path could be discovered for the supply of high-powered domestic money whose pursuance would mean that markets would efficiently estimate the neutral level of rates and guide market rates in line with economic equilibrium. Indeed, equilibrium in a small open economy against the background of huge monetary disequilibrium in the world's largest economy might be a nonsense concept. In any case, demand for the money and the monetary base in the small open economy might be inherently unstable depending on volatile expectations about exchange rate paths and the fluctuating relative attractiveness of larger monies compared to the small domestic one. The neutral level of interest rates in such an economy might also be inherently unstable and highly dependent on shifting disequilibrium monetary conditions in the large economies and especially the US. Any estimation procedure with respect to a neutral level is especially hazardous in the context of the small open economy.

In general, monetary policy in such (small economically advanced) countries even in a situation of monetary stability in the US (or in the biggest regional economy) is likely to involve in some degree the monitoring of the domestic currency exchange rate against the US dollar (or regionally dominant currency). The determining of the ideal monetary path in the small economy is challenging (where independent money is sustained). In the context of Fed QE, it may make sense for the monetary authority of the small country to lean in the direction of accepting a considerable overshoot of the domestic currency in the exchange markets over the short and medium term (relative to long-run sustainable value) rather than putting up no serious defence against the asset price inflation virus.

In those parts of the export sector not at the forefront of dynamism, the strong currency means diminished profitability or even loss, to which management is likely to respond by cutting wages in local currency terms (although not necessarily in US dollar terms). Domestic prices in general are likely to fall widely (most of all in the traded goods sector). Expectations that these prices would rebound eventually when the US QE experiment ended should mean that modestly positive nominal interest rates would be low or negative in real terms, and these might stimulate non-traded goods and services activity (including construction). Even taking account of the fall in import prices and some domestic prices, real wages in parts of the export sector might fall during this period of US-led global asset price inflation, although there would be expectations of these rebounding when such abnormal global monetary conditions eventually came to an end.

The political pressure from the export sector against such a monetary strategy for resisting the Fed QE asset price inflation virus and in favour of some accommodation (importation of the disease) can become intense. Accommodation means the domestic central bank eases monetary policy so as to restrain the amount of currency appreciation. And we should note that even in the case of no accommodation, there would still be considerable real distortions brought about in consequence of the US monetary disequilibrium. In our example here, a period of suppressed activity in the traded goods sector and overactivity in the non-traded goods sector would be two of the distortions.

Even so, under the monetary policy of resistance (to importing the virus of asset price inflation), domestic investors (including wage earners in the export sectors) in the small dynamic economy can benefit from being able to buy foreign assets with the benefit of an exchange rate cushion. This consists of the eventual likely exchange rate gains (in terms of domestic currency) on foreign assets from a fall back of the domestic currency when US monetary conditions begin to "normalize". This cushion may be an important offset to concerns that so many assets globally are at inflated prices as a result of Fed QE.

Who provides this cushion? It is those global investors operating in the opposite direction. In the example of Israel, the providers would be foreigners pouring funds into its stock market or real estate market at a very expensive level of the shekel. These are wearing rose-coloured spectacles which distort their judgements.

The Israeli corporate sector, including exporters, could gain similarly to households, in making foreign acquisitions with the benefit of an exchange rate cushion. Moreover, the cheap level of foreign exchange might make such acquisitions more affordable (given the limits to corporate size in terms of domestic currency, in this case, the shekel). The cheap level might also facilitate Israeli household purchase of foreign real estate for consumption purposes.

Emerging market economies struggle in their response to Fed QE virus

In fact, it has not just been the small dynamic advanced economies which found they faced unenviable monetary choices in consequence of Fed QE. It has also been large emerging market economies and large advanced economies. A big speculative story in the early years of the GME was that the emerging market world would escape the long convalescence of the large advanced economies from the asset price inflation disease of the 2000s and would outperform these on a secular basis. The new dynamic in the global economy was "convergence" between developing and developed countries.

The biggest emerging market of all is China. The Communist Party's policies of huge increases in state sector (local governments, state enterprises) spending alongside the stimulating of a residential and commercial construction boom in 2009–11 brought passingly strong growth in the Chinese economy (albeit that the data on this is notoriously unreliable, not least because of the high proportion of output not valued at open market prices – for example, the third steel mill when already one is inactive) notwithstanding the Great Recession and its aftermath in most advanced economies. Financial institutions, whether in the official banking system or in the shadow banking system, were the conduits of massive credit expansion to the end destinations of state or private sector borrowers. In principle, all of this went along with a neutral level of interest rates in China, which was surely considerably higher than in the US (where market rates at long maturities were plausibly well below neutral level under the conditions of the GME as we have seen in the previous chapter).

Monetary bureaucrats in Beijing and their communist party bosses, though, could not tolerate the potential scope of appreciation by the Chinese currency were rates in China to come anywhere the plausible level of neutral (hard in any case to make total sense of in the Chinese economy in that it is non-market functioning to such a degree). Well below neutral rates in China fuelled asset price inflation most obvious in the real estate sector and in high-yield credit products. There were many speculative stories for domestic (and international – including Hong Kong) investors to chase. Amidst huge capital gains on real estate and credit, it seemed that these were only too true. This was all against the background of financial repression in which Chinese savers faced severely limited opportunities to earn returns from conventional savings instruments (including bank deposits), further encouraging investors to accumulate savings in the form of real estate or shadow banking products. Chinese hoarded empty newly built apartments like gold bars. In turn, the construction boom went along with much issuance of high-yield paper by real estate companies, much of this in the offshore markets which in turn attracted yield hungry dollar-based investors. Official sales of land became a key source of funds to local governments helping thereby to disguise their weak underlying financial situation.

Even though interest rates on the Chinese currency were well below hypothetical neutral, they were also well above US interest rates. Hence, there was a booming carry trade, much of which was in the form of Chinese domestic corporations borrowing offshore (in US dollars) rather than locally (and evading exchange restrictions by a whole range of devices including "commodity arbitrage"). Foreigners became buyers of yuan in offshore money markets (even though interest rates there were not in line with those onshore and generally below due to the regime of exchange restrictions – but this was far from absolutely effective). The story in this carry trade was that as part of the process of economic convergence the currency of China should continually appreciate in real terms (the so-called Balassa principle). In any case, the continuous friction with the US over China's trade surplus and unfair competition pointed in that direction. This speculative hypothesis was not unassailable (see below). There was a related carry trade in credit where global dollar funds desperate for yield (against the background of the GME) poured into high-yield Chinese debt (much of it issued by the real estate development companies) denominated mainly in US dollars. The Chinese borrower converted the dollars into yuan, running thereby a position in the yuan-dollar carry trade.

The credit and real estate binge in China was going along with an underlying shrinking of that country's trade surplus. Indeed, beyond all the phoney export froth which camouflaged capital inflows (largely related to the carry trade) otherwise impeded by exchange restrictions, it is possible that an underlying trade deficit had emerged. Already large real appreciation of the Chinese currency had taken place over the previous decade. For those investors not irrationally exuberant about the yuan carry trade, the future direction of the Chinese currency could well be toward weakness, possibly precipitous.

After all, the appetite of Chinese for foreign assets if and when the yuan eventually became fully convertible was a huge unknown. And meanwhile, capital flight was immense, especially amidst growing repression by the communist party dictatorship. Beijing's military aggression in the South China Seas raised the spectre of war. In the absence of radical economic and financial liberalization, domestic Chinese assets could be unattractive to international investors if US monetary conditions normalized and yield hunger receded. Before then, evident weakness in the Chinese real estate market and related fear of defaults in China's notorious shadow banking system could scare away the foreign buyers of high-yield dollar paper issued by local borrowers. Elements of this picture had already become evident in late 2014 and early 2015. The officially sponsored bubble in Shanghai equities, though, which emerged in early 2015, muddied the picture.

Elsewhere in the emerging market space, countries largely interdependent with booming China, either via direct trade or via the export of commodities whose price was directly buoyed by Chinese economic conditions and amplified by Fed QE, faced similar monetary dilemmas. How could they build their defences against the asset price inflation disease with its origins in US monetary disequilibrium without inflicting serious pain on their export sectors?

The China "growth miracle" was the big speculative story which accompanied the high speculative temperature in many commodity markets during the early years of the GME (2009–11/12) – including oil, copper and iron ore amongst others. One of the biggest US investment banks created a gigantesque business in marketing commodity index funds as a new asset class (based on so-called diversification properties) to investors who should have known better if their judgement had not been adversely influenced by the GME (which induced huge uncertainty and scare about the extent of future dollar depreciation and US inflation, making the salesperson's pitch for real assets seem sensible).

Examples of emerging market countries which attracted huge foreign fund inflows on the basis of the high temperature in commodity markets alongside Chinese demand included Brazil (iron ore and huge new opportunities in oil extraction) and South Africa. The monetary authorities in those countries, by seeking to contain currency appreciation, ended up fuelling domestic real estate and credit booms.

The same dilemma faced the central banks of small advanced economies featuring important commodity sectors – notably Canada and Australia. These countries attracted considerable direct investment interest from China (especially into the commodity extraction industries) whilst their residential and commercial real estate markets enjoyed high demand from Chinese investors. Their currencies (the Canadian dollar and the Australian dollar) became the end destination of a bulging carry trade as yield hungry dollar, yen or euro-based investors poured funds into those higher-yielding alternatives and bet on continuing currency appreciation as the commodity boom intensified.

The mining and real estate booms in Australia and Canada underpinned short-term and long-term interest rates there at relatively attractive levels. The respective central banks tried to contain the rise in their currencies by restraining the climb in market interest rates. These lagged behind neutral level and so generated a powerful asset price inflation evident in the real estate and consumer credit market.

ECB responds to weak dollar by allowing asset price inflation to spread

Turning to the euro-area, the ECB has claimed persistently throughout its comparatively brief history that it has no exchange rate policy. Yet at times, it has bent its monetary policies in a direction of disequilibrium so as to avoid the euro becoming painfully expensive (for many export industries) at a time when the Federal Reserve is following policies of aggressive ease (so tending to depreciate the US dollar).

One critical period for such activity was during the years 2003 to first-half of 2006 when the Greenspan Fed was manipulating down long-term interest rates (relative to neutral level) by incessantly repeating its mantra according to which short-term interest rates (under its control) would rise at only a glacial pace. In response to dollar weakness, the ECB postponed its start to monetary tightening, and when this got underway eventually in late 2005, it was also at a glacial place. And in early 2003, the ECB had launched its own version of a deflation-phobic inflation targeting monetary framework as designed by Professor Otmar Issing (see Brown, 2014). In consequence, the virus of asset price inflation with its origin in the Greenspan /Bernanke Fed, joined with a distinctively European sub-strain (of virus,) made its deadly attack on the European economy – most strongly in various real estate markets (especially Spain), credit markets (Spanish mortgages) and high-yielding government debt markets (Spain, Italy, Portugal, Ireland, Greece).

Greece was the most spectacular example of asset price inflation, with global investors and banks having poured funds into that country during the early and mid-2000s in pursuit of very modest yield spreads (over less risky assets). It was one thing for the government in Berlin to have decided to go along with Paris's insistence that its Hellenic Franco-phone ally (and buyer of French military supplies) should be admitted to EMU (this happened on January 1, 2001), notwithstanding grave reservations about its financial fitness and possible huge fraud in its national debt and other economic data. A hypothetical Truth Commission would surely find evidence of a grand bargain between Paris and Berlin which included admittance of East European countries to the EU. Sober-rational investors surely should have been making a different type of calculation.

The bursting of that bubble in the euro-area in the form of the sovereign debt crisis through 2010–12 meant that the euro depreciated rather than coming under appreciation pressure during the first few years of the Great Monetary Experiment. This was presumably much to the chagrin of the latter's architects, who as we shall see were prone to welcome (in secret!) the devaluation of the dollar. They had their brief day in the sun when eventually the euro rebounded from Summer 2012 (remaining strong until early 2014).

The launch of a potential programme by the ECB for monetizing the debts of the weak sovereign member countries, approved of by German Chancellor Merkel over the head of her disapproving Bundesbank President, together with the swaggering speech of ECB Chief Draghi ("I'll do whatever it takes to save the euro") coincided with Fed Chief Bernanke's rolling out of the QE infinity programme all in late 2012. Speculative temperatures soared in European credit markets, and the hunt for yield there was on in earnest joined by investors from all over the globe.

Once bombed out asset classes, whether Italian and Spanish government bonds or Spanish and Italian equities, became subject to huge global demand pursuing an array of speculative stories, including Draghi's supposed masterly solution to the euro-crisis, renaissance in Spain (and OECD and IMF lauded labour market reform programme albeit introduced by a corruption-plagued government) and Italy (a young so-called reformist PM who had led a successful Socialist party coup against the old guard). And there was the story of German economic miracle reflecting a boom in exports to China and emerging markets (including energy producers, especially Russia) and a strong construction industry upturn amidst a powerful rise in real estate prices in the major German cities (induced in turn by abnormally low interest rates). Foreign labour was flooding into Germany on a scale not seen since the 1970s.

In early 2014, the new Federal Reserve chair, Janet Yellen, managed to surprise markets about the extent of her dogmatic resolve to pursue the Grand Monetary Experiment considerably further. Her pronouncements came against the transitory background of the US economy weakening amidst a very severe winter. The Bundesbank President (doubtless influenced by current strength of the German economy) seemed to be exercising some restraint on ECB Chief Draghi. And so the euro reached levels (close to 1.40 against the dollar and 145 against the yen), which caused some discomfort in Germany – most of all amongst its exporters.

German growth cycle downturn undermines Bundesbank resistance

Such discomfort grew through Spring 2014 as the German economy was negatively influenced by the slowdown in emerging markets and in particular by the Russia-Ukraine crisis whilst optimism faded about economic recovery in France and Italy. Accordingly, speculation grew that the ECB would soon announce its own version of monetary experimentation whose ostensible justification would be the combating of deflation. Yet again the German Chancellor did not back her Bundesbank President (a practical policymaker who had been her chief economic adviser) in his (less than vigorous!) opposition to "non-conventional policy", most particularly quasi money printing, and sided (weakly) with ECB Chief Draghi.

Much later, at a meeting between the Chancellor and ECB Chief in early January 2015, the die was cast – Merkel-Draghi QE subject to the condition that 75% of the government bonds purchased by the ECB would be parked according to nationality in the respective member central bank balance sheets(for example, Spanish government bonds in the central bank of Spain). Speculation had been rife on such an outcome for many months previously.

For the ECB Chief, as for leading US Fed officials, deflation danger meant a serious risk of a prolonged undershooting of the inflation target (set at 2% p.a.). And according to their logic, if real forces were tending to push prices in say Italy and Spain down relative to in Germany, then the latter country should experience inflation at a rate somewhat above the target inflation rate for the whole euro-area. Accordingly, the ECB under Chief Draghi moved in Summer 2014 toward a radical new policy of slightly negative interest rates and a programme of below-market rate lending to European banks linked supposedly to the growth of their loans to SME; on the assumption that the latter were most probably going to grow in any case, this was in fact a QE like operation in which officially subsidized government bond purchases by the banks were financed by an expansion of ECB liabilities (reserve deposits).

In some degree, the asset price inflation which the ECB's growing use of non-conventional policy tools induced in the form of strengthening the credit market carry trade (out of low-risk into higher-risk bonds in the pursuance of yield spread) into once high-yielding European debt in fact ran counter at first to the aim of lowering the euro. The emergence of a boom in Italian and Spanish government debt together with global capital moving into once regarded high risk European bank bonds made not just a few investors wonder whether there had ever really been a sovereign debt crisis in Europe and whether after all the euro was indeed a fine money. It was all reminiscent of that famous Lowe cartoon published on March 13, 1939, in Punch, where John Bull wakes up from a bad dream wondering whether there was ever that war crisis in the previous September (Munich); two days later Germany invaded the remainder of Czechoslovakia.

Yet as long-maturity yields in the German government bond market started to slide in Autumn 2014 under the influences of first, intensified speculation that the ECB might soon purchase Bunds as a main component of a QE operation (alongside other government debts), second, background desperation at negative short-term rates (which the ECB had introduced in Summer 2014) and third, new evidence of falling inflation amidst stalling economic expansion the euro depreciation (from its highpoint of early Spring 2014) gathered some speed against the US dollar. That market move derived support also from the optimism which was simultaneously building on the US economy as this bounced back from its Winter (2013/14) decline, and the US equity market performed strongly. Looming US economic strength had become the dominant speculative story in this phase of the global asset price inflation even though one chapter in the original version – the unique advantages to the US of the shale oil and gas revolution – had become less convincing as energy prices now plunged.

European deflation battlefield an illusion

Understandably, ECB Chief Draghi did not discuss his non-conventional policy choices publicly in terms of how they might depreciate the euro. Currency wars today are fought by stealth not by a series of declarations. Rather, the chief justified the use of non-conventional policy tools (including negative interest rates) in terms of fighting deflation. That battlefield was illusory.

Draghi and his like-minded fellow officials made much of the decline in prices and even wages now occurring in the member countries which had experienced debt crises (especially Spain, Italy, Greece and Portugal) whilst claiming that for the euro-area as a whole the rise in prices was dangerously feeble (meaning below the 2% p.a. target). Yet the decline in prices in those countries was in effect a long delayed retracement from unsustainable levels (when measured relative to the array of prices throughout the European Monetary Union) especially in the "bubble" sectors during the asset price inflation of the mid-2000s. The construction sector and real estate booms had in turn fuelled a temporary boom in tax revenues which governments deployed towards implementing vast increases in public spending which were unsustainable in a longer term context. All of this went together with a climb of wages and prices in the sectors gaining from the public sector spree.

Euro-officials argued that a decline in wages and prices albeit focused on those once bubble sectors whether in Spain or Italy or elsewhere would intensify bad debt problems and so delay economic recovery. Surely it would be better for Germany to accept a dose of inflation so that prices and wages did not have to fall in the "periphery zone". These officials, even if well-intentioned, were missing from their analysis the costs of inducing monetary disequilibrium so as to boost wages and prices in Germany. That monetary disequilibrium would germinate asset price inflation. The symptoms would show up in the German real estate market or the high-yield European corporate debt market or in an intensification of the carry trade boom into the Italian and Spanish government bond market. Asset price inflation would surely impose heavy economic cost in the long run.

This concern of euro-officials about the difficulties of prices falling in some member countries as part of an overall economic adjustment which requires a shift in relative price levels has been evident since the start of European Monetary Union and especially since Spring 2003 when Professor Issing set out a revised monetary framework of which the centrepiece was a 2% inflation target (defined with respect to the medium-term meaning 2–3 years and with undershoots of target being treated as seriously as overshoots). One main argument for the framework has been that it would be better to have a continuing slow inflation at the level of the euro-area as a whole rather than a flat trend for prices over the long-run so that relative price changes between member countries in line with evolving equilibrium conditions would not require absolute price level falls in any one country.

Indeed, in any monetary area – whether a sovereign state or a collection of sovereign states – if there is heterogeneity in real economic conditions across different regions, there are likely to be divergences also in the behaviour of regional prices. Periods of boom in one region – perhaps due to increased competitive advantage or to relative prowess or to the discovery of new resources or other natural advance – might go along with periods of economic disadvantage in another. And then the situations might reverse.

Yet we do not hear from monetary authorities of large sovereign states a defence of inflation targeting in terms of reducing economic frictions in the process of restoring inter-regional balance in the context of nominal wage and price rigidities downward. Rather, the usual lecture is about how a significantly positive inflation target might reduce the extent to which some wages or prices across the particular political jurisdiction as whole could have to fall in absolute terms.

Why concerns about price and wage rigidities are misplaced

Even so, the ECB's concern about regional price level fluctuations is in part driven by the same pessimism regarding frictions impeding price and wage cuts that influence central bankers in a large sovereign monetary union. As we will see in Chapter 4, such concern is misplaced.

The idea that nominal wages (and in some cases prices) encounter much greater obstacle in moving down than up is a legacy from a Keynesian economic doctrine which jars with an age of the microchip. Here economic agents can check continuously a wide range of simultaneous price and wage behaviour. An increase in economic literacy makes the often transitory experience of wage fluctuations downward understandable generally. The attempt of central banks and the Federal Reserve in particular to stand in the way of this "normal experience" has been a key source of those two monetary diseases – goods and services inflation and asset price inflation.

We should distinguish price and wage rigidities in a cross-sectional sense – when some wages and prices are falling and others rising simultaneously but overall they are flat – and across time when the process of the invisible hands guiding the economy continuously to equilibrium means that wages and prices on average are falling during one period and then rising in another. Is it possible that the challenge of cross-sectional downward rigidities in wages (and sometimes prices) including those that show up as regional differences is greater in a monetary union without political union than for a unified jurisdiction?

That could be the case if the divergences between member countries as regards their political economic environment shift considerably over time as might happen under the influence of evolving national fiscal and regulatory policies. Another source could be flawed central bank policy in the monetary union such as to produce virulent asset price inflation. In particular, the ECB in its policymaking has allowed a more serious form of asset price inflation to take hold than ever experienced when the core European economies outside Germany were monetary satellites of the old Bundesbank following monetarist principles.

The virus of asset price inflation might indeed go along with an intensification of relative price dispersion between countries in the monetary area. By its nature, asset price inflation produces great unevenness in investment spending across sectors and industries and firms, with particular speculative stories (based on particular realities) becoming blown up in significance. And so some regions will find themselves with a concentration of economic activity benefiting from such storytelling whilst others will be less fortunate.

Hence, if the ECB were serious about reducing the potential scope of required relative price adjustment through time in the member countries, it should zealously pursue monetary stability. That means abandoning the framework of inflation targeting.

The folly of "permanent inflation" at 2% p.a.

Some advocates of inflation targeting might retort that it is surely possible to construct a monetary regime analogous to the gold standard world – in which a fixed long-run anchor to prices is replaced by an anchor which drifts by 2% per annum. That does not mean prices rise on average by 2% p.a. over each two- or three-year period. Rather, there should be a widespread expectation that over say a 20-year period it is highly likely that the average annual deviation of the "price level" from a path which climbs at 2% p.a. average will be small. And within a 40-year period, the annual average deviation would be even smaller.

Within much shorter time periods, there should be much scope for variations in the pace of price level rise in line with the efficient operation of the invisible hands steering the economy toward equilibrium. The advocates draw the analogy between this regime of permanent inflation and that of long-run price stability such as occurred under the gold standard. In both regimes, considerable flexibility up and down in the short run is consistent with long-run commitment to a stipulated path.

Let us remind ourselves about the purpose of price level fluctuations up and down through time.

First, during recessions, prices fall to a lower than normal level, and then expectations of their subsequent recovery in an ensuing business cycle expansion mean that real interest rates are negative even if moderately positive in nominal terms. Even without strong expectations of business cycle recovery, some impetus for expectations of prices turning up could come from a mild acceleration of high-powered money growth (see below). The negative real rates which emerge under these conditions are a powerful engine of economic recovery.

Second, a secular rise in savings propensities or shrinking of investment opportunity would similarly see prices coming to a lower level amidst expectations that these would re-bound in the long-run . This could happen in the context of an eventual economic renaissance. Or there could be a step up in the pace of high-powered money expansion. (Under the gold standard, the latter would happen through a fall of costs in the gold mining industry stimulating gold production; under fiat money, in principle the same could come through a constitution which stipulated glacial variations in the pace of high-powered money expansion related to changes in the price level). The expectations of price rebound are positive for economic activity in the present.

Can these stabilizing mechanisms be satisfactorily reproduced in a world where the anchor to prices shifts by 2% per annum?

The notion of a variable pace of price level appreciation relative to a long-run climb of constant gradient is a less easy concept for the public to come to grips with than prices fluctuating sometimes above and sometimes below (for a sustained period of time) a flat guide path. (Note this flat path does not apply to prices calculated with hedonic adjustment to take account of quality improvements but to actual prices as quoted. In the gold standard world, it was these unadjusted prices which had a fixed anchor on average over the very long run). The signals given to spending decisions in the context of a constant long-run climb in prices are correspondingly ambiguous.

It is one thing for a business person to bring forward spending to take advantage of prices which now seem depressed also taking advantage of presently very low nominal interest rates. It is another to bring forward spending because prices recently seem to have been advancing only at say 0–1% p.a., likely meaning that far into the next cyclical upturn the pace of price rise would accelerate transitorily to well above the very long-run trend rate of 2% p.a. Assuming that long-term nominal interest rates are tied to the long-run average gradient of climb estimated financing costs in real terms over several years could be significantly negative.

The reliability of an anchor to prices drifting at a constant rate (meaning for example that these rise at 2% p.a. on average over the very long run) turns in some degree on economic agents (households, businesses) having confidence in the corresponding fixed gradient to the guide path. Armed with such confidence, they form their expectations as to the path of prices and wages over time.

Yes, the monetary authority may be applying rules with respect to high-powered money expansion which should be consistent with this constant drift, but there would be no century-long let alone decades-long proven record to demonstrate this framework is solid and dependable. Indeed, the Federal Reserve has only pursued what economists describe as "monetary base control" for two years (in the early 1980s) out of its entire 100-year history. Officials might claim that their clever use of discretionary tools will mean the 2% inflation path can be secured, but who would rationally have confidence in this claim given the Federal Reserve's record?

Moreover during severe recessions and their aftermath when the neutral level for short and medium-term nominal interest rates may indeed be close to zero or negative, there is not much the central bank can do, given the zero rate boundary to nominal interest rates, to counter a present dip in prices. Hence, a steady drift in the long-run anchor consistent with say 2% p.a. average inflation over the very long run would require some years of fairly high actual inflation in the future. That might not be credible to contemporary decision makers. If it seems that the anchor has in fact become stuck for some time, then the confidence in a long-run fixed gradient to the price guide path would start to weaken.

As a practical matter anyhow, the world has never experienced such a monetary regime in the US or abroad – where there is a dominant expectation over decades that the fixed 2% p.a. price trend will hold. By contrast, there has been a long history under the gold standard of a fixed anchor to prices and the self-recovery mechanisms based for example on pro-cyclicality of prices worked well.

Why would any business person in their right mind trust to a whole generation and subsequent generation of monetary policymakers and their political masters maintaining a very long-run anchor with a 2% p.a. drift? During the periods when hypothetically the rate of inflation accelerated to say 4–5% p.a., who could be sure that this would not become the new norm as monetary policy makers balked at allowing nominal interest rates to rise to near double digit levels at some point?

The monetary uncertainty would be negative for economic prosperity. A fixed anchor to long-run prices is one thing, and this might gain such political attractiveness as to make it unassailable. A moving anchor would hardly captivate any popular imagination.

PM Abe exposes Japan to the Fed QE plague

And yet that (an anchor to prices drifting at 2% p.a.) is just what Japan PM Abe sought to achieve in coming into office at the start of 2013. He "cleared out" the existing leadership of the Bank of Japan (BoJ) which had continued to steer Japan along a stable price anchor path (see Chapter 6). Moreover, the new leadership of the BoJ were not talking about prices rising by 2% p.a. on average over 20 to 40 years as detailed above, but within the next two to three years.

The new Japanese prime minister was not expecting to gain popularity from inflation per se but from the short and medium-term promised spin-offs, albeit at the potential cost of a sub-optimal monetary regime for the long-run. Those spin-offs included an immediate depreciation of the Japanese yen, a powerful rise (in yen terms) in the Tokyo equity market, and a jump in long depressed real estate prices. He and his advisers expected that this combination would stimulate meaningfully the Japanese economy.

The fact that such a monetary programme could become popular in Japan was symptomatic of a desperation provoked by the Great Monetary Experiment. This had had the effect of driving the Japanese yen sky-high – as this was the only currency where so far the monetary authority had kept to the path of orthodoxy since the Great Recession.

In principle, a strong case could be made for Japan continuing to defy the GME and the fellow travelling global members of the central bankers' club, counting on the downward flexibility of wages and prices in the short run to moderate the pain in the export industries whilst providing the springboard for stronger activity in the non-traded goods and services. Japanese investors would meantime have enjoyed the cushion of potential future currency gains to make their acquisition of foreign assets – with the cushion provided by foreign investors piling into the safe haven of the yen and willing to accept inferior returns for that.

The case was not made with any vigour in the Japanese political arena. One reason for this was the psychological impact on the population of the triple disasters of Spring 2011 (earthquake, tsunami and nuclear accident). The DPJ government which broadly favored monetary orthodoxy was widely blamed for incompetence in its response to the emergency. Hence Shinzo Abe and his LDP party won the December 2012 elections with a landslide.

It is not clear whether in the sanctuary of their private office, PM Abe and his chosen BoJ chief Kuroda would have ever conceded that they were piloting Japan into a very sub-optimal monetary regime, but pleading innocence on the basis that GME in the US left them with no alternative choice. (There were alternative choices, as detailed above, but let's say they rejected those for various reasons, whether practical or theoretical). In any case, they never publicly assailed GME. Rather, they asked in public – if the US can follow GME to fight the supposed danger of deflation why shouldn't Japan be allowed to pursue the same path without incurring US or global criticism for manipulating down the yen.

This was not wanton manipulation in any case but an attempt to reverse the driving upward of the yen against the dollar by the architects (and pursuers) of the GME. Again, they made no reference to this in public, wanting obviously to sustain good relations with Washington especially at a time of growing geopolitical danger, particularly with respect to the China Seas. And in Washington there was sympathy for the view that "combating deflation" would strengthen the Japanese economy and allow Tokyo to become a stronger ally in holding the line against Chinese aggression.

The architects of the Great Monetary Experiment were currency warriors in disguise

There had been the same silence and indeed denials from Washington on the whole question of whether the adoption of non-conventional monetary policies (in the years 2009–12) were in fact an instrument of currency policy (otherwise described as dollar devaluation policy). When politicians or central bankers from some emerging market countries (especially Brazil or China) were outspoken about Washington's currency war, officials in the Fed and in the wider Obama Administration would vehemently deny that a purpose of the GME was to devalue the dollar. Indeed, they had the chutzpah to turn the table and blame the complaining countries for taking measures that constrained the rise of their currencies against the dollar, suggesting implicitly or explicitly that these were inconsistent with the general obligation to allow currencies to float freely.

Yet one did not have to go much further than the writings of President Obama's chief architect of the GME to realize that dollar depreciation was indeed a welcome aspect, albeit short run in nature, of its implementation. Professor Bernanke provided an up-to-date summary of his views on this point when he addressed an audience at the London School of Economics in March 2013 (see Bernanke, 2013). There, he took issue with the older literature on "beggar your neighbour exchange rate policies":

> Although it is true that leaving the gold standard and the resulting currency depreciation conferred a temporary competitive advantage in some cases, modern research shows that the primary benefit of leaving gold was that it freed countries to use appropriately expansionary monetary policies. By 1935 or 1936, when essentially all major countries had left the gold standard and exchange rates were market-determined, the net trade effects of the change in currency values were certainly small. Yet the global economy as a whole was much stronger than it had been in 1931. The reason was that in shedding the straight jacket of the gold standard, each country became free to use monetary policy in a way that was more commensurate

with achieving full employment at home. Moreover, and critically, countries also benefited from stronger growth in trading partners that purchased their exports.

The lessons for the present are clear. Today most advanced industrial economies remain, to varying extents, in the grip of slow recoveries from the Great Recession. With inflation generally contained, central banks in those countries are providing accommodative monetary policies to support growth. Today most advanced industrial economies remain, to varying extents, in the grip of slow recoveries from the Great Recession. With inflation generally contained, central banks in those countries are providing accommodative monetary policies to support growth. Do these policies constitute competitive devaluations? To the contrary, because monetary policy is accommodative in the great majority of advanced industrial economies, one would not expect large and persistent changes in the configuration of exchange rates amongst these countries. The benefits of monetary accommodation in the advanced economies are not created in any significant way by changes in exchange rates; they come instead from the support for domestic aggregate demand in each country or region. Moreover, because stronger growth in each economy confers beneficial spill overs to trading partners, these policies are not "beggar-thy-neighbour" but rather positive-sum, "enrich-thy-neighbour" actions.

Where to begin in the critique of those views from the architect of the Great Monetary Experiment? Well, let's start with the history in the first paragraph. On examination this turns out to be historical folklore rather than historical reality.

Architects of GME based their designs on historical folklore not fact

The gold standard world of pre-1914 was not re-established in the 1920s. Rather, at the start of the 1920s, the US alone amongst the big or medium size economies had a gold money (in the sense that gold coins were in circulation and the national money was fully convertible into gold – meaning that the national authorities would pay out gold coin at par against the national currency unit and also mint all gold offered to it into gold coins of given weight equivalent at no charge). The other large and medium size monies were freely floating or dirty floating against the dollar with none convertible into gold.

Then in 1924, the pound was effectively pegged to the US dollar. At the time and in the history books, this is described as the return of the UK to the gold standard, but in fact it was no such thing. Gold coinage had ceased to circulate in 1914 and had subsequently been sequestered by the government for war financing (see Brown, 2014). Given this wartime depletion of UK gold stocks (due to the sequestration described, which extended to gold held by the banks and individuals whether in the form of coin or bullion), the UK was not in a position to restore a gold currency in the pre-1914 sense where the monetary base would be largely gold coins, and its path over time set by automatic mechanisms intrinsic to a global gold coin standard.

Technically, in the 1924 "return of the pound to gold", the UK authorities were obliged to sell 400oz gold bullion bars at a given price in Sterling, and in line with this, the pound could move within a band against the US dollar determined by the so-called "gold points" (if the pound strayed outside these, then a profit could be made from shipping gold between the UK and the US).

Gold stocks (and flows) were not the continuously dominant element in determining the monetary base in the UK after its "return to gold" or in the bloc of countries whose currencies were fixed to the dollar or to gold. Rather, monetary base growth in the UK was determined by the Bank of England, albeit subject to the constraint of maintaining the fixed link of Sterling to the US dollar (the gold points which limited the band of fluctuations for that exchange rate could move around very slightly depending on relative tightness of gold markets in the US and UK or elsewhere). When the pound came under attack, gold arbitrage outflows as described (via 400 oz. gold bars) could cause the Bank of England to slow the growth of or reduce the stock of high-powered money.

In the US also, for different reasons, there was no continuous strong link between the stock of gold and the supply of high-powered money (monetary base) as had been the case pre-1914. There was normally such a surplus of gold over legal requirement that for most of the time, the growth of high-powered money was set implicitly by policy decisions of the Federal Reserve (which on occasion used aggressive open market operations in this connection).

In 1924, Germany linked its currency to the US dollar in accordance with the so-called Dawes Plan concluded in the aftermath of the hyperinflation. In 1926, France "returned to gold", but at a par for the French franc which meant that this was now worth only 20% of its 1914 value. As with the UK, this was not essentially a return to a gold coin standard, although there was a small continuous issue volume of the high-denomination "Poincare gold coin". Japan "returned to gold" in early 1930, but left a year later.

The political will in the UK to defend the new regime of a paper pound (albeit with a gold bullion window) fixed to the US dollar was never strong and continuously sabotaged by the polemics of John Maynard Keynes. It is understandable that the paper pound camouflaged as gold never found great popular appeal.

The automatic mechanisms of the gold coin standard which depend on a large and stable demand for gold reserves by the banks and gold coin by the public did not function such as to silently sustain the pound dollar exchange rate within its gold points. Instead every change in interest rates for that purpose became an issue of political conten-tion. The widespread lack of conviction about the future of the fixed parity between the pound and dollar interest rates (both short and long) meant that UK prices (including wages) did not adjust flexibly down-ward to a level consistent with internal and external balance for the UK economy as would have been the case under the pre-war international gold standard.

It was this uncomfortable and economically damaging hybrid pound regime which came to an end in September 1931. The political will just did not exist to raise interest rates in the midst of the German and mid-European debt crisis (with UK banks big lenders there) to defend the pound dollar parity. The mark dollar regime had effectively crumbled a month earlier when Berlin imposed exchange restrictions on capital outflows in the context of a collapsing banking system. The official mark dollar rate remained unchanged, but this was no longer a free market price. German "liberation from gold" meant a descent into Nazi economics.

In France, meanwhile, the link of the currency to gold was no constraint on the ability of the authorities there to allow monetary conditions to remain very easy as the Great Depression formed in the world outside given the huge stock of gold and dollars which the Bank of France had amassed given the stabilization of the franc at such a cheap devalued level back in 1926.

The US remained on a full gold coin standard until President Roosevelt took office in March 1933. Yet the Federal Reserve had ample scope under that regime to have pursued an aggressive expansion of its monetary base as Milton Friedman and Anna Schwartz have demonstrated (see Friedman, 1963), albeit that a potential limit could have been imposed by France were that country to have insisted in converting its massive dollar reserves into gold (never plausible despite some bluster). In the wake of the Roosevelt Administration "liberating" the US "from the gold standard" – an action which included almost doubling the yellow metal's official US price – the monetary base of the US grew exponentially from 1934 in view of massive gold inflows (the US Treasury stood ready to buy all gold offered to it from outside the US at the official price, albeit that private gold holdings had been made illegal within the US). These came mainly from France and the remainder of the gold bloc in Europe (which did not break up until Summer 1936), whose currencies had experienced effectively a big revaluation against the US dollar in consequence of the rise in the official US gold price.

That swamping of monetary base – an early widely unrecognized example of monetary experiment very similar to the Obama GME – generated a powerful asset price inflation which culminated in the Great Crash and Great Recession of 1937–38 as we shall see in Chapter 7. What Bernanke describes misleadingly as the "US liberation from gold" by the Roosevelt Administration was no such thing, and whatever its name, it did not have a happy ending even in the context of the contemporary business cycle.

Phoney "monetary liberation" claims by the chief architect of Fed quantitative easing

If Bernanke had been telling history rather than historical folklore, the Federal Reserve was "liberated" from the gold standard not in 1933 or 1934 by President Roosevelt but within a few months of opening its doors in Summer 1914. The founders of that institution had in mind the continuation of a monetary system where high-powered money in the US or internationally was determined by the automating functioning of a global gold standard as known at that time not by the discretionary judgement of officials whether targeting prices or employment or both.

It seems that the leading officials in the Federal Reserve at that time did not realize that liberation had taken place and continued to behave as if nothing had happened, allowing massive gold sales by Britain (to finance its participation in the Great War) during the US period of neutrality (up until March 1917) to passively swell the monetary base and create virulent inflation (both goods and assets) (see Brown 2014). Having passively ploughed on with rapid monetary expansion even after the end of the war for a further year (made possible under its then rules of operations because of huge excess gold position in its balance sheet) and then suddenly stopping (due to concern about the extent to which the excess was dwindling), the consequence of which was the Great Recession of 1920, the Fed then started to construct a policy framework for its new liberated condition. Effectively it pursued price level stability despite an economic miracle featuring rapid productivity growth putting downward pressure on prices. The result was the Great Asset Price Inflation of 1924–29 – the root cause of the Great Depression about which Bernanke is strangely silent.

Bernanke's folklore about the Great Depression and the "liberation from gold" mutates into illusionism about the Great Monetary Experiment. Essentially, this chief architect maintains that radical monetary policy in the US and in other countries may have caused a sequence of temporary large currency devaluations which could have brought some passing short-run benefits at the point of implementation. But in the bigger picture, Bernanke claims that the combination of all countries jettisoning monetary orthodoxy and joining in the GME (adopting various versions of QE or non-conventional policy tools) benefited everyone.

A first critique is the phoney egalitarianism. This was no case of countries of equal economic size deciding independently to free themselves from "the yoke of monetary orthodoxy". This was the US giant deciding to initiate a GME which presented a huge dilemma to a host of economies whether in the emerging market world or amongst the most highly developed. Did they remain on the path of orthodoxy and suffer a big appreciation of their currencies or did they reluctantly fall into line and either corrupt their own monetary principles or follow the same path as the case may be, acknowledging sometimes that there were likely huge long-run economic costs for doing so.

A second critique is that the "freedom from the yoke" in the case of the US was spectacularly unsuccessful in stimulating economic expansion. The Obama GME has gone along with the slowest economic recovery ever recorded from Great Recession as we saw in the last chapter.

Rather than accepting the Bernanke fairy tale of countries one by one resolving to join the GME and everyone becoming better off as a result, the astute monetary student of the 2009 Great Recession and its aftermath should consider an alternative narrative. The Obama Federal Reserve embarked on QE first in 2009 knowing full well that this would most likely trigger a devaluation of the dollar which should stimulate the US economy for some time. The devaluation, though, might well not endure as other countries felt constrained to introduce similar policies.

There most likely was some considerable disappointment within the chief architect's inner circle about the failure of the dollar to fall against the number two currency in the world, the euro, on account of the eruption in EMU of the sovereign debt crisis. And the chief architect joined with other officials in the Obama Administration in persuading "the Europeans" to take policy paths which would salvage EMU and bolster the euro rather than decide to break up their monetary union which could mean a global strengthening of the US currency. Bernanke and his co-officials within the Fed and the White House were also paranoid about a crisis of EMU becoming another Lehman crisis.

The phase of high speculative temperatures in commodity markets

Whilst Professor Bernanke and the White House may have been frustrated by the European obstacle to dollar devaluation, they showed no concern about the extent of speculative temperature rise which was occurring simultaneously in commodity markets and in asset markets related to emerging markets (see p. 43). Superficially, the high economic tides there, reflecting the speculative fever infecting those countries, were arguably of some stimulus effect for the US – first of all, through lifting demand for US exports and second, through buoying the US equity market where profits from emerging markets are an important source of overall earnings.

The counter argument is based on several observations. The commodity price speculative fever which accompanied China and the wider emerging market asset price inflation squeezed real disposable incomes in the US and so undermined the recovery in consumption. The fever also induced mal-investment or overinvestment into commodity extraction industries and more generally emerging market investments (including real estate and consumer credit). This mal-investment and overinvestment was doubtless exacerbated by the rising speculative temperatures in the high-yield credit markets through which much of this was financed. Although all of this may have provided some short-run economic stimulus in the US, would it not have been better to have allowed global spending to have taken a more efficient path with less waste even if this meant a slower upturn in global profits of US companies? And alongside this question, there is the issue of the boom which was developing in the US shale oil and gas sector and related sectors – driven in part by the sky-high energy price and the asset price inflation in the high-yield credit markets. In itself this could be counted as a stimulus but at what future cost in terms of mal-investment.

Shareholders in those companies whose revenues were buoyed by this stage of asset price inflation disease should not have expected this to last through all the future stages and would not react well (in terms of implication for the share price) to management who took the cue from this to plough funds into long-gestation investment especially within the US rather than paying out higher dividends or buying back equity (see p. 24). Indeed, business investment in the US arguably experienced less dynamism than otherwise as investors put some considerable probability on an eventual bust in those emerging market economies now enjoying the heat of speculative fever and in any case realized fully the long-run monetary uncertainty also afflicting the US economy in consequence of the GME. At a geopolitical level, GME added to the dangers by lavishing fantastic revenues (from high commodity prices, especially oil) on a range of ugly political regimes from Russia to Latin America to the Middle East. Lofty land and real estate prices together with high commodity prices generated high levels of economic rents – the fuel of crony capitalism – internally in the emerging market world.

In hindsight, we can now say that a range of commodity markets peaked in late 2011 or early 2012, although there was no immediate plunge. The China economic boom (in terms of growth rate) also peaked around the same time. The real estate and credit boom in emerging markets continued in many cases though some deceleration was perceptible ahead of the QE tapering tantrum of Spring and Summer 2013. Before then, by late 2012, the QE asset price inflation fever had spread to various markets in the euro-zone (once high-yield sovereign debt, bank debt, equities) and Japan (equities) as well as infecting important segments of the US market (high-yield corporate debt, private equity, momentum stocks including biotech and social media). The range of speculative stories in the euro-zone and Japan have already been outlined, including Draghi's "solving of the EMU crisis", German mini-miracle, Southern European renaissance and in Japan there was the promise of Abe economics and national reawakening.

The plague of market irrationality moves into a new stage 2012/14

In the US equity markets, there were the stories emanating from Silicon Valley, the explanations for the boom in financial sector profits (in fact strongly connected to the private equity, mergers and acquisitions and ultimately driven by the same desperation for yield amidst monetary disequilibrium as described already for so many markets). Meanwhile, the carry trade in high-yield corporate credits across the globe boomed. A frequently told big speculative story was the amassing of huge riches, in many cases stemming from vast global monetary disequilibrium and related asset price inflation, in "grey" areas of global finance.

The owners of this wealth were desperate for safe havens where growingly intrusive national tax authorities (in particular the IRS or European fiscal authorities) either acting on their own or together could not penetrate. Any asset class said to be in strong demand from the new hoards of grey and black money around the world enjoyed a speculative halo. Examples include top-end real estate in metropolitan centres where the local authorities appeared not to cooperate seriously with the OECD-orchestrated pursuit of grey funds. Another sub-plot in this big speculative story was the role of Chinese and Russian elites scurrying ill-gotten gains out their country of origin and finding havens where these could not be traced or frozen (whether by the country of origin or the host country).

All such speculative stories contained important grains of truth. At issue in the diagnosis of asset price inflation is whether monetary disequilibrium around the globe (as led by the Federal Reserve) was causing many investors to be putting an irrationally high probability on the "lead scenario" (or speculative story) turning out to be reality. If indeed asset price inflation were present then at some stage in the future, there would most probably be a plunge in speculative temperatures due either to an ending of the Obama GME (reversal of QE and phasing out of other non-conventional tool use) or to a discrediting of the various speculative stories by harsh contradictory reality (or by some combination of these two).

It would be likely that as the asset price inflation progressed, there would be a period during which speculative temperatures started to fall (sometimes violently) in some asset classes whilst simultaneously rising in newly infected asset classes. Further ahead, there could be a more general and violent fall in temperatures across all hot asset classes leading on to Great Recession.

At the time of writing (early 2015), the progression of the asset price inflation disease is largely a matter of conjecture. From 2013 onwards, there has been some evidence of plunges in speculative temperature in some asset classes – starting with the emerging market currencies, for example, in Summer 2013. This particular plunge was in part related to the arrival of evidence suggesting that the Chinese economy was indeed cooling and possibly headed for a "hard landing", and also that serious slowdowns were occurring across several large emerging market economies (also including danger of real estate and credit busts).

A serious slowdown in many emerging markets became more recognizable through 2014 including not just China but Russia, Brazil, and

Turkey. In China, a lead story was the downturn in the real estate sector and related construction activity. More generally, across many emerging market economies, there had been a vast boom in real estate and consumer credit during the early years of Fed QE under the impetus of huge pressure from carry trade related capital inflows. A widespread bust was not yet evident outside China, but there was widespread pessimism at last that Brazil and Turkey in particular were headed to that destination. Indeed, some commentators raised the possibility that the looming speculative bust in Turkey would send greater shock waves through global markets than any new developments in the long playing Greek sovereign and bank debt crisis. Elsewhere, speculative temperatures in the commodity space plunged, bringing for example iron ore prices to one third of their 2011 peak by early 2015. From Autumn 2014, oil prices joined the downturn. Previously hot equities in the commodity extraction industries fell sharply as did the commodity currencies.

The middle stage of asset price inflation disease includes some market busts

It is a familiar feature in the progression of the asset price inflation disease that well before a general late stage is reached speculative temperatures fall in some markets infected early on whilst at the same time they continue to rise in markets infected later or as yet not infected.

For example, back in the Great Asset Price Inflation of the mid and late 1920, the Berlin stock market (arguably the biggest "bubble") already burst in 1927. Also in that year, the Florida land bubble burst whilst the following year domestic US real estate markets peaked in general. Alongside the speculative temperature in Wall Street equities continued to soar.

More recently, in the asset price inflation of the mid and late 1990s, the emerging market bubble including South East Asia and Russia already burst in 1997–98. Speculative temperatures continued to soar in the IT equity markets and some high-yield credit markets (think of Enron and Worldcom) for another two years or more.

In the next episode of asset price inflation disease (2003–08), big quakes had already occurred in the sub-prime and other high-yield credit markets in Summer 2007, and yet in early 2008, there was a spike of speculative temperatures in the commodity markets and most of all oil. It is only in the final deadly stage of the disease that speculative temperatures are falling everywhere.

In the plague of market irrationality with its origins in Fed QE, the same pattern seems to be occurring. It is still a matter of conjecture at the time of writing (April 2015) whether the bubble in the Shanghai equity market, which seemed to emerge in early 2015, is similar in timing (with respect to the course of the disease) to the oil bubble of early 2008.

In Spring and Summer 2014, the Draghi ECB's new journey into unconventional monetary policy (small negative interest rates, renewed balance sheet expansion) stimulated a new wave of carry trade business, although this petered out soon in some important emerging market and commodity currencies, given the gathering pessimism about emerging market economies and commodity markets. Very likely, the ECB's actions also helped sustain high temperature across an array of high-yield credit markets globally and in the periphery euro-zone government bond markets. It may also have contributed to the high temperatures in the US equity markets.

Negative interest rates, the new element in the ECB's monetary experiment which had not been tried in the US (or Japan), may have had a more powerful effect on strengthening irrational forces in the global markets than the tiny drop below zero might have suggested. It could be that zero is a key benchmark to cross in explaining how mental processes veer away from sober rationality.

The counterpart to the ECB embarkation on its new journey – in response to growing evidence that the hoped-for European economic recovery had stalled – at the same time as the Federal Reserve was halting further expansion of its balance sheet amidst evidence of apparently stronger economic activity brought a powerful rise of the US dollar. This got more impetus in November 2014 from the Abe BoJ doubling down on its QE policies.

A powerful rise of the dollar underscored by a relative and sometimes absolute tightening of monetary conditions in the US has been a theme of previous mid or late stages of the asset price inflation diseases (always with their origin in the Federal Reserve), although they may predate the final stage by a long and variable lag. In the case of the plague of market irrationality with its origin in Fed QE, we could say that the dollar strengthening and accompanying monetary shift got under way already in Spring 2013.

That is when the GME architect-in-chief Bernanke announced the plans for a tapering of Fed QE (meaning a slowdown in the rate of balance sheet expansion) to start soon, contingent on incoming economic data. The tapering started in fact at end-2013 just prior to the architect's retirement.

Beyond the Emperor's New Clothes moment

The announcement of Spring 2013 – that Fed QE could start to be tapered from the end of that year – turned out to be the "Emperor's New Clothes moment" in the long-term US interest rate market. The conjurer architect-in-chief had told all that the power of the QE weapon was measured by the size of the bond inventory held by the Federal Reserve. According to the tapering statement, inventory would remain huge and indeed continue to grow for some considerable time further.

A big and sudden decline in the price of long-maturity US T-bonds revealed to investors that the Fed's QE tool was not all that its architect had boasted. Maybe after all the manipulation of long-term rates on a sustained basis was not possible, and the chief architect's defiance of past conventional wisdom including Paul Volcker's observation that "he couldn't outsmart the markets" was just posturing.

This moment did not mean that the US monetary forces essential to the spread of the QE plague had become impotent, but they did lose some considerable effect. The situation where forward-forward interest rates in the US term structure beyond five years were barely above 2% and substantially negative in real terms (given the inflaming of inflation expectations by the contemporaneous surge of speculative temperatures in commodity markets) had fostered much of the frantic "search for yield" and had powered the capital gains which were intrinsic to the positive feedback loops sustaining a succession of speculative stories.

Yet short-term rates in the US still were pinned at close to zero by the Obama Fed, and this made clear that the rise of these from zero would be slower than glacial. A regime of zero short-term interest rates is an abnormality; it never occurred in the context of the gold standard.

And so the Fed's tapering of QE, completed in Autumn 2014, was accompanied at its start by a victory for market forces in the determination of long-term forward-forward rates but not in the markets for spot short and medium-term rates. Even so, how did these far-off forward-forward rates remain so low by recent historical standards, and why did they actually decline substantially through 2014 (with the five-year forward five-year rate in the US Treasury market falling from a peak above 4% at the start of that year to around 2.4% by February 2015)?

A first explanation is that the GME had in fact so lowered confidence in the long-run future amongst business decision makers and their shareholders (all concerned at the dangers of the final phase of the asset market inflation disease which would emerge at an uncertain date) that the neutral level of interest rates in real terms was now indeed abnormally low. The simultaneous slowdown in the emerging market economies and the evaporation of apparent investment opportunity there (amidst some degree of asset price deflation) also played a role (see chapter 1).

A second explanation was a decline in inflation expectations prompted by evidence both from Europe and the US that actual inflation was undershooting significantly projections. Indeed, consistent with this explanation was the fact that real yields in the inflation-indexed US T-bond market remained significantly positive and well above their previous low points (substantially negative) back in 2012. A key fact in this undershoot could have been the powerful real forces bearing down on prices (including wages), some related to the nature of present technological change. This latter was fuelling the supply of unskilled or low skilled labour as many previously skilled individuals found their human capital destroyed by the progress of intelligent machines and other forms of digitalisation (some of which facilitated substitution of cheaper labour in the emerging markets for onshore labour).

Unlike in the second industrial revolution when low or unskilled workers from the South of the US could move North and undergo training to join the high-paid assembly lines in the automobile industry, the present era of technological change was much more elitist, fanning the rental income of human talent with no quick and easy advantage for broad segments of the labour market. Yes, the invisible hand did a great job through 2014 in producing a bulge of low paid low productivity jobs for the mass of labour whose human capital had been eroded by mal-investment of the previous cycle or the nature of present technological change and for the individuals affected by the elimination of long-term unemployment benefit at the end of 2013. The pity was that monetary uncertainty had so maimed the forces in the capitalist economy which would generate a powerful upturn in business investment (see p. 23) that real living standards stagnated at best.

A third explanation was that the GME by ultimately bearing down on the neutral level of interest rates in the various ways described here – in particular by having created so much pessimism about the looming final stage of the asset price inflation disease – had eliminated the prospect of nominal interest rates falling far if at all below neutral level given the zero rate boundary. Yet it is the divergence between those two for short or medium-term maturities which is a deep root of monetary inflation, especially goods inflation (asset price inflation more sensitive to long-maturity divergence).

A fourth explanation was the launch of negative interest rates by the ECB in Summer 2014 and the related plunge in long-term European interest rates. This triggered a strengthening of irrational forces also in the US long-term rate market as European investors sought a way out from income famine. They were joined by Japanese investors alarmed by the Abe-Kuroda's intensification of quantitative easing in Autumn 2014. In rational mode European and Japanese investors would not have turned to speculating heavily on the long side of far-out forward-forward US interest rates as would occur in strategies involving the purchase of long-maturity US Treasuries, for example, rather than taking say short positions in the far-out euro forward-forward rates or simply taking no position at all. Most plausibly, the purchase of Treasury debt would take place on a currency hedged basis, otherwise the investors in question would be assuming huge currency risk in their scramble to escape European or Japanese interest income famine. And indeed, it is not evident at all that the amount of new demand from Japan or Europe for long US Treasuries was substantial as a proportion of the total stock of actual or potential long-term interest rate exposure in US dollars (whether in Treasuries, swaps or other paper). It could be that the story about Japanese and European demand based on present flows gained an exaggerated importance in the market-place influencing expectations beyond the limits of rationality as occurs in monetary disequilibrium.

The plunge of oil prices in late 2014 did generate some optimism in economic and market commentaries based on a boost to consumer spending and business investment which could drive up the neutral level of interest rates in real terms. According to simplistic Keynesian narratives, the gainers from the price plunge (most of all consumers) would increase their spending by more than the losers (OPEC, Russia and more generally those sharing in oil producer wealth including, for example, US households whose main source of wage income was in the shale oil and gas industry) would cut back theirs at least in the short or medium term. Such narratives, though, lacked plausibility.

In the past, oil shocks and reverse-shocks had tended to be at most small components in a much bigger economic story. Even the biggest shock – the jump in prices during late 1973 and early 1974 – was a sideshow in the unfolding Great Recession of 1974–75. That economic downturn and the accompanying great asset market crash was the end phase of a powerful asset price and goods inflation disease which had been long in the making (from the early-mid-1960s onwards) and intensified under the rule of the Nixon/Burns Federal Reserve.

Uncertain arithmetic as to effects on aggregate demand at a global level palled in economic significance compared to the revelation of gigantesque mal-investment in the energy sector and related sectors this time round. And in any case, economic theory would suggest that if consumers regarded the oil price plunge as transitory, they would not adjust spending by much. The plunge in the oil price indicated that there had been much irrational exuberance regarding the potential profit from capital spending in energy extraction and likely in much energy-saving activities. Desperation for yield and associated high temperature in high-yield credit markets had contributed to the mal-investment (with private equity and high-yield credit finance playing big roles in the commodity extraction boom in particular).

Back in 2010–12, marketing commodity funds to investors (in which oil was a large element) on the basis of the speculative story of a super cycle in commodities, huge growth ahead in emerging market and especially Chinese demand, alongside dubious "thought pieces" on how investors should hold a permanent significant share of their portfolios in these (commodity funds) toward achieving more efficient overall diversification, had been big business for several leading Wall Street firms. Positive feedback loops seemed to justify those hypotheses and make business decision makers in the commodity (including energy) extraction business more confident in bullish long-run price projections.

If market signalling in capital markets had not been so distorted by the GME then surely the invisible hands would have done a much better job of stimulating entrepreneurship and deploying funds into projects which on sober assessment would have been superior (in terms of likely investment outcome) and at a macroeconomic level gone along with higher productivity growth. Yes, some consumers might use their income bonus (from lower gas prices) on filling up their cars to buy an iPhone or more modestly a cup of coffee. But the wealth of nations depends on savings, entrepreneurship, risk-taking, growth in the forest of investment opportunity and the avoidance of squandering scarce capital (as in the oil bonanza) not on such transitory blips in consumption.

The revelation of mal-investment might well be followed by emerging strains in the global financial system as bad debts piled up related to the oil market bust. And it could jump-start investors and commentators becoming more conscious of other potential areas of mal-investment which could end up badly – whether the automobile sector boom in which the private equity run (and financed with high-yield credit) subprime credit financiers were playing such an important role, the vast construction booms across the emerging market world or the aircraft boom (Boeing and Airbus) fuelled by ultra-cheap leasing terms available courtesy of the high-yield credit markets and so on. A plunge in a key price (energy and energy investment) which so many investors had regarded as almost certain to remain at high levels could undermine their confidence in other prices, especially in asset markets, where there had been similar consensus on the justifications for sky-high valuations based on popular speculative stories. There was no evidence of such contagion by Spring 2015. Indeed a wave of speculative funds into oil-related investments (futures, equities, high-yield credits) had developed causing their price to re-bound substantially from their late 2014 lowpoints. Pessimists saw a repeat of the normal pattern in speculative markets for bottom-fishers to enter prematurely. Interest income famine as generated by the continuing GME could be accentuating that pattern. The most spectacular example historically of badly timed bottom-fishing had been the huge re-bound of Wall Street in the first few months of 1930 following the Crash of the previous Autumn – only to be followed by a much more devastating collapse.

3

A 100-year History of Fed-origin Asset Price Inflation

Great monetary experiments in the US did not start under the Administration of President Obama. In the 100-year plus history of the Federal Reserve, there have been several big experiments, although arguably these were not launched with such deliberation. Often the lead actors did not even realize that they were designing or administering an experiment. The triggers to experimentation have included transition from peace to war or war to peace, Great Depression, and public dissatisfaction at economic outcomes (high inflation, weak and volatile growth) for which monetary policymakers have been held responsible by the American public and their elected representatives.

Historical irony

The historical irony in all of this is that the founders of the Federal Reserve did not imagine that the new institution would be responsible at all for setting up a monetary framework or implementing a monetary policy, let alone pursuing monetary experiments. They assumed that the US would continue to "enjoy" a monetary environment defined by the functioning of the international gold standard in which London was the "leader of the orchestra", and the global growth of high-powered money was determined to a large extent by above ground stocks of gold.

Milton Friedman in his "A Program for Monetary Stability" (1960) described the pre-1914 monetary situation of the US as follows:

> A small country on a commodity standard that is common to much of the rest of the world – or, what is economically the same thing, that seeks to maintain fixed-rates of exchange between its own currency and the currencies of most other countries – has little leeway with respect

to internal monetary policy. Its stock of money must be whatever is required to maintain external equilibrium. Internal policies and events affect internal monetary conditions primarily through their effect on the demand for and supply of foreign exchange and hence on the behaviour of the stock of money that is required to maintain external equilibrium. For most of the period prior to World War 1, the US was in that situation. Since World War 1, the situation has been very different.

Indeed, when the Federal Reserve Banks opened their doors for business in mid-November 1914, the Great War had already started. The Federal Reserve Act had been signed into law by President Wilson the previous December. Friedman maintained that during the war years (including both the period of US neutrality and then its participation), the creation of the Federal Reserve made little if any difference to the monetary outcome compared to what would have happened under previous institutional arrangements. Only in the immediate aftermath did a big difference first emerge:

> The expansion of the money supply during the active phase of the World War I requires little attention: until our entry into the war it was produced by the gold inflow from the belligerents to purchase war supplies, thereafter, by the use of the equivalent of the printing press to finance some war expenditures. Up to late 1918 or early 1919 the experience was the same as in earlier wars and the existence of the system made little difference to the general course of events. But then a difference emerges. In earlier wars, prices reached their peak at the end of the war, when government deficits were sharply reduced or eliminated. They would have again if the system had not been in existence. As it was, the mechanism developed to create money for government use continued to operate even after government deficits came to an end. Under Treasury pressure, the Reserve System maintained re-discount rates at their wartime level. From early 1919 to mid-1920 the money supply rose by over 20% and prices by nearly 25%. This post-war rise in money and prices would almost certainly not have occurred under the earlier system.

The origins of the great goods and asset price inflation 1915–19

There are two big caveats about Friedman's "the Fed made no difference until early 1919" case. The first is that the administration and Wall

Street's ability to facilitate the flow of finance to the Entente would have been highly constricted in the absence of backdoor support (via trade acceptances and bills eligible for discount) by the newly created Federal Reserve. The second is that all of the leading officials within the Fed, whatever their divergent views on the first point (financing the Entente), were united in welcoming the accumulation of gold on their new institution's balance sheet (for their reasoning, see p. 79). This ruled out an alternative policy, which might have been adopted otherwise (in the absence of the Fed) – the suspension of official gold purchases – and which could have arrested the growth of high-powered money during the period of neutrality.

During the crisis of late July 1914, in the days immediately before the eruption of war in Europe, it had been the dollar itself which was most under pressure, as US businesses, active in international trade, could not renew trade credits in the London market; thus, they had to obtain funds from the US and convert these into Sterling for the purpose of repayment. Amidst a crisis of liquidity and gold loss, Treasury Secretary McAdoo, in close consultation with the New York Federal Reserve President Benjamin Strong, ordered the closing of the New York Stock Exchange (which lasted eventually for three months) and took emergency measures so as to prevent any formal suspension of the dollar's convertibility into gold (see Silber, 2007). McAdoo prevailed against the contrary opinion of Secretary of State Bryan, a powerful figure on the liberal wing of the Democratic Party, who had argued in favour of an immediate suspension of the gold standard. (Bryan had critically swung his supporters behind the nomination of Woodrow Wilson as presidential candidate at the 1912 Democratic Convention; in 1913, he had provided essential support to the Federal Reserve Bill in its passage through Congress). McAdoo and Strong saw continued gold convertibility of the dollar as essential to building up New York as a great financial capital in competition with London.

Benjamin Strong stemmed from the Morgan empire, having been the right-hand man of J.P. Morgan during the 1907 financial panic. Morgan later put him at the head of Bankers Trust. Murray Rothbard (see Rothbard, 2002a) makes much of the importance of the "Morgan club" as a factor in understanding Federal Reserve policy in its early years. Strong, in taking the position as head of the New York Federal Reserve, had confidently expected that in this role he would be the most powerful official in the new system, although there were some ambiguities about how power would be divided between New York and the board in Washington. At the head of the board was Charles Hamlin, also in the Morgan sphere, as was the Treasury Secretary McAdoo, whose railroad company had been bailed out personally by J.P. Morgan.

Under the initial organization of the Federal Reserve, the Treasury Secretary was an ex-officio member of its board, and McAdoo (now son-in-law of President Wilson) regularly attended its meetings. The main counterweight to the Morgan empire within the Federal Reserve was Paul Warburg, who stemmed from the German banking family of that name and was close to, having married into, the New York banking house of Kuhn Loeb. Warburg has been seen by many historians as "the father of the Fed" in the light of his powerful intellectual and political advocacy of a US central bank, derived from his experience and admiration of banking arrangements in the German Empire and his dismay at the "primitive state" of monetary arrangements which he perceived on arrival in the USA. Strong himself described the Federal Reserve as Warburg's "baby".

The importance of the Morgan connection was soon to play out in Federal Reserve policy debates and decisions about a whole range of key issues during the period of US neutrality (August 1914–early 1917). One theme through much of the literature about this period (see Roberts, 1998; Rothbard, 2002a) has been the huge business (and profit) that the Morgan empire derived through arranging finance for the Allies and how this may have swayed US policy at all levels. Even so, historians concede that Benjamin Strong had strong beliefs, which may have happily coincided with what turned out to be good for Morgan. He belonged to an East Coast upper class and Anglophile elite fully in tune with his view of the war as a "global struggle between the forces of good and evil – Prussianism, Kaiserism, and autocracy against freedom, civilization, and Christianity" (see Roberts, 2000).

Warburg, by contrast, in common with many other prominent figures on the political and economic scene in the US at that time, believed that the best outcome from the dreadful war in Europe would be a negotiated settlement, which would be most likely achieved by the US remaining strictly neutral. They warned that facilitating war financing in forms that jarred with strictly legal interpretations of neutrality made a negotiated outcome less likely and increased the risk that the US would eventually be drawn in as a protagonist on the Entente's side.

The arguments within the Federal Reserve about how far to facilitate allied financing turned on such issues as whether trade acceptance credits, which were obviously war financing bills (related to ammunitions and other war materials, rather than to normal commercial trade), should be discountable. In practical terms, the question was whether the New York desk of the Federal Reserve could buy them in the market or lend against them as collateral. (Note that prior to the creation of the Federal Reserve, there was no official institution providing liquidity to the commercial bill market in this way. Hence, the trade acceptance market in New York had remained narrow. In this sense, the new central bank's launch was timely for Entente war financing).

The protagonists discussed the issue in terms of banking risks versus developing New York as a financial centre (and all the bankers, Morgan and Kuhn Loeb, had supported the creation of the Federal Reserve in considerable part because of its potential to enhance their international business). But the real issues of war and peace were not far below the surface. Strong often used the independence of the New York Fed to defy, in effect, rulings from the board in Washington. On one occasion, in April 1915, the board was able (due to skilful moves by Warburg and Miller and the absence of Treasury Secretary McAdoo caused by ill health) to get through a tough ruling against acceptance financing which was camouflaged lending to the belligerents. But then Strong, with the support of McAdoo, struggled successfully to get this regulation diluted (see Roberts, 1998), which was in the wider context of the Wilson Administration drawing closer to the Entente.

Already in Spring 1915, Wilson's chief political adviser, Edward House (known as "Colonel House"), on a visit to Europe, had telegraphed that "we can no longer remain neutral spectators". This comment had been read out approvingly by Wilson to his Cabinet (see Bobbit, 2002). In June 1915, Secretary of State Bryan, the leading anti-war member of the Cabinet, had resigned in protest at the Wilson Administration's drift toward aggression and away from strict neutrality.

Wilson's brief peace diplomacy triggers market crash end-1916

Toward the end of 1916, the Wilson Administration did briefly rein back financing for the Entente Powers, notwithstanding the stance of Benjamin Strong and his Wall Street friends, as part of its diplomatic efforts (in December) toward forcing a negotiated peace. The Battle of the Somme had underlined the military stalemate amidst a holocaust of youth. It is doubtful, though, whether anyone in London saw the move as more than an irritating temporary interruption in US financing or anyone in Berlin seriously interpreted it as a possible precursor to Washington abandoning its pro-Entente stance.

According to Fischer (1967), President Wilson himself had intended to offer that the US would throw its full "financial might behind which-ever side made a genuine effort to reach peace, meaning the setting of realistic terms for negotiation", but he was dissuaded from doing this by Colonel House (who was already by this point solidly with Great Britain, having an excellent relation with its Foreign Secretary Grey, even though in Summer 1914 he had warned Wilson about how Britain and France were fanning war risks). Indeed, the brief collapse in the New York stock exchange, where speculative temperatures had soared as asset price inflation disease spread, in response to the Wilson Peace Note may well have added to scepticism in Berlin about whether Washington would seriously curb the booming wartime export trade with the Entente (see Baruch, 1962).

Meanwhile, the high rate of goods and services inflation, which appeared in 1915–16, deeply concerned all the senior Federal Reserve System officials, whatever their stance on the war. The huge shipments of gold to the US by the Entente Powers (this stemmed in part from the mandatory handing in to the authorities of gold coins and the banks similarly exchanging their gold reserves for central bank deposits), against which they received dollar deposits at the official gold price of $20.65, fuelled growth in the US monetary base. In effect, the Entente Powers were levying an inflation tax on US residents toward financing their war expenditures with the US authorities acquiescing in this either deliberately or by default.

The wholesale price level rose by 65% between June 1914 and March 1917 (the date when the US entered the war), with the stock of money rising by 46%. Over the subsequent period to May 1920 (when the price level peaked), wholesale prices rose a further 55% and the money stock by 49%. Benjamin Strong used concern about inflation as an argument for extending war credits to the Entente Powers, in that the latter would in consequence ship less gold to the US and there would be less monetary expansion. A rising concern about credit risks of British and French bond issues in New York, though, would have surely curbed investor appetite for such paper, even though the Federal Reserve was promoting its liquidity in many cases (by its interventions in the bill and accept-ance markets).

Indeed, if the US had suspended or slowed official gold purchases, so allowing the Fed to gain tight control of the monetary base, the virus of asset price inflation would have been less powerful. That would have meant in turn less irrationality (in particular yield seeking behaviour) in the now high risk wartime market for French and British government

dollar debt markets in New York. If Strong had been successful in indi-
rectly slowing down the rate of gold purchases, he would surely have
undermined the demand for such paper. His idea that sales of the latter
could be promoted as an alternative to gold purchases did not make
sense in principle or in practice.

Why did the US not suspend official gold purchases?

Strangely, there is no evidence of any discussion within the Federal
Reserve about recommending (to the US Treasury) a suspension of
official gold purchases. Such action has not been an issue taken up by
Friedman and Schwarz or other monetary historians. Yet this would
have stopped the monetary source of inflation – albeit at the same time
starving the Entente of its US inflation tax revenue ("collected" from US
citizens). Under suspension, the Entente Powers could have used their
gold to acquire dollar funds only by selling this in a free market where
its price would have plunged far below the official price.

A floor to the price would have been set by speculators in the now free
gold market judging that the likely profit to be made from an eventual
return of the price to its official level sometime after the end of the war
was greater than the loss of interest in the meantime. The British pound
would have slumped against the US dollar as the UK government would
no longer have received huge proceeds from gold sales to support its
currency. In Europe, Switzerland, with a small neutral currency swamped
by gold inflows as soon as 1915, had taken such action, and correspondingly, the Swiss franc had risen far above its gold parity against the US
dollar (see Brown, 2012).

So why was there such silence on this obvious policy step? The most
plausible explanation is that it was a non-starter in terms of politics
both within and outside the Federal Reserve. Suspending the official
gold purchases would have hit Entente financing hard. Strong was
hardly likely to put forward the suggestion of suspending official gold
purchases in total contradiction of his war sympathies, of Morgan interests, of ambitions to make the New York Federal Reserve all powerful
within the Federal Reserve or of promoting New York as a world financial centre to compete with London.

Paul Warburg and his sometime ally on the board, Professor Adolph
Miller, might have seen some considerable advantages of suspension in terms of tackling inflation and constraining the amount of
war finance for the Entente Powers (hence, making a negotiated
peace more likely) – although there is absolutely no evidence on this

point. Even so, Warburg shared Strong's enthusiasm for building up gold reserves within the Federal Reserve. Both had been concerned from the start that the Federal Reserve Act had opened the door to fiat money creation (in that Federal Reserve notes were the liability of the US government) and saw a strong gold backing (in terms of gold reserves within the Federal Reserve being in excess of the legal minimum specified in relation to notes outstanding) as a bulwark (see Silber, 2007). Yet both Warburg and Strong would have been deluding themselves if they indeed viewed wartime floods of gold into the US as providing a basis for monetary hardness, especially when viewed in a global context.

If a much larger share of global gold stocks were now finding their way into the US to permanently back (at an unchanged gold dollar parity) an inflated supply of Federal Reserve notes matched by a permanently higher US price level, how could Europe ever return to a pre-war type of gold standard, where gold – including gold coins in circulation – would be a high proportion of the monetary base. Of course, the Entente Powers were similarly to blame for the recklessness with which they were destroying any likelihood of a return to a full gold coin standard for their monies by sequestering gold from banks and individuals for the purpose of war finance. A full resumption of the international gold standard after the war would require their governments to reverse the sequestration by re-accumulating huge amounts of gold perhaps by floating international loans. In turn, the drain of gold from the US at that point would have created severe monetary deflation there. In total, none of this was a plausible scenario.

There is no evidence that Strong or Warburg were looking ahead with any insight to the post-war order. Both shared ambitions for New York as a financial centre. Both saw the sustaining of global faith in the continuing gold convertibility of the dollar (at a fixed price throughout) as fundamental to realizing these ambitions. Perhaps they had some intuitive awareness that the gold sales by the English were corroding the foundations of British financial hegemony in the pre-1914 world and implicitly welcomed that fact – but who knows for sure? There is no evidence they realized that the depletion of private and public stocks of gold (including gold coin) in Great Britain would mean that a full international gold standard could not be restored after the war (as against the truncated gold system including the UK's adoption of a gold bar standard – effectively a dollar pound peg – in 1924, see p. 60). In any case, they continued to worry about inflation without proposing any real solution.

From Great Recession 20/21 to monetary base "stimulus" and rate manipulation

As a practical matter, the still considerable amount of free gold within the Federal Reserve (in excess of minimum legal requirement relative to its liabilities outstanding) at the end of the war surely played some role in its readiness to continue holding down interest rates during the first year of peacetime. Federal Reserve officials did not anticipate the further surge in prices which occurred through 1919, although this surely revealed negligence given the extent of new money creation occurring on top of pre-existing huge excess.

Only in early 1920 did the Federal Reserve take restrictive action, with a dwindling in the amount of free gold apparently the trigger to its severity. A stock market crash and wider financial market distress as the long asset price inflation transitioned into its final stage including Great Recession was the consequence with the wholesale price index declining by 50%. Eventually, in response to this downturn, the Fed used for the first time tools of contra-cyclical monetary management, pumping the monetary base by open market operations in government bonds. Rothbard cites two powerful doses of "controlled reserve" increases by the Federal Reserve. These were effected in late 1921 and 1922.

In the pre-1914 gold standard, automatic mechanisms operating at a global level would have caused some gradual rise in world high-powered money under the circumstances of depressed prices (via lowering gold mining costs). And prices of goods and services would have followed a powerful pro-cyclical path (falling far below their long-run average level amidst expectations of a subsequent climb in the recovery phase) in turn inducing recovery by encouraging firms and individuals to bring forward spending. There would have been no man-made policy application of contra-cyclical tools at a national or global level. Grant (2014) in his eloquent narrative of "The Forgotten Depression" analyses how the invisible hand did a great job of pulling the US economy into a recovery in this historical instance, although a full account would include the role of Federal Reserve monetary manipulations in creating the preceding boom (1919–20) and exacerbating the recession whilst also accelerating the recovery (see Rothbard, 1972).

The Federal Reserve had no great understanding of its new tool – piloting the growth of US monetary base growth (no contemporary official would have seen it in this way). Benjamin Strong and Paul Warburg had never cast themselves as monetary experts who could in a moment devise a framework for stable money no longer secured by a gold pivot. In practice, the Fed through the 1920s improvised using their new degree of monetary freedom – at times focusing on cyclical stabilization (via open market operations) and at some points on exchange rate stabilization vis-à-vis the British pound. Overall, in line with the fashionable doctrines of Irving Fisher, the US economist most prominent on the public stage at this time, leading Fed officials worked with the concept that the Federal Reserve should be guided by the aim of "price level stability" assessed implicitly over just a few years. Strong's position on this was ambiguous. His overriding goal was the restoration of an international gold standard. In a 1921 meeting, he had expressed the view that it was not the duty of the Federal Reserve System to "deal with prices" (see Meltzer, 2003). That view likely evolved in subsequent years at least in terms of practical policy making. Miller and others in the board were more sympathetic to the Fisher doctrine. This was flawed in not recognizing that there should be considerable fluctuations of the price level (sometimes over multi-year periods) both upward and downward, consistent with stable prices over the very long-run under a regime of monetary stability in its fullest sense (meaning no monetary inflation either in goods markets or asset markets) (see Chapter 4). And at a time of rapid productivity growth as in the 1920s, prices should have been falling.

Milton Friedman and Anna Schwartz give the Federal Reserve high marks for their monetary management in the seven years following the Great Recession (up until mid-1928), calling this the "high tide of the Federal Reserve". Austrian School economists totally disagree.

For example, Rothbard (1972) details the periods of rapid monetary base expansion which the Federal Reserve induced in bursts of policy activism (buying bonds mostly), especially in late 1921 and 1922 (in response to perceived economic weakness and deflation), the second half of 1924 (linked to Benjamin Strong's efforts to help Britain return to the gold standard) and the second half of 1927 (again motivated by help for Sterling). Meltzer (2003), in his epic history of the Federal Reserve, maintains that the growth of monetary base was fairly stable throughout, with spurts being later counterbalanced by slowdowns.

Thus, a four quarter moving average of the monetary base was growing at 6% per annum in early 1923, slowed to 2.5% per annum in early 1924, blipped up to 4% per annum in late 1924, decelerated to 2% p.a. in 1925–26, slowed further temporarily down to zero in late 1926, reaccelerated to 2% per annum in 1927 and then decelerated to sub-zero from 1928 onwards. But this four quarter moving average defence for the Federal Reserve against the charge of inducing monetary instability falls flat.

In the pre-1914 gold standard, global above ground supplies of the yellow metal increased at a 1–3% p.a. rate (average 1.5% p.a.), never getting outside that range even during the period of gold mining boom in the late 1890s and early 1900s related to new technology (cyanide process) and discoveries. The large fluctuations over fairly short periods in the early and mid-1920s had much to do with the Federal Reserve's efforts to stabilize money interest rates at a low level.

Under the regime of the pre-1914 gold standard, money interest rates had fluctuated violently in line with day-to-day shortages or surpluses in the market for reserves. Short-term rates in the pre-1914 world played little or no role in long-term interest rates determination. By contrast, in the new world of stabilized short-term rates, these began to have considerable influence on long-term rates. Investors began to anchor their expectations of interest rates far into the future on where the Fed was stabilizing short-term rates today. Hence, long-term interest rates in the mid-1920s did not rise sharply despite buoyant demand for capital and a growingly voracious appetite of the public for equity under the then economic miracle conditions (rapid technological change). The misalignment of long-term rates played a crucial role in the growingly serious asset price inflation disease.

Neither Friedman and Schwartz nor Meltzer consider possible distortion of the long-term interest rate market as a channel of monetary disequilibrium. Rather, both focus on measures of aggregate money supply broader than the monetary base and argue that these reveal no disequilibrium.

Friedman and Schwartz do concede (unlike Meltzer) that monetary policy during the years 1921–25 was somewhat expansionary if viewed according to the metric of the monetary base – but they choose to focus on wider measures of money. In measuring the expansiveness of monetary base, Friedman and Schwartz point out that the advent of the Federal Reserve System led to an economization in demand for excess reserves (the development of a market in the early 1920s for Federal Funds encouraged this trend). They do not go into all the details behind this key insight, but the big point is that bankers (and their deposit clients) would now see a reduced danger of liquidity crisis. After all, the founding purpose of the Federal Reserve, conceived in the aftermath of the 1907 panic, was to eliminate the periodic liquidity crises of the past by introducing a lender of last resort which could add to the supply of monetary base under such circumstances. The bolstering of short-term bill and acceptance market liquidity via continuous Federal Reserve intervention in those presumably would make banks somewhat more complacent and ready to hold a lower ratio of reserves to deposits than in the past.

The fall in demand for high-powered money (relative to past experience for given level of important variables such as deposits outstanding, size of the economy) would surely mean that the observed apparently low rates of increase in this aggregate could be stimulatory to a considerable degree. Friedman and Schwartz back away from that conclusion, even though these authors make the further point that a shift in public demand away from sight deposits to time deposits (stimulated by the new differential reserve requirements on the two, much lower on the latter) lowered overall demand for reserves. But their preferred wider monetary aggregate throughout those years was growing in line with their econometric estimates of money demand at stable prices.

This turning of attention away from monetary base to a wider definition of money, nearest to M2 according to present-day terminology, is not strange given that the authors, Friedman and Schwartz, do indeed stress broad money rather monetary base in their analysis of US monetary history in the gold standard years before 1914. Yet under the pre-1914 gold standard, these wider aggregates had little relevance to understanding the monetary forces at work. The big mover was the global monetary base as determined by increases in the stock of above ground gold.

Now it is possible that in the truncated gold system after World War I in which there was a blurred distinction between high-powered money held by the banks and other short-term debts now liquefied by the Federal Reserve, the monetary base (as defined in the national US context) was no longer as pivotal as in the pre-1914 system. But the authors do not make that case. Moreover, they do not deal with the criticism that even wider monetary aggregates (for example, an aggregate specified by Rothbard) show a much more expansionary path than their selected aggregate. Finally and most importantly, they succumb to the trap of measuring inflationary excess by looking at the short or medium behaviour of the prices. But during a period of rapid technological change accompanied by well above average productivity growth, stable prices might actually mean considerable monetary inflation in the present. And the 1920s were just such a period given the innovations of automobile assembly line production, electrification, telephone and radio.

Staging the disease of asset price inflation 1922–29

Hence, monetary inflation as generated by the Benjamin Strong Federal Reserve during the early and mid-1920s did not show up in a rising trend of goods and services prices. But the disease of asset price inflation was spreading and intensifying. Indeed arguably the disease was initially present in 1922 as US equity markets responded strongly to the Federal

Reserve's monetary stimulus amidst a surge of inflows from Europe. But then there had been a remission as Germany in 1923 faced economic and political breakdown (hyperinflation took off as French troops occupied the Ruhr) and the US economy passed through a shallow recession (May 1923 to July 1924). Then the emergence of economic miracle both in the US and Germany coupled with global détente (the Kellog Pact) could well have justified the high stock and other asset prices through 1925–6. The path of this disease is notoriously hard to diagnose, especially in its early stages. By the time central bankers or other officials responsible for economic policy become convinced that the disease is present, it may already be on the point of endogenous transition to the stage where speculative temperatures drop violently, and actions which they take might only make its end phase even more deadly.

The transition does not usually occur all at once, but there is a first stage where speculative fever continues to build in some asset classes even though it is receding in others. (see p. 65). There is no mention in the histories of the Federal Reserve in the mid and late 1920s of any official joining the dots between the Florida land bubble bursting, the crash in the Berlin equity market, the peaking of the broader US real estate markets and realising that the US or global economy were already in an advanced stage of asset price inflation where speculative temperatures fall in some areas whilst still rise in others. And all of this was occurring before the late deliberate raising of rates by the Federal Reserve to counter stock market speculation.

The whole experience is a cautionary tale for economists who believe that the way forward for the design of monetary frameworks is for central banks to target low inflation over the "medium term" (meaning around two years) whilst being "ready" to discretionarily tighten policy (beyond the requirement of price level stability) if there are evident signs of asset and credit markets forming. By the time those signs were evident to the policymakers in the late 1920s, many parts of the credit and asset universe were near or already past their peak temperatures, and most if not all of the mal-investment to match had already taken place.

Friedman and Schwartz suggest that if Benjamin Strong had still been alive in the final phase of the stock market bubble (from late 1928 onwards), he would have had better judgement than to tighten at that point. Perhaps, but they do not address square on the long list of criticisms concerning Strong's earlier monetary misjudgements – and in particular his role in generating the virulent asset price inflation disease of the mid-1920s which spread globally. A particular focal point of such criticism has been the Fed rate cut and high powered money boost of mid-1927 undertaken as part of Strong's agreement with Bank of England Governor Norman to support Sterling. Indeed, the authors overlook asset price inflation disease altogether, most plausibly because difficulties in empirically diagnosing and measuring its severity are hard to reconcile with Friedman's emphasis on "positive economics".

A key symptom of US monetary disorder: boom in German carry trade

Yet in choosing to stick so resolutely to empiricism, Friedman and Schwartz miss out the crucial spread of the asset price inflation disease (which in any case they do not diagnose) to the Weimar Republic and how this played such a deadly role in the final panic and collapse of 1931 onwards. In modern terms, we would describe the huge flow of capital into Germany in large part from the US (but also from small European creditor nations and the UK) as a boom in the carry trade driven by monetary disequilibrium in the US where short and long-term rates were well below neutral.

As we have seen earlier in this volume, the carry trade is often a feature of the asset price inflation disease. The speculative story which drove this trade was economic miracle in the Weimar Republic in the aftermath of war and hyperinflation. The high yields on German bonds – whether in mark or dollar denomination (the mark dollar rate was fixed) – attracted carry trade both in the form of credit risk arbitrage (funds moving out of safe dollar paper into higher risk dollar-denominated German bonds) and currency arbitrage (funds moving out of dollars into Reichsmarks to earn the higher interest on the latter). The New York Fed in fact boosted this carry trade in its attempt to build up New York as the global number one finance centre.

Rothbard (1972) makes the cynical suggestion that the Federal Reserve's big support (via rediscounting and other liquidity operations) of the foreign acceptance market (much of which was German credits) may have been in line with the contemporary business interests of Paul Warburg. Even though the latter had resigned from the Federal Reserve Board in 1918, stung by President Wilson's delay in putting him forward for reappointment in view of Congressional attacks on his German connections (see Ferguson, 2010) – including the high-up position of a brother in the German secret service, he continued to exert considerable influence within that institution. Warburg had now become head of the International Acceptance Council and chairman of the International Acceptance Bank of New York.

In mitigation of Rothbard's harsh criticism, Warburg's support for the New York Fed's "subsidization" of the trade acceptance market was also consistent with his long-held view that an overriding US foreign policy objective in terms of global peace should be a rebuilding of war-crippled central Europe, and this also made good economic sense. Warburg did not succumb to the irrational exuberance found in the US with respect to investment in Germany, as generated under the glow of growing monetary disequilibrium created by the Federal Reserve, even though eventually the descent of the Weimar Republic into the economic and political abyss was to cost him dearly.

Ferguson (2010) relates how Paul Warburg's nephew, Sigmond Warburg, working in the US during the mid-1920s, wrote (in 1927) that he was "well aware that American confidence in Germany was in part a function of ignorance. In New York I had been struck by how remarkably optimistic people were about the German currency; there was no real appreciation of the economy's underlying weaknesses. As I saw when back in Germany the tax burdens had grown so enormous that an accumulation of capital and thus of new means of production had become practically impossible; businessmen thought they were lucky if they could keep their heads just above water".

There is nothing new under the sun! Who could not have made the same comment about "function of ignorance" when examining the various forms of carry trade especially into emerging market currencies as ignited by the Great Monetary Experiment. The difference, if any, is one of economic size. Germany in the mid-1920s was the second largest economy in the world, and the US (and some foreign) banks had exposures which could bankrupt them if the worse scenarios became real. Today, the so-called fragile five do not loom nearly as largely – although there is the huge issue of camouflaged or indirect exposures in various forms of carry trade to the largest emerging market economy of all (the second or third largest economy in the world), China.

In the mid-1920s, the flood of foreign loans into Germany (whose currency was tied to the dollar) did contribute directly to the emergence there of asset price inflation disease in an ultimately deadly form. Real estate prices in Berlin multiplied by several times in five years amongst a frenzied nationwide construction boom. In principle, the German authorities could have sought to defend the economy against the importation of the asset price inflation virus by suspending the fixed exchange rate between the mark and the dollar, allowing the mark to float temporarily to a much higher level (the dollar cheaper against the mark) and tightening domestic monetary conditions (meaning market interest rates would have risen).

That was unthinkable under the exchange rate regime established at the end of the hyperinflation which had been inscribed in an international treaty arrangement (the Dawes Plan). In any case, the forces of irrationality as powered by monetary disequilibrium in the US can penetrate the defence of a floating exchange rate, causing speculative fever to rise in the equity market and in the currency market (in particular, the Reichsmark might have risen to a fantastic extent), even though the domestic real estate market would plausibly have become insulated in some degree allowing domestic investors the opportunity to make bargain purchases of foreign assets (see Chapter 1).

Historians have debated whether the Second World War was an inevitable consequence of the Treaty of Versailles and in particular of the reparations bill imposed on Germany. To reach such a conclusion we would have to include under the heading of "inevitable" the huge monetary disequilibrium which was generated by the Benjamin Strong Federal Reserve through the 1920s. Was it indeed inevitable that the newly created Federal Reserve administered by bumbling officials who had no reliable concept of monetary stability and who looked to current monetary wisdom as dispensed by Irving Fisher would end up creating the most serious asset price inflation disease ever known up until that time with global reach – in this case infecting most of all Germany? That is a lesson to be written in counterfactual history.

The Friedman and Schwartz counterfactual history of the Great Depression

Also a matter of counterfactual history are Friedman and Schwartz's comments about how the Federal Reserve could have performed better during the Great Twin Recession of 1929–31 and 1931–33 (the incipient recovery of Spring 1931 snuffed out by the German banking and sovereign debt default crisis which started to erupt at that time). In their monetary history (1963), Friedman and Schwartz suggest that the Federal Reserve could have taken various actions to ameliorate the violence of the economic downturn.

Their starting criticism relates to the Federal Reserve's failure to act forcefully during the first banking crisis of late 1930, which they suggest was primarily a liquidity rather than solvency crisis stemming from a crop of bank suspensions in the farming stats and spreading to New York, culminating in the collapse of the Bank of the United States in December

1930. According to the authors, this was just the type of liquidity crisis which the Federal Reserve was set up to solve and which in any case rarely proved deadly (for the banking system or the economy) under the pre-Federal Reserve regime. Indeed, the authors suggest that the Bank of the United States was solvent and should have been saved and would have survived (albeit with a temporary suspension of 1:1 convertibility of deposits into banknotes) under the pre-Federal Reserve regime.

The second of several criticisms by the authors (Friedman and Schwartz) relates to the Federal Reserve's failure to aggressively expand the monetary base during 1931–32, in particular in the wake of the German and Central European banking and sovereign solvency crisis of Summer 1931. The aim of such aggressive expansion (according to the authors) would have been to resist a powerful decrease in the wider money supply which emerged and to even turn this round. The authors praise the brief aggressive open market operations of Spring 1932 during which there was a boost to the monetary base and even link this to the trough in the equity market that summer and short-lived stirrings in the economy.

Here we have the intellectual origins of the Obama Great Monetary Experiment as designed by Ben Bernanke – the idea that powerful quasi money printing could indeed stimulate the US economy out of a Great Recession or Depression. Friedman and Schwartz remind their readers of how Benjamin Strong had boosted monetary base aggressively in response to the Great Recession of 1920–21. They do not deal with the historical analysis of that episode by Austrian School economists, such as Rothbard, who argue that this aggressive action in fact created an eventually powerful virus of asset price inflation and the Fed should have allowed the strong forces of recovery which were already taking hold to do their job without interference.

These forces included the pro-cyclical fluctuation of the price level (prices falling to a low level during the Great Recession amidst expectations of a subsequent upturn in prices during the economic expansion which would follow) and a recovery in the equity market (led by expectations of profits rebound into the cyclical upturn and helped on this occasion by powerful capital inflows from Europe where the German reparations issue was triggering massive capital flight). Albeit with the benefit of hindsight (derived from the experience of QE after the 2008–09 Great Recession), we can say that Friedman and Schwartz did not acknowledge that in a situation where short-term market interest rates (on default-free paper) are zero and the neutral level of interest rates very low (and possibly at zero or below zero for short or even medium-maturities), high-powered money is not the hot potato. In fact, during the recession of 1920–21, there was no period when market rates were at zero and plausibly the neutral level for all maturities was substantially positive – reflecting expectations of price rebound and strong trend productivity growth.

There were other key factors (not mentioned in the Friedman and Schwartz history) beyond monetary base growth patterns and Federal Reserve politics (the authors praise Benjamin Strong for activism in expanding the monetary base in 1920–21 and criticize political bickering within the Fed of 1931–32 for standing in the way of such action then) to account for the differences between 1921–22 (strong economic recovery from the Great Recession coupled with rebound of money supply) and 1931–32. In the earlier episode (1921–22), a severe price fall had taken place in a very short time (during 1920).

That fall, when coupled with expectations of a rebound of prices in the subsequent cyclical upturn (as had always occurred in previous cyclical history under the gold standard) helped to generate spending. With increased spending and economic activity came increased demand for bank loans and bank deposits. This was not the situation in 1931–32. Then the Hoover Administration joined with business leaders and unions in an effort to hold up wages so as to "prevent a fall in general purchasing power" (see Shlaes, 2007), so interfering with the normal recovery mechanisms operating in a capitalist economy in a well-functioning stable monetary order. The decline in prices, though, large over the period as a whole (1929Q4–33Q1), was not as concentrated in time as in 1920.

Of course, there was no stable global monetary order in 1920–21 or in 1931–33, but the latter period was particularly unstable. When Britain abruptly unpegged the pound from the dollar in September 1931 (the so-called departure from gold, albeit that Britain had never really returned to gold – see p. 59), the Federal Reserve responded swiftly to a drain of gold triggered by investors seeking safety against a possible break of the dollar with gold. It raised interest rates sharply even though there was no immediate lack of "free gold". Federal Reserve notes still had ample gold backing relative to the minimum legal requirement – which in any case could have been suspended temporarily in an emergency according to the present law (see Meltzer, 2003; Butkiewicz, 2007). Researchers find that Federal Reserve President Meyer was particularly (and excessively) sensitive to warnings from Paris (Bank of France Governor Moret) about a potential flight out of the dollar and crash of the "global monetary order".

Later in the depression after the election of Roosevelt as President (in November 1932) and ahead of his inauguration (March 1933), there was a renewed bout of speculation on the US leaving the gold standard (even though Roosevelt had denied any such intention during the election campaign!), and this in turn led to a tightening of monetary conditions in the midst of economic declines. The rumours were of course correct and when he took office, the dollar's convertibility into gold was suspended. Around a year later, the administration fixed a new official price of gold against the dollar at $35 per ounce; but in the meantime, private holdings of gold by US citizens had been outlawed. There followed massive foreign inflows of gold to the US as funds fled the remaining gold bloc in Europe (centred on France), and capital inflows to the US equity market gained strength. The gold inflows were matched by a creation of high-powered money as the Fed and Treasury coordinated their operations so as to prevent any sterilization of funds used in the official purchase operations. In effect, this was a type of QE 70 years or more before Obama's Great Monetary Experiment. The history of this QE including the great asset price inflation which it produced (leading on to the Crash of 1937 and the subsequent Great Recession) is the subject of Chapter 7.

A decade of the international dollar standard (1960s)

Let's fast forward to the decade of the international dollar standard – the 1960s. During the Second World War and its immediate aftermath, the Federal Reserve had become subservient to the US Treasury in carrying out the policy of pegging government bond prices so as to keep long-term yields in nominal terms at around 2.5%, never mind the consequences in terms of inflation. Any plausible estimate of the neutral level of rates was far above that level – for example, during periods of peak military spending or of a surge in investment opportunity alongside pent-up consumer demand in the aftermath of military conflict.

The return of active monetary policy (independence from the Treasury occurred with the accord of March 1951, but unofficial support for the bond market continued for a further two years) came fully by early 1953. William McChesney Martin, the Federal Reserve's newly appointed chairman (he held office between April 1951 and January 1970) was intent on following "independence within government" (Meltzer, 2009a). There was no broad guiding concept of monetary stability. Federal Reserve policy was subject, though, to two legal constraints.

First, there was the pivotal role of the US in the international dollar standard as established by the Bretton Woods Treaty. This standard only started to come into effective operation when the Deutsche mark became fully convertible (all exchange restrictions scrapped) in 1958, and other leading currencies dropped many of their exchange restrictions. Second, Congress, taking its cue from Keynesian economics, had passed the Employment Act (1946), which exhorted the Federal government and its agencies (including the Federal Reserve) to pursue "maximum employment, production and purchasing power" through cooperation with private enterprise. As Meltzer points out, the Federal Reserve faced an inherent contradiction in following both the Bretton Woods Treaty and the Employment Act.

Essentially, under the international dollar standard (as established by the treaty), countries pegged their currency to the US dollar on the (implicit) understanding that the US would run a monetary policy such that on (weighted) average across the countries participating in this system there would a fixed stable anchor to prices over the very long run. The treaty commitment of the US to convert dollars into gold bars for the accounts of any non-residents at the official price of $35, in principle, was a confidence booster globally in the Federal Reserve following policies consistent with the stable anchor commitment, although there was no automatic mechanism at work here. By contrast, under the pre-1914 gold standard, there was such a mechanism in that the supply of high-powered money globally was closely related to above ground gold stocks.

At best, there would have been a set of rules for expanding the monetary base inside the US so as to be consistent with a fixed stable anchor for global prices in dollars. Also, there would have been a set of institutional arrangements such that the monetary base could function as an effective pivot for the US monetary order – a subject to which we return in Chapter 5. Essentially, this means forgoing those props to the banks (wide-ranging deposits insurance, too big to fail, lender of last resort), which shrink the demand for high-powered money and undermine its distinctiveness as an asset.

Given the abnormally high rate of productivity growth in the US during the late 1950s and early/mid-1960s, prices would have been falling slightly there so as to be consistent with the fixed stable anchor as defined for the dollar standard countries as a whole. That conclusion is reinforced by the tendency of Germany and Japan, in particular, during this period to be gaining in competitiveness vis-à-vis the US as they experienced economic miracles periods concentrated in their export sectors.

According to the famous Balassa-Samuelson hypothesis, countries experiencing such a miracle record a real appreciation of their currencies; if these are pegged to the dollar, then this comes about through prices in the US falling and those in the miracle countries rising. Given that the US was by far the largest economy, most of the relative price adjustment would come through prices rising in Germany and Japan rather than prices falling in the US.

In fact, the evidence does not suggest that Federal Reserve Chairman Martin had any grand vision about the requirements of monetary stability, whether in narrow US terms or in global terms. Well connected to the Democratic Party (which won all elections, Congressional and Presidential, from 1932–52), President Truman had appointed him to the chair of the Federal Reserve in 1951. Prior to that, his career had included episodes as top securities regulator, as President of the Export-Import Bank and as top monetary official in the Treasury (in the Truman Administration). Meltzer describes Martin as having an intuitive and practical sense to "lean against the wind". That is euphemistic.

Yes, Martin tightened monetary policy when inflation rose or a balance of payments crisis threatened (meaning a drain on the gold reserves). As Martin put it, the art of the central banker was to take away the punchbowl just when the party was going well. All of this smacked of reacting to symptoms of monetary disorder when already it had been in the making for a considerable time. The gaps between disorder and the first suspected symptoms appearing, and the gap between that and a definitive diagnosis being made by the Fed officials even one as "intuitive" as Chief Martin, are long and variable. As we have seen, diagnosis of asset price inflation is particularly difficult – and in any case Chief Martin did not recognize that this particular type of monetary disease existed.

It was no wonder that the Martin Fed, through the 1950s, generated a succession of three nasty business cycle downturns even though the trend economic growth rate was in a miracle zone. And the average inflation rate was just under 2%, far from being consistent with prices in the US, let alone the global economy, having a stable fixed anchor. Richard Nixon, Vice-President in the second Eisenhower Administration, blamed his wafer-thin defeat by John Kennedy in the November 1960 election on the third of those downturns. Arthur Burns, Nixon's economic advisor and Eisenhower's chief economic advisor, attacked Martin for his inflationary policy, arguing that there should be no inflation (see Burns, 1957).

The repeated monetary stumbles of Chief Martin paved the way for the Keynesian economists to make their popular claim that they could produce a much better outcome with their fiscal fine-tuning tools and by finding a better trade-off on their illusionary Phillips curves relating unemployment and inflation. Specifically, they claimed that by aiming for a higher inflation rate, unemployment could be permanently reduced. These Keynesian economists enlisted in the Kennedy Campaign and pioneered the "new economic policy" under the Kennedy and Johnson Administrations. Implicitly, the opting for inflation so as to lower unemployment would undermine the dollar standard, although once in office these Keynesians would strenuously deny the obvious. In the early Martin years, there had been no standard to undermine. And in the early years of the 1960s, inflation actually fell as productivity growth surged.

Martin had no qualms about working closely with the Keynesian policy advisers around the new president or with the Keynesian officials who were gradually appointed to the Federal Reserve Board. He lacked any clear intellectual or ideological basis to challenge their policy proposals (in particular pursuing a trade-off between higher inflation and lower unemployment). Martin saw the Federal Reserve as still playing a role in government financing – in particular maintaining an "orderly" Treasury bond market. And under the new Keynesian economic policies, the Federal Budget deficits started to widen. The deterioration in government finances became more serious under the influence of the new social programmes and the Vietnam War. Martin delayed "aggressive" action on the promise that a tax rise would be implemented. When the tax rise was finally introduced, its temporary nature contributed toward its having much less cooling effect on "aggregate demand" than had been forecast. Belated efforts by the Martin Fed to tighten policy in the midst of the war brought a public rebuke from President Johnson.

Asset price inflation, crash and the 1974–75 Great Recession

Eventually, the Federal Reserve implemented fairly aggressive tightening (less than Martin imagined because of this failure to distinguish nominal interest rates from real interest rates: see Meltzer), with the Federal Funds rate reaching almost 10% in Summer/Autumn 1969. As Martin hung up his coat in early 1970, he admitted failure in that inflation had risen so far (with CPI inflation peaking at 5%). The Keynesian economists who had boasted their policies would permanently banish the business cycle now had some explaining to do when the US economy plunged into recession (end-1969). The virulent virus of asset price inflation, which their monetary policy had created, moved on to its deadly phase of violent fall in speculative temperatures. In the 5-year period 1962–6, the S&P 500 equity market index had risen by around 250% (the index had been volatile around a flat trend through 67–8, peaking in late 1966 and returning to that peak in late 1968 having been far down in the interval). This was the glory period for the "nifty fifty". It was when the real estate titans emerged and Warren Buffett amassed his fortune and stardom. It was also the age of periodic financial scandal – for example, Bernie Cornfeld's mutual stock selling enterprise (see Aliber, 2001).

The abrupt monetary tightening in the dying days of the Martin Fed brought a near 35% collapse of the US stock market during 1969 and the first half of 1970. Warren Buffett exited the fund management business returning capital to all those who had entrusted it to him. There followed a brief Indian Summer in the equity market as Arthur Burns, the new Fed chief (from January 1970), followed the instruction of his political boss (President Nixon) and created massive monetary stimulus even though reported goods and services inflation had barely fallen back. In late 1972, the US stock market had risen to 15% above its nominal peak in late 1968 – although it was virtually unchanged in real terms. This time a powerful asset price inflation virus attacked the commodity markets, where a terrific boom developed through 1972–73. The commodity bubble turned to bust but not before the newly powerful OPEC cartel had taken advantage of the monetary situation (including the strong depreciation of the dollar from Summer 1971 onwards when the Nixon Administration "closed the gold window") to ramp up its official price of oil in the aftermath of the Yom Kippur War (October 1973). Spot oil prices had been soaring for many months before that. The aggressive monetary tightening of the Burns Fed from Spring 1973 onwards culminated in the violent stock market downturn through 1973 and the first half of 1974 – a fall of 50% in nominal terms and much more in real terms – a decline which ranks with the worst in US history including 1907, 1929 and 1937. The commodity bubble turned to bust. The recession of 1974–75 ranks as one of the Great Recessions in US history.

There followed an economic upturn (1975–81) through which there was little evidence of asset price inflation disease in the US real estate markets (except for agricultural land where there was a boom and bust) or in the US equity market (apart from financial equities). The disease was also present in the US bank bond market as we shall see. There was much and growing evidence of the asset price inflation virus having entered the veins of the global economy, especially as regards the emerging market economies (then called the less developed economies), most of all in Latin America. Wider evidence of US monetary disorder included the weakness of the US dollar against the Deutsche mark and Swiss franc, whose central banks were pursuing strict monetarist policies. And in the US, goods and services inflation started to rise again after a brief easing during and immediately after the Great Recession.

Asset price inflation in the late 1970s

The asset price inflation during these years stemmed from the Burns Federal Reserve following a highly stimulatory monetary policy. Nominal money market rates were substantially positive but below the rate of inflation. Investors around the world desperate for real returns on their dollar funds and having already suffered real loss during the recent year of high inflation, were willing to plough these into the growingly popular (and innovatory) floating rate capital notes issued by the leading money centre banks. Some of these took the form of perpetuities. In the irrational world which characterizes asset price inflation, they did not ask fundamental questions about their possible exposure to loss should the booming loan business to the developing countries turn out badly. (Eventually, when the asset price inflation moved into its phase of steep speculative temperature fall, those floating rate note issues slumped in price).

In similar irrational mode, equity investors became captivated by bank stocks whose current reported earnings were booming in reflection of the international lending boom (with fees and margins in the booming syndicated loan market boosting current earnings, and bad debts, meanwhile, running at very low levels). According to the popular speculative story chased by yield hungry investors, the recycling of giant current account surpluses from the OPEC countries to governments and state agencies in the non-oil developing countries was a benign and safe process. Recycling was approved of and blessed by the IMF and the global central bankers' club (albeit that the Bundesbank was not an insider in those years). At the end of the 1970s, however, the OPEC surpluses had virtually evaporated, yet the lending continued unabated.

The end phase of this asset price inflation disease almost bankrupted the big US money centre banks. Latin American borrowers suspended their debt servicing and in subsequent years worked out revised schedules of repayment and interest. In some big cases, pain for the lenders was eased by US Treasury and IMF interventions. The IMF made mega packages of finance available on strict conditionality to the distressed borrowers so that they could restart to service their debts to the banks.

The trigger to the transition from boom to bust was the monetary tightening in the early years of the Volcker Fed (1979–82), which has become legendary.

Two years of monetarism and on to a new plague of irrational exuberance (1980–89)

This was the brief period when the First Monetarist Revolution and its advocated framework of monetary base control arrived in the US. Volcker already abandoned the revolution in late 1982, reverting to the direct pegging of the overnight Federal Funds rate. The level of the peg was changed frequently with the ostensible purpose of achieving the "intermediate target" for wider money supply growth, in turn set to be consistent with ultimate objectives of a path back to price stability and full employment. This method of piloting monetary policy was effectively the same as that of Arthur Burn's, albeit that Volcker had the reputation for greater independence and hawkishness in not tolerating high inflation even transitorily and for his conviction that inflation is essentially a monetary phenomenon.

Yet Volcker, like his predecessors, did not explicitly recognize the monetary disease of asset price inflation. His focus was on goods and services inflation. He also kept his eye on the US trade balance. After all, he had been the top official under Treasury Secretary John Connolly (a Texan Democrat) in the Nixon Administration responsible for driving through the devaluations of the dollar at that time on the argument that the US trade deficit had become "unsustainable". As the trade deficit again ballooned through the mid-1980s, Volcker swung behind the view that a dollar devaluation was again essential to economic equilibrium and that invisible hands of market forces could not do the job on their own.

In the notorious Plaza Accord (September 1985), Volcker committed the Federal Reserve to following policies consistent with dollar devaluation. The sharp slowdown in the US economy which had emerged in late 1984 and persisted through the next two years or more brought intense political pressure on the Fed from the Reagan Administration (especially the new Treasury Secretary, James Baker) to ease policies and foster a weaker dollar (the latter so as to dent the growing protectionist mood in Congress), especially in the run-up to critical Senate elections in November 1986 (which in fact the Republicans lost).

In sum, we could say that the Volcker Fed in the years following the abandonment of the monetarist revolution became overly concerned about fine-tuning the economy, over-impressed by the short-term path of inflation (as when it dipped far under the weight of crashing oil prices in the mid-1980s) and under-impressed by symptoms of monetary instability in the form of speculative temperature rising in credit and asset markets. And so the Volcker Fed in its late years did not view such phenomena as the junk bond bubble, the plunge of the US dollar, the global real estate and credit booms, the S&L bubble or the growingly feverish speculation in equity markets as symptomatic of US monetary disequilibrium.

The asset price inflation virus as generated by the Volcker Fed went global, infecting a range of markets, including, for example, Japanese equities and real estate, European real estate (most spectacularly in Scandinavia and UK), in addition to several real estate markets and the equity market inside the US. The depreciation of the dollar played a key role in the export of the virus in so far as the monetary authorities in the countries whose currencies were appreciating sharply (in particular Japan) followed disequilibrium policies so as to limit the appreciation.

Asset price inflation started to move on to its next phase of steep falls in some speculative temperatures already in October 1987 with the equity market crash of that month, the trigger being the tightening of US monetary conditions which started in the spring simultaneously with the US entering into the Louvre Accord (of which Volcker approved) so as to bring the dollar's already fantastic depreciation to an end. The new Fed chair, Alan Greenspan, (from August 1987) was able to extend and delay the final bust across all asset classes around the globe by aggressively easing policy through late 1987 and early 1988. The bust nonetheless followed as rising goods and services inflation forced the Greenspan Fed to reverse course.

The Greenspan Fed generates two asset price inflations

Alan Greenspan was even more distant than his predecessor from any concept of monetary stability which embraced asset price inflation. Even though he had been a protégé of Ayn Rand (whose political views were in line with radical laissez-faire) and had written an early article advocating the gold standard, he never demonstrated any awareness of the Austrian School ideas (according to one biographer, he attended, with Ayn Rand, one lecture by von Mises; see Sechrest, 2005). Greenspan, like Burns, was hugely concentrated on fine-tuning the business cycle, and he had an encyclopaedic knowledge of all current indicators about the state of the economy (plus full access to a huge arena of contacts for assembling anecdotal information).

In some respects, the monetary disequilibrium under Greenspan was a throwback to the disequilibrium generated by the Strong Fed in the 1920s. Then, as in the mid-late 1990s, there were downward pressures on prices in consequence of a spurt in productivity growth driven by technological revolution (now IT). These lulled the Federal Reserve into pegging short-term rates at a low level – far below the span of neutral rates across short and long maturities which corresponded to this miracle period. The low stable short-term rates promulgated irrational forces which held down also the long-term rates, suppressing them far below neutral level. The big speculative story of this age was the boundless opportunity stemming from information technology. And as "new economy stocks" spiralled upward in price, positive feedback loops reinforced irrational exuberance.

As we have seen, asset price inflation goes along with booming carry trade. Earlier, in 1993, there had been the carry trade boom into Mexican bonds. The speculative story chased was the economic liberalization occurring and the opportunities presented by the North American Free Trade Agreement. The Greenspan Fed was holding down interest rates out of concern at the apparently fragile nature of the business cycle upturn from the 1990–91 recession. The Mexican carry trade moved into its bust phase as the Greenspan Fed belatedly allowed a sudden climb of interest rates to take place through 1994. At the same time, Mexico political instability suddenly increased with the eruption of the Tequila crisis.

The Fed responded to the Mexican crisis and a mild growth cycle downturn in the first half of 1995 by administering a further dose of monetary stimulus. In the mid-1990s, a new carry trade boom flourished in the East and South East Asian currencies linked to the US dollar but offering substantially higher interest rates (either due to higher credit risk or residual currency risk). The speculative story was economic miracle in the Asian tigers, several of which were becoming key parts of the production chain in the manufacture of IT hardware and software. The story began to sour, especially once the yen fell sharply in 1996–97, as US interest rates climbed and as real estate booms in those countries revealed huge excesses. A wider collapse in the carry trade boom occurred in Summer 1998 centred then on Russia's descent into default.

These steep falls of speculative temperature in the carry trade were symptomatic of asset price inflation having transitioned into a late stage, not a final stage. The NASDAQ bubble and bust was still to come in 1999–2000, culminating in a steep fall of speculative temperature in some sectors of the credit market amidst the criminal bankruptcy scandals of Enron and Worldcom amongst others.

The great monetary disequilibrium which developed under the Greenspan Federal Reserve beyond the recession of 2001 (which followed the NASDAQ bubble's burst) and particularly during 2003–05 was driven by the extraordinary impatience with the potentially slow recovery process from the excesses of the IT spending boom – explained in part by the hits to confidence from the terrorist attack on New York (September 11, 2001) and the gathering concerns about looming military action in Iraq. It would have taken time for the combination of entrepreneurship, discovery of new opportunities for profitable investment, relative price and wages adjustments and return of healthy risk appetites to reroute the US economy onto a path to enduring prosperity.

The newly arrived (2002) Governor on the FOMC from Princeton University, Ben Bernanke, had an extraordinary influence on policymaking through raising the spectre of potential "deflation" and a Japanese-style "lost decade". Even though Greenspan vetoed Bernanke's suggestions for direct intervention in long-term T-bond markets, he went along with new procedures to strengthen Fed influence (downward) on long-term rates – in particular the virtual pre-announcement of a long period ahead during which short-term rates would rise at a glacial pace only and tying changes in the Fed Funds rate to the achievement of a low positive inflation rate (at around 2% p.a.) rather than to some intermediate money supply target.

As US medium and long-term rates were dragged down far below neutral, a virulent germ of asset price inflation formed. Its contagious spread to Europe and Japan gained strength as monetary authorities there sought to prevent their currencies appreciating unduly. Moreover, the newly created European Central Bank (ECB) had embraced the same deflation-phobic inflation-targeting monetary framework as that now adopted by the Federal Reserve. Peak infection rates (highest speculative temperatures) were recorded in an array of asset and credit markets. In the US, these included residential real estate and sub-prime mortgage markets, private equity-related high-yield debts and financial sector equities. The overall US equity market index in real terms, though, even at its peak in 2007, did not reach the heights of March 2000. In Europe, speculative temperatures rose to high levels in Spanish, French and UK real estate, high-yield sovereign debt, financial equities especially in the new mega banks for which the speculative story (as for high-yield sovereign debt) was the wonders of European integration. And there was the fantastic boom of the yen carry trade.

Then, even as the asset price inflation virus transitioned into its late stage, there was a big rise of speculative temperature in oil and other commodities during Spring 2008. As the ECB and Fed responded to this late appearance of commodity inflation they added to the forces of asset price deflation elsewhere already well advanced, almost certainly making the final bust phase of the asset price inflation virus in the global economy even worse than otherwise.

4
How to Cure Deflation Phobia?

Under monetary stability, there would be short periods and some longer periods during which many prices and some wages would fall significantly. Symmetrically, there would be some short and some long periods during which the overall thrust of prices would be upward. This would all be consistent with a fixed anchor to prices in the very long run. These fluctuations in "the general level of prices" over time are essential to the invisible hand of the market operating powerfully and efficiently.

If the monetary regime in place (US and globally) has the effect of suppressing these fluctuations, it runs serious risks of creating an asset price inflation disease. That undermines economic prosperity – first by generating much mal-investment and overinvestment during the stage of feverish speculation; second, by sapping the long-run appetite of investors to bear risk, given their knowledge about the deadly end phase of the disease, which is endemic to this regime.

"Sapping the appetite" has two dimensions. Investors lower their expectations for future returns over the long run as they take account of the possible slump in corporate profits during the end phase of the next asset price inflation disease. Also, these returns in the far-off future could be depressed by the ultimate political consequences of the disease –legislative innovations which permanently cramp the invisible hand. (Think of the Federal Reserve Act in the aftermath of the 1907 Crash and Great Recession, the New Deal legislation following the Great Depression, the Dodd-Frank Act after the 2008 Panic and subsequent Great Recession). Investors may also require a higher premium for bearing risk – whether defined in terms of variance of returns or in more complex fashion.

Examples of such resistance on the part of the US monetary authority (Federal Reserve) to accepting the natural rhythm of prices when in a downward direction have included Benjamin Strong in the 1920s, Alan

Greenspan in the 1990s, Greenspan together with Ben Bernanke in the 2000s, Bernanke and Janet Yellen in the 2010s. In every case, including most recently the architects of the Great Monetary Experiment, leading Fed officials and their political bosses were seemingly blind to the dangers of suppressing the natural rhythm of prices. Their mantra (since the 1990s) has included much about the danger of deflation. By this, they have meant periods of a sustained fall in prices as measured in the indices compiled by official statisticians, which now include "hedonic adjustment" to take account of quality improvements.

According to the present doctrine of the Federal Reserve and like-minded foreign monetary officials who belong to the exclusive global central bankers' club, the ideal monetary framework should be built around the aim of stable positive inflation at 2% p.a. in each and every 2–3 year period, eliminating any prospect of even a temporary dip in prices. And under the circumstances in which the Great Monetary Experiment was launched – a Great Recession which had started with a Great Panic – an absolute priority of the architects was to prevent any fall in prices in the immediate or short term whilst producing a rise in prices as quickly as possible. The purpose was to solidify expectations that inflation would indeed run at the declared target over the next few years even though economic activity could still be subpar. This was all truly extraordinary.

Five reasons why the Fed QE architects suffered from deflation phobia

How can we explain the blindness of the architects of Fed QE to the benign economic role of price fluctuations through time and their emphasis on targeting a stable positive inflation rate?

A first point is that in the neo-Keynesian economic texts which guided the architects (some authored by themselves) there is not even a passage about the alternative viewpoint according to which episodes of price fluctuations both downward and upward through time should be viewed as evidence of a well-functioning capitalist economy under conditions of monetary stability.

Second, the architects of GME have been very much influenced by "the zero rate boundary problem" widely discussed both by themselves and other neo-Keynesian economists (see, for example, De Long, 1998 and Bullard, 2010). The essence of this problem is that interest rates may not be able to fall to equilibrium levels which are negative in real terms (such as in a recession or during periods of unusually poor investment

opportunity or elevated savings or when risk aversion is unusually high)
if inflation is very low or negative. For if nominal interest rates fall
significantly below zero, depositors would pull funds out of the banks
and hoard banknotes instead.

Third, the architects have been keenly aware of the so-called danger of
"balance sheet recession". This describes a situation where prices of real
assets (buildings, commodities, inventories, equities, for example) are
falling whilst debt claims are fixed in nominal terms. In consequence,
firms get driven toward insolvency, and in this perilous condition,
they become reluctant to undertake any new capital spending. Surely,
it would be better in weak economic conditions (as in or after a Great
Recession) to use monetary policy to inflate, thereby lowering the real
value of debt and raising the prices of goods rather than the reverse?

The short answer here is no. Asset price deflations are usually the
consequence of prior attempts of monetary authorities to suppress a
downward rhythm of prices (whether stemming from cyclical forces or
from other factors such as above-trend productivity growth, a bulge in
savings relative to investment opportunity or severe downward pressure
on wages across big segments of the labour market). Why go down this
same route again? In any case, if there is a fixed stable anchor to prices
in the long run, then any present fall of prices would be expected to
be reversed in the long run. And there is much scope in a sophisticate
finance system anyhow to substitute equity for debt.

Fourth, some Keynesian campaigners against deflation have chosen
the soft target of radical views amongst a few of its advocates (see,
for example, Hulsmann, 2008) who have argued that deflation helps
"cleanse" the economy of big government, crony capitalists, bankers
and other undesirables that have gained from inflationary finance. Yes,
it is good to cleanse, but why in one big almighty deflationary depression far more severe than if the invisible hands were working efficiently
under monetary stability? By quoting views of such deflation advocates
and the notorious "liquidationists" during the Great Depression (for
example, Treasury Secretary Mellon who supposedly advised President
Hoover – according to the latter's records – "liquidate labour, liquidate
stocks, liquidate farmers, liquidate real estate; it will purge the rottenness
out of the system. High costs of living and high living will come down.
People will work harder, live a more moral life. Values will be adjusted,
and enterprising people will pick up from less competent people", some
neo-Keynesians believe that deflation in general has become discredited
sufficiently not to have to consider the much broader issues of monetary
equilibrium raised here.

Fifth, the Keynesians stick to the common sense of "social frictions" in the way of nominal wage cuts such as occurs in deflationary episodes. Such cuts, they argue, promote bad feelings in the workplace, can trigger industrial strife and most likely lead to less work effort. And they may be counterproductive in that they reduce worker purchasing power and, hence, consumer demand.

Here is a snapshot of the rebuttal to such common sense (as in the fifth point). No one employer will find that he or she is the only one effecting wage cuts. Many will be in the same situation at the same time. The price cuts which accompany the deflationary phase will also be evident to all, including those whose nominal wages are cut, especially in today's age of information technology. Therefore, all will realize that real wages are falling (if at all) by less than nominal wages. In an enlightened economic and political climate, there would be a widespread realization that transitory nominal wage cuts in the depths of a recession are part of an overall benign economic process (rather than their being picked on by a harsh employer).

Moreover, if the deflation does indeed lead to a quicker economic rebound (see p. 53) – and this is a central expectation – then the news of widespread nominal wage reductions can indeed boost economic confidence in the future (compared to a situation where this recovery mechanism is frozen). In many highly cyclical industries, wage fluctuations both up and down are the norm (especially when taking account of bonus payments) and expected by all. Transitory falls in nominal wage rates related to cyclical downturn should have no traumatic effects. Indeed, in so far as such cyclicality occurs, it reduces the intrinsic risk of equity investment in those industries, thereby promoting overall investment and prosperity on a secular basis.

Historically, Keynesians composed their doctrines based on nominal wage rigidities in the UK of the 1920s during the years of the "return to gold". As we have seen (see p. 60), this return to gold was a myth. The pound did not become gold money in its full sense, and the stock of high-powered money (or its destruction) in the UK had no strong automatic link to gold flows or to the above ground supplies of gold. Everyone and their dog could see that it was far from certain that the official peg of the pound to dollar would hold. And powerful trade unions in particular might make this assumption part of their negotiating strategy (the belief that ultimately their refusal to accept wage cuts would be met by a dislodging of the anchor to stable prices). Keynes himself was the leading polemic on why the pound should be devalued throughout these years. Why would labour accept nominal wage cuts if the leading economic populist of the day, buttressed by many politicians and trade unions, is saying that the system under which these would make sense is broken and cannot be fixed?

Keynesian textbooks omit Austrian School thesis on deflation

Let's revert to a fuller consideration of the earlier points (one to four above) explaining the phenomenon of deflation phobia. Take the first point first.

What are the missing passages which at a minimum should be entered in the neo-Keynesian textbooks so that the student of these could become aware of alternative viewpoints?

These do not feature at all in the textbooks which the Great Monetary Experiment architect-in-chief Bernanke authored or co-authored – see Bernanke (2014 and 2013). Of course, the authors would dispute those viewpoints, but why are they not mentioned in the best traditions of teaching?

A key example of deliberate oblivion is the silence about the thesis discussed by economists writing in the Austrian School tradition. This describes how resistance to a lengthy initial phasé of price falls induced by rapid technological change (as during the 1920s or 1990s) on the part of the monetary authorities generates highly economically destructive asset price inflation (see, for example, Rothbard, 2002 and White, 2013).

These same neo-Keynesian texts studiously make no reference to work by Austrian School economists on definitions of deflation and inflation (see Salerno, 2003). Some of these fall into line with popular usage and say that falling prices equate to deflation and rising prices to inflation. Others prefer to stick to "monetary deflation" meaning that there is a shortage of money (relative to demand) putting downward pressure on prices. Price declines which are consistent with monetary stability (such as may occur for example during a period of rapid productivity growth) should not count as deflation.

Ideally, there would also be a note (in the Keynesian texts) of the debate about whether optimally in the long run prices should be declining. Should the anchor to prices be shifting downward albeit glacially in line say with productivity growth or should it be fixed? The Austrians disagree amongst themselves on this, and indeed, one famous non-Austrian, Milton Friedman, sided with those who argued for a trend decline, as we shall see.

The Keynesian textbooks ideally would go beyond the Austrian School literature to older accounts on the practical and theoretical workings of the gold standard. These would open their readers' mind to the possibility that periods of falling prices could be consistent with a fixed anchor to prices in the very long runs. References to gold standard history in any positive sense – conflicting with Keynes's description of gold as a "barbaric relic" – may be anathema to most neo-Keynesians. But nonetheless, there is much to be learnt at both at a theoretical and practical level from such consideration.

Under gold standard prices rise and fall but no permanent decline

In the world of the gold standard the stock of high-powered money (in aggregate for all countries on gold) was largely determined by the above ground stocks of the yellow metal. These climbed at a very slow trend pace (of 1–3% p.a.), with fluctuations in the pace explained both by technological changes (specifically in the mining industry, including new discoveries) and shifts in prices of goods and services on average relative to the official fixed price of gold ($21 per ounce pre-1933). And so, if there was a significant fall in goods and services prices over a period of time (perhaps related to a business cycle downturn, sudden acceleration in productivity growth or bulge in savings relative to investment opportunity), this would tend to be reflected in lower mining costs which in turn would induce a transitory increase in the rate of gold production (as this would become more profitable). Under these circumstances, the slightly quickened pace in high-powered money growth would help fortify the pull of the fixed anchor on prices over the long run.

Variations in the rate of gold production induced by economic variables as described was not the only force operating so as to fortify the fixed anchor to prices in the long run. One should also consider natural rhythm – the pro-cyclicality of prices, "seven years of plenty to be followed by seven years of famine" (meaning a period of economic miracle might well be followed by a period of stagnation) or bulges in the savings surplus followed by contraction. Moreover, the shifts in pace of high-powered money growth induced by dips in prices were slow in coming into effect, fairly glacial and typically quite long lasting.

In sum, the automatic mechanisms functioning to fortify the fixed anchor to prices were subtle. They were at first provisional, then slow and yet flexible – a far cry from the fine-tuning policy changes advocated by the priests of fiat money! And the sluggish pace of variations in the supply of high-powered money (mainly made up of gold) to changes in demand could mean that there were periods when short-term rates in the money markets were far out of line with the neutral level of interest rates as estimated for medium or long maturities. Excess demand would bring a spike in money rates, which would stimulate banks and individuals to economize on their holdings of cash or other components of high-powered money.

In principle, if short-term rates spilt over into influencing far-out rates (within the term structure) in various irrational ways (see p. 28), there could be a serious misalignment between market rates and neutral in the longer maturity range and the disease of asset price inflation could germinate (in the case of market rates being misaligned in a downward direction relative to neutral). Yet because under the gold system short-term rates were typically highly volatile – as determined by fluctuating conditions in the market for reserves rather than by central banks fixing the price and adjusting the supply – long-term rates were not dragged away from neutral by passing episodes of glut or famine in the market for high-powered money.

Even so, the possibility existed under the gold standard that a multi-year spurt of productivity growth (which would bring prices in general down relative to the gold price) would induce a sustained increase in the growth of high-powered money (the stock of above ground gold would be buoyed by now cheaper to extract metal, reflecting a fall of unit labour costs in the gold mine industry), which would in turn germinate asset price inflation. In effect, the automatic mechanisms of the gold standard which held the anchor stable to prices in the long run could create monetary disease in that form. This possibility, though, was not a serious defect as first, multi-year spurts as described tended to be followed by pull backs in productivity growth (seven fat cows followed by seven thin). And second, even a long period of below neutral short-term interest rates in money markets did not mean that long-term rates would be far below their respective neutral level, given the volatility of the short-term rates and the barriers to pass through (into the long-term markets) as described above.

Nonetheless, the possibility has been viewed as significantly serious for some authors to conclude that the ideal monetary regime would abandon the fixed anchor to prices in the long run and instead replace it with one which drifts lower in the long run. Such persistent tendency to price decline, though, is inconsistent with the workings of the gold standard for good economic reason.

For once we break confidence at large in the fixed anchor to prices in the long run, a whole range of economic frictions emerge, Most importantly, the zero rate boundary problem emerges. (Note that the fixed anchor to prices in the gold standard world was to "raw prices", not to today's "hedonic prices" taking account of quality improvements). So long as a present fall in prices is expected to be reversed eventually (as is the case with a stable anchor to prices in the very long run), then interest rates in real terms can indeed reach substantially negative levels, even though nominal interest rates on money are zero or positive. Indeed, the present fall of prices is the means by which the capitalist system produces negative real interest rates under such circumstances. Let's give some illustrations of this point.

Pro-cyclical fluctuations in prices key to stability

During a business cycle recession, many firms find they are facing weak demand. Each on their own could respond by cutting prices in the expectation of boosting turnover and cutting their losses (so long as they can cover variable costs). In weak labour markets, they can also cut back wages without suffering a harmful shrinkage in the amount or quality of input required. As prices and wages fall across the economy, real wage declines are considerably less than nominal. The wage declines are concentrated in cyclical industries where labour always anticipates that there would be just this flexibility of wages. And if indeed there is a fixed anchor to prices in the long run, labour would expect nominal wages to pick up further ahead and see present nominal wage cuts as transitory only. By the same token, business decision makers realize that present low prices are only transitory and expect higher prices in the future. This should induce some bringing forward of spending. Households with available means would act similarly in bringing forward consumption. In essence, expectations of prices recovering in the future coupled with low prices now mean that zero or low nominal interest rates are in fact substantially negative in real terms.

Why should there be any confidence in the stable anchor to prices holding firm and indeed being strong enough to mean a substantial likelihood of price rises within a time-horizon relevant to present business or household decision making?

Confidence turns partly on experience. Historically, under the gold standard, such experience was ingrained into expectations. The same experience could become ingrained under a fiat monetary system constructed so as to be stable and which proved to be stable. An essential property of such as system must be high-powered money which is a firm pivot of the monetary system. That means (as shall be discussed in greater detail in Chapter 5) high-powered money must be a highly distinct asset (in terms of liquidity and ideally in terms of physical property) for which a large and stable real demand exists (related to incomes). And it must be high-powered. That means no interest paid on it and so it functions as the proverbial hot potato, which banks and individuals are highly motivated to economize on and not manage sloppily (allowing non-equilibrium holdings to build up without any quick reaction).

These qualities held for gold as the high-powered money. It is indeed possible that they might be recreated for a fiat money system increase in high-powered money supply in response to lower prices such as occurred under the gold standard – meaning a temporary quickening in the pace of growth under such circumstances – would also reinforce expectations of prices rebounding from cyclically low levels.

Even so, is it possible that during the severe recession phase a pattern of continuing price declines (and wage declines) could emerge which would be detrimental to economic stabilization? If price cuts are still to come, why spend now? Yes, today's price might be lower than where it is likely to be in several years' time. But it could still be higher than where it is likely to be in three months' time. So hang on! This possible scenario is fortunately less plausible than at first sight. As a statistical matter, price declines are most likely bigger and quicker than caught in the statistics. Many firms might give discounts secretly or concede buyer's incentives, which are not traceable by the methodology of the official statisticians. By the time officially recorded prices fall, they may already have been down at that level for some time in effective terms. Indeed, it is in firms' interests in stimulating demand to make bold price cuts rather than give the appearance of these coming in dribs and drabs. Prices fall to a point from where rises are more likely than falls in the long term.

Moreover, big price cuts are not synchronized. So in some industrial sectors, a big cut might already have occurred and that be regarded largely as final, whereas in other sectors there might still be speculation about price cuts to come. And that speculation is not a sure thing. It could be that there is a likelihood of further price cuts. But it may also be that recovery is already starting, albeit unnoticed, and in fact, the next move in prices could be up. And so, in probabilistic terms, now might be a good time to plan a purchase programme over the medium term even though there can be no certainty that prices are at their low point. Just because we can observe a trend of falling prices in hindsight does not mean that this was what the rational economic agent would have expected on the basis of averaging all possible future scenarios. It may be that the recession just turned out to be more severe than the central scenario would have had it. And so, at each stage in the decline of prices as viewed in retrospect, a stabilizing mechanism could have been at work in the form of an expectation of higher prices in the future.

Stabilizing price fluctuations under secular stagnation

Turn to the fall in prices which occurs during a period of bulging savings and diminished investment opportunity on a secular basis. Weak overall demand might indeed go along with some initial dip in prices and cuts in some nominal wages. Under a gold standard, this in turn would give some transitory spur to gold production (high-powered money creation). A rebound of prices and wages would be expected in a longer term perspective. In a fiat money system, appropriate rules regarding high-powered money creation could produce the same result.

In fact, the weakness of real income growth in a state of secular stagnation would mean under the automatic mechanisms of the gold standard or under the constitutional rules of an ersatz gold standard some tendency for high-powered money supply to outstrip real demand. Therefore, prices would tend to recover over the long run. Accordingly, nominal interest rates which are low and positive could be negative in real terms. This would be consistent with the depressed secular state of the economy. Even during the period of weak prices, far-out expectations would be for these to recover, meaning that medium-term interest rates could also be negative in real terms at that point.

There is a symmetrical situation for the high-tide economy in a secular boom (productivity growth above long-run trend, buoyant investment opportunity, much risk-taking). The bulge in productivity growth would indeed be accompanied by some prices falling. High-powered money supply would at first lag real income growth meaning no immediate pressure from the monetary side to reverse that decline in prices. Yet raised productivity growth over the medium term would go along with an accelerated growth of high-powered money (either an increased rate of gold production as spurred by increased efficiency and lower costs in the mining industry under a gold standard regime or high-powered money creation in line with constitutional rules as set in a fiat money system organized as an ersatz gold regime). This would eventually introduce some upward pressure on prices, although this cumulatively may well not reverse the initial fall before this particular phase of economic evolution comes to an end. Hence, long-term nominal interest rates within a normal range might appear very positive in real terms when compared to the initial falling trend of prices. But they are less positive when taken together with the far-out expected recovery in these.

Why Adam Smith's baker would not like Friedman-ite deflation

Those economists who have argued that prices in the long run should fall in line with productivity are defying the natural rhythm of prices such as would occur under a gold standard regime or an ersatz fiat money regime which mimicked this. A prolonged spurt in productivity growth should not mean permanent downward adjustment of prices, although there may well be such a fall (in prices) for some considerable time during the early phase. There should be some gentle and sustained acceleration of high-powered money creation, although this would carry a very contained risk of inducing mild asset price deflation. This is very different from the blatant price stabilization of Benjamin Strong or inflation stabilization of Alan Greenspan, which prevented any early fall in prices during the productivity spurts of the 1920s and 1990s respectively and led to rampant asset price inflation.

If the monetary system did not automatically operate such as to sustain a fixed anchor to stable prices as described then the ability of the capitalist economy to self-stabilize is impaired. Such impairment would characterize a regime where prices fell in the long run in line with productivity growth. Moreover, such a system would reinforce the zero rate boundary problems about which the neo-Keynesians write so much. If the expectation is for prices to fall at a significant pace over the long run, then even low nominal interest rates are substantially positive in real terms. It is true that there could be big dips in prices during recessions, for example, followed by smaller recoveries during booms, but this would stretch the limit of the automatic mechanisms which depend on exercise of common sense rationality.

Adam Smith wrote about the baker who, in making bread for profit, is guided by the invisible hand of the market. But it would have stretched credibility for him to cite, as an example of the invisible hand, a business person who decides to bring forward spending today because prices have fallen so much below a long-run declining trend (which no one knows for sure) that some substantial rebound over the medium term appears plausible. It would be no stretch, though, if the bringing forward were in the context of a stable fixed anchor to prices in the long run.

This same point of criticism is relevant to Milton Friedman's suggestion (2006) that in the optimal monetary arrangement, prices would be falling such that the holder of non-interest bearing fiat money would earn the natural rate of interest. As fiat money costs nothing to produce, it is economically optimal that households expand their holdings of money (non-interest bearing) up until that point at which marginal convenience yield (in particular savings in transaction costs) from money is also zero. And they should not face an opportunity cost in the form of interest foregone which causes them to economize on money holdings. Let's assume the natural rate of interest (in real terms) is around 2% p.a. That would mean the aim should be long-run price level decline at 2% p.a., and the nominal interest rate would be zero.

The generation of pro-cyclical price fluctuations under such a regime (rebound of prices in cyclical recovery) would require steep price declines at some times. In principle, we could have fluctuations in the pace of price decline over the cycle rather than absolute falls and rises, but how would such positive and negative variations relative to downward trend generate negative real interest rates consistent with the zero rate bound? And would economic agents discriminate well between different paces of price decline? There is a further weighty problem with Friedman's permanent deflation suggestion. For much of the time, market nominal rates of interest would be zero. And so, the rate of return on high-powered money and these other short-term risk-free debts would be equal. Under such circumstances, high-powered money loses its unique functions and it loses its power as we have seen (p 9), meaning that there is no good pivot to the monetary system.

Flawed non-orthodox routes to negative real interest rates

Neo-Keynesians, including the architects of the Great Monetary Experiment, have implicitly sought to engineer the negative real interest rates which pro-cyclical price fluctuations produce during the weak phase of the business cycle without the economy experiencing any "deflation" (meaning here cyclical fall in prices) as part of that process. Instead, they rely on shock and awe to induce price expectations that are strongly positive even without an initial period of price decline as would occur in a well-functioning economy under monetary stability.

Hence, the Obama Fed under its first chief, Bernanke, undertook a "bold" expansion of the Fed balance sheet, thereby raising the spectre of mega money printing (the possibility that present quasi money printing could mutate into actual money printing). The procedure inflamed price expectations amongst economic agents such that there would be no price cuts and wage cuts at least on average overall.

The experiment generated in the immediate a depreciation of the US currency and a flight into commodities (including oil) which also stimulated expectations of inflation and thereby depressed real short-maturity interest rates into negative territory. One downside of this experiment was a squeeze on real disposable incomes of many households. Another downside was the creation of an asset price inflation virus, of which commodity price explosion was one early symptom. That virus would likely impose ultimately heavy economic cost.

And there could still be a dip in prices further ahead if the commodity "bubble" were to burst and if the dollar were to rebound (perhaps because other countries responded to dollar weakness by introducing even "bolder" monetary experiments than in the US). On the other hand, there could be some passing "stimulus" to the US economy via the disease of asset price inflation in its early and mid-phases buoying mal-investment in the US energy sector and fuelling credit-driven demand for autos and airplanes for example (see p. 27).

This particular asset price inflation virus stemming from the Obama Fed was a novel virus in that everyone and their dog realized that the Fed's intent was to deliberately create it and spread it. And so, there was also widespread concern about the eventual next stage in which speculative temperatures would fall. That would almost certainly also bring goods and services inflation to a lower or even negative level. Hence, the QE experiment was unsuccessful in convincing many economic agents about a sustained strong rise in prices from a level which had never fallen. The scope for real interest rates to fall was correspondingly limited (to much less than what would have happened had a normal rhythm of prices been allowed to emerge albeit meaning initial "deflation").

Some neo-Keynesian critics have argued that it would have been better if the Obama Great Monetary Experiment had taken the form of administering a powerful negative interest rate regime, rather than blowing up the Fed balance sheet (see Mankiw, 2009). From the viewpoint of the Obama Administration and its chief monetary architect, there was obvious lack of appeal to this alternative. Passing legislation to allow the Fed to pay negative rates on deposits could have been politically explosive – hurting the small saver and benefiting Wall Street and the private equity barons amongst others. And any procedures for taxing banknotes such as described above so as to discourage hoarding would offend libertarian sensibilities amongst a wide section of the population. Blowing up the balance sheet on the basis of paying above market rates to the banks on their reserves at the Fed and using the proceeds to buy massive amounts of long-maturity Treasury debt and mortgage backed securities had big perceived advantages.

First, the balance sheet expansion as described should mean (at least according to the architect's reasoning which included suppression of term risk premiums – see p. 30) cheap funding for the federal government suiting well with the Obama Administration's plans for expanding big government. (Arguably, negative interest rates via the fanning of irrational processes in the market might have produced the same or better result here).

Second, an important price support to home mortgages would help revive the housing market and mitigate potential loan losses (related to residential real estate) at the banks. Yes, some economists might argue that it would be better to let house prices find a much lower free market level and that this could indeed boost the real spending power of younger households who had not previously acquired properties. In reality, though, bolstering the banks, their shareholders and older households who had made bad investment decisions regarding homeownership took effective priority in practical policymaking. And so, if balance sheet explosion of a given amount had the same overall stimulatory effect as negative interest rates to a given degree without Fed balance sheet expansion, then the Administration would choose the former policy option.

Two hypothetical negative interest rate regimes and their particular defects

In fact, there were wider grounds for considerable doubts about the negative interest rate proposals. Many of these were allied to proposals to finally scrap or tax banknotes in circulation and thereby penalize any anonymity which remained in money transfers, hardly consistent with a politically liberal (in classical sense) agenda. Moreover, interfering with the demand for high-powered money (of which banknotes are a substantial component) and destabilizing this was hardly compatible with any long-run objective of restoring high-powered money to the pivot of the monetary system – a requirement of any serious agenda to abandon central bank manipulation and fixing of interest rates (see Chapter 5). In addition, negative interest rates could produce an asset price inflation virus even more deadly than what was now germinating under Fed quantitative easing, especially if rates falling below zero had a discontinuous impact on human psychology such as to induce a dangerous new stage in the plague of market irrationality.

One proposal for negative interest rates as discussed previously (see Brown, 2002) has been to start with an announcement of a conversion for banknotes at a fixed date in the future – for example, 100 old banknotes equals 90 new – and in the interim, there is a sliding scale for converting banknotes into deposits or conversely. In the retail economy, there would be two-tier pricing – one set of prices for payments in cash (banknotes) and one for payment by any other means (with cash prices progressively higher relative to cheque payments the closer we get to the conversion date). ATM machines would dispense cash at a rising premium to deposit values. All of this would send a below zero limit to interest rates (around –2% p.a. in this example), but where market rates were at any time relative to this limit would be determined by the central bank. There is the drawback here of no automatic equilibrating mechanism at work. We are in a world of total discretion by the central bank as to where to position market rates, when to suspend the 1:1 conversion rate of deposits into notes and when to ultimately fix the conversion date. Finally, when the time came to dismantle the negative rate regime, who would have the least idea about the equilibrium demand for high-powered money?

An alternative device for solving the problem of cash hoarding under a negative interest rate regime is for the central bank to ration the supply of new banknotes as soon as interest rates are driven into negative territory (see Pollock, 2009). Hence, banknotes jump to a premium value over bank deposits. The size of that premium reflects a combination of expectations regarding the duration and extent of negative interest rates and also the convenience yield of banknotes to a wide variety of users (especially in the grey or black economy). This aspect – a transitory bonus to holders of banknotes – might make the particular negative interest rate regime described less objectionable than the alternatives to political liberals (in the classical sense) who would object to the penalties imposed under these on users of anonymous medium of exchange. Yet even this salvaging of some political principle pales in comparison to the overall damage potential.

Whereas the price level falls during the severe phase of cyclical downturn under a regime of monetary stability brings a wealth gain for the holders of money, the reverse is true for the negative interest rate regimes described here. Not only would there be a jump in prices as the regime is introduced (commodity spot prices would rise, foreign exchange value of the domestic currency would fall), but there would be the cumulative real income loss for money holders during the period of negative rates (analogous to the income loss which money holders would suffer after their initial windfall real gain in the stable money regime). This doubled up real loss for money holders under the negative interest rate regime would very likely trigger a desperate search for yield and create a powerful virus of asset price inflation.

One aspect of this virus would be a boom in carry trades using the given currency now at negative interest rates. Yes, there would be immediate wealth gains for equity and real estate owners rather than these being delayed (in a more moderate form consistent with market rationality) until an initial broad fall of goods and services prices can generate expectations of price level recovery and so negative real interest rates. But many economic agents would also realize that these early wealth gains (under negative interest rate regimes) are transitory and likely to be reversed (when the negative interest regime comes to an end if not earlier). And so this well-known and well-advertised asset price inflation might not generate an upturn in business spending in particular (see p. 23).

The above discussion of negative interest rates is in the context of a regime where these would indeed become substantially negative and for a long period of time. That is different from the negative interest rates introduced by the ECB originally in Summer 2014. A tiny negative rate imposed on bank reserves with the ECB was not inevitably the start of a radical new monetary policy. Rather, it could be viewed as a throwback to the situation under the gold standard where banks implicitly incurred safekeeping fees with respect to their holdings of high-powered money whether in the form of gold bullion, gold coins or banknotes. That was the sum of the small extent of the throwback! And when the ECB moved to full-scale QE in January 2015, there were grounds for anxiety that the negative rate regime might become more radical further ahead. The Swiss National Bank had already blazed that trail when it lowered money market rates to –0.75% in January 2015 in the hope that this would limit the rise of the franc in the aftermath of lifting the cap to its exchange rate against the euro.

Would Milton Friedman have opted for negative rates on his "daylight saving time principle"?

Yet advocates of a negative interest rate tool being available for monetary policymakers could take their cue from the writings of Milton Friedman's "Case for Flexible Exchange Rates" (1953). In that essay, he writes:

> If internal prices were as flexible as exchange rates, it would make little economic difference whether adjustments were brought about

by changes in exchange rates or equivalent changes in internal prices. But this condition is clearly not fulfilled. The argument for a flexible exchange rate is, strange to say, very nearly identical with the argument for daylight saving time. Isn't it absurd to change the clock in summer when exactly the same result could be achieved by having each individual change his habits? But obviously it is much simpler to change the clock that guides all than to have each individual separately change his pattern of reaction to the clock, even though all want to do so.

Well, Friedman did not contemplate the monetary chaos which accompanies a floating exchange rate system in which the dominant power, the US, is freed from all constraints to unleash huge waves of monetary disequilibrium on the globe. The advocates of negative interest rates are similarly blind who argue that it is simpler for central banks to guide rates below zero under conditions of savings glut or business cycle recession than have wages and prices fall to below a long-run trend coupled with expectations that they would recover in the subsequent business cycle expansion. That pro-cyclical pattern of prices is how interest rates became negative in real terms under the gold standard and this patter guided the invisible hand in a way which allowed economies to recover from recessions without the Keynesian "fine-tuners" in finance ministries and central bankers pulling the appropriate strings.

Introducing daylight saving time in the form of negative interest rates rather than relying on a decentralized and highly flexible capitalist system of price and wage formation means that humanity must suffer the plague of market irrationality.

Deflation phobia leads to exaggerated view of balance sheet recession danger

Let's turn to a further (third) source (see p. 104) of Keynesian phobia about deflation – balance sheet recessions. In severe cases of deflation phobia, this concern might even extend to the essential rhythm of prices both in a downward and upward direction which would be evident in a well-functioning capitalist economy under conditions of monetary stability (including a fixed anchor to prices in the very long run). Balance sheet recessions were first analysed by Irving Fisher in the context of the Great Depression and have been made much of by some inflation target proponents such as Bernanke (2000). Their trumpeted fear is that the fall in the price level would bring an increase in the real indebtedness of businesses which would hinder their prospects of weathering the recession and moving forward to take advantage of new investment opportunities.

The antidote to this fear is the realization that the recovery of the price level further ahead (beyond the present fall related to recession or start of secular stagnation) will go along with a decline in the real value of the debt (or equivalently there will be a period of substantially negative real interest rates) offsetting the rise in real value during the price fall. Hence, in the context of a fixed anchor to prices in the very long run, cyclical deflation would not permanently redistribute wealth between shareholders, bondholders and other creditors or affect financial risk (of the corporation). And less dangers of asset price inflation virus under a policy of monetary stability (meaning that prices sometimes fall) is a positive for financial stability. Even in the short run, the equity shareholders should not be at risk from balance sheet recession if the prospective fall of, say, medium-maturity real interest rates into negative territory (made possible by the pro-cyclical rhythm in prices) also goes along with a fall in equity capital costs (equivalently a rise in P/E ratios). Note that the fall of real interest rates to negative levels (as expectations of price recovery over the medium term gather) does not necessarily bring capital gain for bondholders, as rates in nominal terms can remain well above zero.

In sum, the harmful balance sheet effects of deflation (rising real indebtedness) only appear where markets fail to put any significant weight on a possible later price level recovery – meaning that substantially negative real interest rates do not emerge. Even in that case, there is the potential for companies to lower their leverage ratio back to a more comfortable level (in terms of bankruptcy risks) by issuing equity to retire debt. The problem with such a deleverage strategy could be that it involves driving up the price of now risky debt (in that higher leverage due to price level fall means that the same bonds, outstanding as before, become riskier) and thereby handing a windfall gain to the bondholders (at the expense of equity holders). In some situations, this problem can be solved, in part, by direct negotiations between bondholders and equity holders so that the gains from deleverage can be more equally shared (private equity groups, for example).

Deflation, social justice and illusory "real balance effects"

Distorted views about the danger of balance sheet recession are tangential to a further (fourth) element sometimes present in deflation phobia (see p. 104). This is the charge of social "unfairness". The allegation is that deflation favours the rentier (an investor whose income mainly comes in the form of interest payments on low-risk nominal debt securities or equivalent) and the salary earner in safe employment (especially government) where nominal wage rates are fixed (and public sector unions are powerful) and disadvantages the risk-taker – whether the equity owner or the worker in risky employment (where wage rates may be cut in nominal terms). Surely this type of redistribution is "undesirable", especially at a time of economic hardship, as would be the case during a severe recession? Keynes, who wished for the "euthanasia of the rentier", would have had no liking for "good deflation" even if he had been persuaded of the economic rationale.

In fact, as we have explained here (see p. 109), where long-run price level stability reins, the rentier does not make permanent gains from the decline in prices which occurs during a business cycle downturn. His or her gains during the period of falling prices are subsequently eroded. In principle, we could say the same about incomes of persons in safe employment whose wages are fixed in nominal terms (not subject to any possible wage cuts such as those occurring in other parts of the labour market). The safety of nominal wage income in some employments should be reflected in lesser upward potential during good economic times and a lower level of income overall than otherwise (to reflect an implicit premium for safety). In practice, though, this may not happen if public sector unions exert great power over the wage determination process.

Some economists have pinpointed the real wealth gains which the fall of prices during a cyclical downturn brings to holders of money (and bonds where the principal and interest are fixed in nominal terms) as one key source of recovery. They do not point out that the gains are fleeting, as in their models there is no basis for expecting a subsequent rebound of prices. This is the basis of the so-called Pigou effect, which also features importantly in the work of Patinkin (1989). The idea is that the fall in prices boosts the real spending power of holders of money and bonds. The Pigou theorists admit some offset to these real gains in the form of real losses suffered by equity holders in leveraged businesses or by households with debts outstanding (of which the real value rises as prices fall). Hence, they focus instead on "outside" money and bonds which are matched by the government on the other side.

In fact, more important to the economic upturn process than this initial "real balance effect" are the negative real rates that go along with expected recovery of prices and the lowered cost of equity capital which accompany these. The most important aspect, in fact, of the initial real balance effect is that it provides the investor with a "cushion" against a subsequent period of negative real returns on money and safe bonds, making him or her less prone to the irrational yield seeking behaviour which emerges when negative real interest rates are generated in various artificial ways by monetary experimentation as described above.

The transitory fall of prices during the business cycle downturn or the fall of prices during the early years of a spurt of productivity growth or the fall of prices during the first years of a phase of depressed investment opportunity and enlarged propensity to save, all against the background of monetary stability with a fixed anchor to prices in the very long run, have something in common. They would not be described as deflation by those Austrian School economists who defined this phenomenon in terms of monetary disequilibrium.

When falling prices do not mean deflation

According to this subsector of the Austrian School (see Bagus, 2003), deflation is a sustained monetary disequilibrium in which a "shortage of money" drives "the price level" downward. (Note, however, that Austrian School economists are adverse to using aggregates such as "price level", stressing instead the huge heterogeneity of economic life). Mises defined deflation not as declining prices per se, but as a "diminution of the quantity of money which is not offset by a corresponding diminution of the demand for money so that an increase in the objective exchange value must occur" (Mises, 1981). Money shortage in the Austrian definition's sense would go along with market rates of interest rising far above so-called natural or neutral level.

Deflation in its full Mises definition, actually meaning a fall in the price level driven by monetary disequilibrium, did occur on a sustained basis on several occasions in the decades before 1914. In the era of the international gold standard, episodes of Mises-type deflation for the gold bloc as a whole were characterized by a contraction in the supply of new gold or a sudden increase in demand (for gold) as occurred after the Franco-Prussian War, when the newly formed German Empire adopted the gold standard. Otherwise, one or more countries within the gold bloc might have experienced downward pressure on their prices due to a crisis of confidence in their continued adherence to the gold standard causing local monetary conditions to become very tight. Yet this could not be described as deflation within a well-functioning gold monetary order. And relative shifts in "price levels" between countries under the gold standard – some downward and some upward – in line with economic equilibrium should not be described as indicative of monetary deflation (or inflation) which in any case is defined for the gold bloc countries as a whole not just one part. In the hybrid US domestic gold standard and global dollar standard of the interwar years, episodes of monetary deflation included the attempts of various central banks in succession to defend their gold or dollar parities by shrinking the supply of monetary base as defined for their political jurisdiction.

In sum, according to Mises and other Austrian School economists mentioned here, we should distinguish episodes of statistical deflation which are symptomatic of monetary disequilibrium (what Mises describes as deflation) from episodes of statistical deflation which are quite consistent with monetary equilibrium (Mises would not describe these as deflation). But according to modern usage, deflation has become a statistical concept dislodged from economic meaning and refers to a broad price index falling over a given period specified by the data analyst.

Symmetrically, we should consider the meaning of inflation and distinguish statistical inflation symptomatic of monetary disequilibrium from statistical inflation which is consistent with monetary equilibrium. As an example of the former, consider the rise in prices which occurs due to a shortage in the supply of natural resources or more generally to a disaster, natural or otherwise (for example, war). Under such circumstances, the demand for money might not fall relative to supply in broad terms. Although the rise in prices would squeeze real incomes, the demand for money would be underpinned by its use for transaction purposes. It could be the automatic mechanisms in the monetary control system which respond to prices rising well above the long-run average level that would adjust down the rate of growth in high-powered money under such circumstances, and this could induce monetary deflation (in the sense of monetary shortage).

For example, under the gold standard, higher prices would mean less profit in the gold mining industry and a curtailment of output. The same could occur under a fiat money system where constitutional rules set the growth in supply of high-powered money to mimic the situation under a gold standard.

In a similar vein, we can analyse the rise of prices in the boom phase of the business cycle. At that stage, prices may indeed reach a level well above (away from) their long-run average – consistent with expectations that they would fall back from these levels in a subsequent post-boom period including probably a recession. That long run expected fall in prices would act as a brake on the extent of the boom as some consumers and businesses would hold back spending in anticipation of lower prices at a later date. No one knows the extent to which a currently observed rise in prices is non-monetary and purely cyclical as business cycles are notoriously hard to chart in real time and even in retrospect. And so the automatic control mechanisms in monetary systems make phased adjustment to the supply of high-powered money when sometimes these are not ideally appropriate.

Under a gold standard regime, the presently higher prices (in the boom phase of the cycle) would squeeze the gold miners meaning a slowed pace of high-powered money expansion and gently induce some monetary tightening. The same effect could be generated in an ersatz gold standard where the rate of high-powered monetary expansion would slow when prices were above their long-run anchor level, with the amount of slowing depending on the extent to which prices were adrift from the anchor level.

Expectations of price declines from present elevated levels would mean that monetary systems designed to sustain a fixed anchor to prices in the very long run should experience less swing in long-term nominal interest rates. Expectations of price decline from the vantage point of the boom would mean that a given nominal interest rate was higher in real terms. This is the mirror image of the symmetric point that in a recession under such a monetary regime interest rates can remain significantly positive in nominal terms and yet be negative in real terms, meaning no zero rate boundary problems.

Turning to the rise in prices which would typically occur in the aftermath of recession during which prices fell to a low level, this should not be viewed as symptomatic of monetary inflation (inflationary disequilibrium). It could be that under the rules of the monetary system, though, that a monetary inflation element joins itself to the process. That could be the case if the fall of prices to well below the anchor level during recession leads to some automatic gentle acceleration in the pace of high-powered money expansion, which in turn could be corrected by reverse mechanisms at a later date. This is what occurred under the gold standard regime. After all, the automatic mechanisms do not have perfect comprehension, and they cannot distinguish how much of say the present fall of prices is likely to be reversed by the course of the cycle as a whole and how much may need a monetary kick. And so, the gold standard mechanisms in fact provided for a continuous process of mini-kicks until more information become available. Then they could go in the reverse direction if necessary.

All of this reinforces the earlier tentative observation that the defining of inflation or deflation in terms strictly of monetary disequilibrium cannot provide a practical guide to the official statistician. In real time, we do not know the extent of monetary disequilibrium with any precision that would allow us to "decompose" statistical price changes into monetary and non-monetary in origin. The critical observation is that the attempt of the Federal Reserve to suppress the natural rhythm of prices which would occur under a regime of monetary stability leads directly to monetary instability, often showing up in a virus of asset price inflation. It is not possible to measure that rhythm with precision in real time. Yet we can recognize whether a given monetary framework tolerates such a rhythm or tries to suppress it.

In this sense, there is no doubt about the regime as designed by the architects of the Great Monetary Experiment. The rigid application there of inflation targeting as specified for just two years into the future meant no toleration for rhythmic price changes down and up through time. Correspondingly, the danger of severe asset price inflation disease became severe.

Architects of the Great Monetary Experiment misunderstood deflation

There was an additional factor beyond just cyclical weakness bringing downward pressure on prices during the Great Recession of 2008–09 and its aftermath. This was the nature of the secular adjustments taking place in the US labour market.

The process of introducing "intelligent machines" into the workplace was leading to a hallowing out of middle-class jobs which had been routine in nature. All of this meant downward pressure on nominal wages across a big segment of the US labour market as once middle-class job occupants moved into low-paying non-routine jobs, which are often part-time.

This was a different type of industrial revolution from earlier ones where a blossoming of new job opportunities which could be seized at fairly modest human capital investment occurred alongside. The advance of the intelligent machine did not boost aggregate productivity at the economy-wide level as the spectacular gains in small subsectors went along with a shift of labour to low productivity occupations.

If this rhythm of falling nominal wages had been allowed to play out, the US economy would have continued to experience some downward drift of prices through the economic expansion which followed the

Great Recession. Yes, a gold standard-type rule would have meant some slow and measured acceleration in the pace of high-powered money growth in response to this – such as to be consistent with a fixed stable anchor to prices in the very long run. But the massive expansion of the Fed's balance in the course of its mega quasi money printing went well beyond that.

It may be that historians will conclude that the GME was "successful" in limiting the extent of downward pressure on nominal wages, but at the price of squeezing even further both in the short and long run the real living standards of labour on the wrong side of the intelligent machine revolution. That squeeze did not just come from the upward pressure on commodity and real estate prices as already described. Also, we should consider the deterrent of "perfectly recognized" asset price inflation to business spending and entrepreneurship (see p. 23).

With the passage of time, it seems that the chief architect of the GME, Professor Bernanke, became growingly concerned that the US economy could indeed have entered a long period of difficult adjustment following the Great Recession and Panic, meaning a prolonged tendency toward savings glut, even though he disagreed with the hypothesis of secular stagnation, expressing confidence that in the long-run investment opportunity would flourish and productivity growth accelerate.. In turn, this perception of long difficult economic adjustment went along with an intensified phobia of deflation – the fear that long-time savings glut could result in a perpetually falling price level which would mean given the zero rate boundary to nominal interest rates that real interest rates would stay far above neutral level.

Yet in the scenario of threatened prolonged savings glut (a term which makes no sense in a well-functioning capitalist economy under conditions of monetary stability), the best recipe for preventing the emergence of in-built deflationary expectations stretching into the long run is for there to be a prompt fall of prices in the early stage, coupled with a gentle acceleration of high-powered money expansion (in a regime where monetary base is indeed the pivot of the system). Monetary uncertainty should in no way be fanned as this would deter already weak investment spending and add to equity risk premiums (meaning even more negative neutral interest rate in real terms).

The prompt fall in prices would stem from weak demand conditions coupled with entrepreneurs trying to get ahead of expectations of further price declines by making bold price cuts in the present. Expectations that prices would be more likely to rise than fall from that level – perhaps bolstered by the gentle quickening of high-powered money expansion, perhaps influenced by the realization that seven fat years often follow seven lean – would mean that medium and long-term rates would become negative in real terms even with nominal interest rates slightly positive. That would be the kicker to wider monetary growth along with lending and spending. The architects of the GME did the opposite – shoring up present prices and hugely adding to monetary uncertainty.

5
A Manifesto for US Monetary Reform

"A Manifesto for US Monetary Reform" hardly sounds like a winning banner in an election campaign. And that is a big problem. The ideal of a free society – where capitalism, a competitive market economy and political liberalism in combination build prosperity for all – is continually at peril in an environment of monetary instability. And so long as US monetary conditions are unstable, the rest of the world cannot hope to build monetary stability, although individual countries may have varying degrees of success in partially insulating themselves.

Yet how can campaigners in the US galvanize public support for monetary stability in its full sense given that the concept is so abstract, and there is absolutely no consensus amongst the so-called experts as to what this means? Even the great conservative leaders who sought to turn back the tide of state intervention and regulation – whether Ronald Reagan in the US or Margaret Thatcher in the UK – failed to seize the moment for reform and build a system of defence against the forces of monetary instability. In part, this failure was due to no ready-made agenda for them to follow, in part the explanation lies in their becoming corrupted by power. Ultimately under challenging conditions they proved ready to seek electoral and other advantages from the monetary authority stimulating currency devaluation and easy credit.

How does monetary instability imperil the ideal of a free society? The peril which has featured most of all in popular economic discussion has been goods and services inflation. There is a point at which this becomes so troublesome to most citizens that politicians can actually hope to win elections on a fairly easy to understand message of restoring monetary stability, and they may turn to a leading academic with a popular message for that purpose. That was the opportunity for the monetarists and Milton Friedman in particular during the 1970s. In Germany, the

Bundesbank became the most popular public institution on the back of pursuing monetarist principle and thereby building the hard Deutsche mark. In the US, first Carter and then Reagan briefly hoped to gain popularity by backing Paul Volcker in his very brief monetarist experiment. As soon as goods and services inflation fell to moderate levels, the Reagan Administration became steadily less supportive.

As we have seen, Volcker strayed from monetarist principle in which his belief had been shaky at best to a more eclectic position in which he supported deliberate dollar devaluation for the purpose of reducing "unacceptably" high trade deficits. He was a prominent member of the Reagan Administration's "High Command" in the currency war whose first act took place at the Plaza Hotel in September 1995 (see p. 98). In Germany, the Bundesbank monetarists were swept aside by the greater causes of German and European Monetary Union, and the growingly powerful bank lobbies which resented the high reserve requirements on which the German version of monetary order was based. Continuing low goods and services inflation in the US and Europe through the 1990s helped to build a climate of complacency in which monetary dangers seemed to have vanished. The central bankers waxed about their skills and success and announced the new age of moderation in which unpleasant violent business cycle fluctuations and high inflation had been banished.

Asset price inflation peril for free society

Yet there is another peril besides goods and services inflation emanating from monetary stability and also dangerous for the survival of a free society. This is the disease of asset price inflation as described in earlier chapters. Asset price inflation is a monetary disease which is most often accompanied by some presence of goods and services inflation. But the latter may be at low level or even camouflaged by real forces transitorily bearing down on prices at the same time as the former has become virulent. Moreover, asset price inflation at various stages, and even during its virulent stage, may be broadly popular.

Asset price inflation is the lifeblood of a vast and powerful private equity industry which has spread its crony capitalist tentacles deeply into the US political economy and wider afield and is deeply inimical to monetary stability which would cause it wither away. Overpriced risky debt – where the high prices are powered by the asset price inflation disease – is the essential condition for the private equity industry boom (see p. 26). The industry depends on multiple tax privileges and lack of transparency, which a heavy flow of top officials from Washington DC to the industry helps to sustain. Private equity suffered near death in the 2008 crisis. A lasting crash in the junk bond market and a sober equity market (no asset price inflation virus) would have meant a big shrinkage. The Great Monetary Experiment came to its rescue. No wonder the leading private equity industry barons (including a one-time presidential candidate – see below) are opposed to any serious monetary reform agenda.

When the ultimate stage of steep drop in speculative temperatures, financial crisis and recession arrives, leaving in its wake much economic destruction, it remains largely unclear to the population at large that the responsibility for this lay with the promoters of monetary instability. Rather, the popular targets become the bankers, the brokers and the criminal fellow travellers. The central bankers and their political masters who unleashed the forces of monetary instability may actually become heroes for having plugged the dams during the crisis which their policies caused and for acting imaginatively so as to stimulate recovery. They may weep crocodile tears about the fate of the unemployed and bankrupts and the plight of the small saver without admitting (perhaps even to themselves) that they were ultimately responsible.

The crisis, the Great Recession and the weak economic expansion, together with the general erosion of living standards, could have produced a demand for monetary reform. But who would lead the call? Some conservative candidates mouthed phrases such as scrapping the Fed's dual mandate and focusing on price stability or the benefits of a strong dollar or even setting up a commission to examine an eventual return to a gold standard, but why would the population take head of these calls when there seemed no current inflation problem, albeit that some scare could be engendered by the quasi money printing which featured in the Great Monetary Experiment. Yet with only low inflation at present that all seemed like a distant and possibly phantom threat. The monetary reformer could have hoped to rally the anti-Wall Street sentiment to his or her cause by demonstrating how much the big banks were gaining from the Federal Reserve and the depth of crony capitalism in the private equity industry, but this was difficult given that the conservative presidential candidate in 2012 was himself a private equity baron and there was a risk of messages getting mixed with left-wing populists attacking the same targets and calling for tougher regulations. Yet the perils of asset price inflation are for real and remain menacing.

In our earlier discussion, we have seen that the two big economic costs of asset price inflation are first mal-investment and second an enfeebling of risk appetites, which means that the progress of the given economy into the forest of opportunity is slower and shallower (less economic prosperity over the long run). Yet we should also consider a third cost alongside these which is the enfeebling of the free society.

We should also keep in mind that the inflation viruses – goods and services inflation and asset price inflation – are not the only channels through which monetary authorities endanger the free society. There is also the whole question of the use by the Federal Reserve of its powers to boost the liquidity of particular asset classes to engage in crony capitalism and further the power of government not just in the economy but more broadly. A monetary reform programme should engage that aspect – and in some ways, that is the easiest part of a populist agenda to formulate.

A first illustration of that process was during World War I. A follow on was in the German lending boom of the mid-1920s. Fast forward to the present, we have the links presented in the research of, for example, Haber and Levine (2014). They quote a growing body of empirical findings that the stock market values bank-Fed connections. Recent academic papers make similar points – see, for example, Acemoglu, Johnson, Kermani, Kwak and Mitton, 2013 or Cieslak, Morse and Vissing-Jorgensen, 2014.

The perils of asset price inflation for a free society are both more insidious and subtler than the examples which could be cited of crony capitalism. The diminishing of economic prosperity makes it more difficult to maintain popular support for free markets and competitive capitalism. Nothing succeeds like success. Great recessions, panics and laying to waste of human capital all amidst the heightened wealth inequality which asset price inflation induces reduces such support for free markets.

The aftermath of asset price inflation is highly dangerous for the free society. The political elites scramble to assemble control and alarm systems to prevent a recurrence of the disease (that they refuse to recognize as monetary in origin). They rush to identify popular scapegoats rather than undertake the more difficult and likely unrewarding task of designing and implementing monetary reform (an enterprise which itself holds huge dangers if this is badly flawed). One only has to think of the maze of regulations introduced in the wake of financial panic and the increase in the powers of government to intrude on what was previously regarded as private. Government finances whose underlying deterioration was previously camouflaged by bubbles suddenly dive into the deep red. In consequence, the fiscal authorities obtain new powers to reach far into the affairs of its citizens in ways which trample on long-regarded rights of privacy and without due restraints on abuse of individual freedoms.

Historical examples of asset price inflation as enemy of freedom

There are several historical episodes to demonstrate the vulnerability of free societies to asset price inflation. Take the most catastrophic example of all – the descent of the Weimar Republic into the political and economic abyss, culminating in World War II. None of this was pre-programmed by the Versailles Treaty and the Reparations Issue as some historians and populist commentators taking their cue from John Maynard Keynes would have us believe. If the US had been a zone of monetary stability during the early and mid-1920s rather than a fermenter of perhaps the most powerful global asset price inflation virus ever seen, the outcomes would surely have been much different. The giant carry trade boom into German bonds fuelled by the monetary disequilibrium created by the Benjamin Strong Fed and abetted by its crony capitalist connections was the engine of destruction. Domestically, the assault in the US of the 1930s on the free society – at first on competitive capitalism and then more widely on free markets – by the Hoover and subsequently the Roosevelt Administrations came as a direct response to the disastrous economic aftermath of the Strong monetary instability.

Turning to the post World War II era, we have already seen (p. 93) how the monetary instability generated by the Martin Fed during the 1950s (the Eisenhower Administration years) paved the way for the New Age Keynesians to carry out their great experiment. The hypothesis was that lifting inflation would boost employment growth and smooth the business cycle. First, there was the Great Asset Price Inflation, then the Great Goods and Services price inflation. The end phase of the Great Asset Price inflation included two great crashes: the first in 1969 and the second in 1973.

In response to the first crash and related recession (1969–70), the Nixon Administration appointed its Fed Chief (Arthur Burns) who would abort a monetary policy programme aimed at bringing down goods and services inflation and would turn instead (when next inflation risks increased) to extending government intervention into direct setting of wages and prices. In practice, these new controls were launched simultaneously with a devaluation of the US dollar (Summer 1971) amidst a threat to free trade which rocked the global order. The Great Recession of 1974–75 left in its wake enfeebled public finances stretched by the great new social spending programmes. The fiscally conservative Carter Administration did work toward lower deficits but largely via cuts in defence spending facilitated in part by the US withdrawal from Vietnam.

That was a background catalyst for the Soviet Union to move a new generation of medium-range nuclear missiles into its East European satellites including East Germany, which in turn stirred a wave of passivism in the then front line state of West Germany.

It was in response to this worsened Soviet menace in Europe that the Reagan Administration stepped up military spending (concentrated on nuclear rearmament) in the early 1980s. It took a gamble in cutting taxes at the same time, counting on the success of its supply side economic programme to generate prosperity on such a scale that the bulge in the federal budget deficit would disappear over a decade as additional revenues flowed into the Treasury. That gamble may have proved successful if it had not been for the Volcker Fed and the early Greenspan Fed in their pursuance of the weaker dollar as desired by the Reagan Administration in its late years creating the Great Asset Price inflation of 1986–89, which culminated in another crash (equities in 1987, real estate from 1989) and difficult recession. As estimates of the economy's productive potential were revised down and the underlying budget arithmetic became even more worrying, the Administration of WH Bush raised taxes, thus, turning its back on the supply side ethos of the early Reagan years and breaking its election promises. This dispirited the conservative movement in the US and was an important factor in the loss of power by the Republicans in 1992. The US economic pessimism in the aftermath of the 1990–91 recession was a key factor in the launching of the Clinton currency war through 1993–95 and the accompanying trade offensive against Japan – penalties on Japanese exports if Tokyo failed to comply with demands by Washington for structural reforms and macroeconomic policies designed to favour the US Administration's important backers (for example, the automobile labour union).

Let us move fast forward to the Great Asset Price inflation of 1996–2000 (featuring in its late stage the NASDAQ and related dotcom bubble) culminating in the 2000 Crash. This was followed by three years of cyclical weakness (2001, 2002 and early 2003). The response of the George W Bush Administration to economic pessimism was the launching of a currency war (a key event was the Dubai G-7 Summit of September 2003 at which the Asian dollar bloc was broken up) and installing leadership in the Federal Reserve that would veer US monetary policy even further away from monetary stability. Greenspan was reappointed as Fed Chair in Spring 2003 (for a shorter than usual term), and it was plain to all that he was expected to "stimulate the economy", keeping rates far below neutral. In 2002, Bush had appointed Bernanke to the Federal Reserve Board, an academic renowned for his advocacy of inflation targeting coupled with aggressive use of non-conventional monetary tools in the countering of deflation and recessionary dangers.

The culmination of all this was the Great Asset Price inflation of the mid-2000s and the subsequent panic and Great Recession which in turn ushered in the most left-wing administration in US history, with its agenda of widespread regulation, higher taxes and state health provision. Again, the huge gap which opened up in the federal budget as the economy enfeebled by the further episode of asset price inflation – revealing that previous spending plans based on higher growth estimates in the long run were unfunded – brought a new ratcheting up of taxation reinforced by new powers for US fiscal authorities to police offshore transactions of their citizens and override bank secrecy laws.

Some conservative thinkers ignore the imperative of monetary stability

So what is to be done? Some leading conservative thinkers still do not address the monetary challenge even after so much damage has been done to the free society by monetary instability. For example, University of Chicago Professor Zingales wrote (2012) a highly stimulatory and imaginative book on how to resell the message of capitalism and freedom to US voters based on the overriding message that free competition will bring a new prosperity whilst shrinking or eliminating the scope for widely hated crony capitalism. It is a pity that the private equity industry does not even get a mention – an omission which is explained by a lack of focus on monetary stability. Zingales, in fact, has no prescription for monetary stability except to break up the monetary authority into one entity responsible for price stability and the other for financial stability: "My proposed architecture calls for having a fully independent monetary authority board and a politically accountable financial stability board".

This misses the crucial point. Monetary stability is a necessary and sufficient condition of financial stability. The latter cannot be achieved if there is monetary instability. And monetary stability, appropriately defined, prevents the emergence of the asset price inflation disease responsible for financial instability. Financial stability cannot be achieved independently of monetary stability.

It is not possible for monetary stability to emerge under a regime where the Federal Reserve is manipulating interest rates based on its ever changing views about the state of the economy and its supposed special knowledge about the appropriate level of rates. Rather, monetary stability depends on the existence (birth is not immaculate!) of high-powered money whose supply is determined by automatic mechanisms (as in the gold standard) or constitutionally enshrined rules (as to be described in this chapter) and whose special attributes mean that it enjoys a high and stable demand. Then all market rates can be determined in free markets without any official fixing. Under such a regime, individual decision making by market participants will lead to these rates coming closer on average to neutral level than could ever be achieved by monetary Bureaucrats execrcising their discretionary judgement.

Those Republican politicians who in Summer 2014 endorsed the so-called Taylor Rule as the basis for their monetary reform programme just did not get the point either. We should surely have learnt by now that neo-Keynesian steering of interest rates even if constrained by some econometric based rule ends up generating monetary disease. Of course, Professor Taylor may argue that if the correct coefficients were used in the implementation of this rule and policymakers made well-educated estimates of key inputs (including the neutral level of interest rates and the natural rate of unemployment), the most recent monetary disequilibrium would not have occurred. But "correct" and "well-educated estimates" are terms which should make us concerned about likely dupery.

Milton Friedman in his *Capitalism and Freedom* (1962), unlike Zingales, has no doubts about the absolute importance of monetary stability to the existence and survival of the free society. In a prominent chapter, he advocates his famous monetary rule – that the Federal Reserve should set a fixed rule of x% p.a. for the expansion of the money supply. He means by the latter, an aggregate which includes both cash in circulation and transaction deposits with the banks. The tool for achieving this set rate of monetary expansion is adjusting the supply of high-powered money, meaning principally the supply of reserves to the banks. The central bank should not set interest rates in the money market, but leave these to be determined such as to be consistent with the amount of reserves which the central bank has created. With the central bank signalling nothing about the level of interest rates, long-term rates would be free of official manipulation (by forward guidance or in any other way).

At the time, Friedman provided a message that conservative politicians could sell. The gist was that we can end the hated inflation by firing those lousy bureaucrats at the Federal Reserve and replacing them with an automatic growth of the money supply at a low fixed-rate of x% p.a. That is certainly a powerful message. But reformers seeking to lead the US into an era of monetary stability, which in turn re-invigorates economic and political liberty, should not rest on such rhetoric.

Identifying a gap in Milton Friedman's guidance to reformers

Demand for the money as defined by the aggregate which Friedman identified (nearest to M1 using present statistical terminology) has been highly volatile in its relation to the path of the US economy. Hence, strict adherence to a simple fixed rule based on this definition of money could have induced considerable macroeconomic instability including episodes of severe monetary disease. Further, the relation between monetary base as partly determined by prevailing reserve requirements together with other institutional factors and the chosen monetary aggregate (M1) has been highly variable. Hence, tight control by the central bank of the monetary base does not mean that money supply can be steered reliably along a stipulated path (for example, the x% p.a. rate as consistent with long-run demand growth at stable prices).

Friedman does not consider explicitly the disease of asset price inflation – perhaps because this would be hard to analyse within the methodology of positive economics which he espouses. Instead, he takes as the ultimate aim of monetary policy the achievement of "price level stability". He argues that this aim is best achieved via the setting of an intermediate target for money supply (M1). In recent decades that recommendation has been undermined by the apparent instability in demand for such a monetary aggregate (albeit researchers have tried with varying degrees of success to identify alternative broader aggregates for this purpose). Friedman does not take up the issue raised by the Austrian School that monetary stability, in fact, requires sustained periods when prices on average come to a level well below the long-run flat guide path and sometimes well above; otherwise, the disease of asset price inflation forms, perhaps virulently. And in his other writings (see p. 108), Friedman espouses ideas such as permanent gentle decline in prices or interest rate at market levels being paid on reserves which are inconsistent with monetary base being the powerful pivot to a stable monetary order in which all interest rates (including money rates) would be determined without central bank manipulation (including "pegs" and "corridors") in any form.

A big challenge for monetary reformers is how to securely pivot the monetary system. That means designing a form of monetary base (high-powered money) such that we can set a simple rule for determining the supply of this which would mean prices are well-anchored (a firm fixed anchor) over the long run, though, able to fluctuate upward and downward through time consistent with efficient operation of the invisible hand (meaning considerable flexibility in the line linking the anchor to prices). In principle, this means that the demand (in real terms) for high-powered money (as designed) should be a recognizable stable function of real income and wealth. Demand for high-powered money should be substantial relative to both (income and wealth).

Moreover, it should also be the case (in an ideal design) that short-run shifts in demand for the high-powered money in the nature of statistical white noise (no fundamental factor behind) cannot undermine the stability of a regime based on a simple set of rules determining its growth in supply. The self-limiting device here tending to suppress interference from white noise is volatility of short-term rates. High volatility means swings in those short-term rates as caused by random short-lived shifts in demand for high-powered money do not play much of a role in the determination of those medium and long-term rates which are critical in consumer and investment decision making.

It is also helpful toward monetary stability that there are substantial rewards to the public (whether banks or households) in pursuing optimization procedures on a continuous basis with respect to their holding of high-powered money. If there is no big opportunity cost with respect to sloppy optimization, then for much of the time aggregate holding of high-powered money could deviate substantially from the path of equilibrium demand, meaning considerable scope for cycles of disequilibrium to form (in which, for example, interest rates may get driven further from neutral level) even as the supply was piloted by automatic mechanisms or constitutional rules. For example, if reserves at the central bank are hardly distinguishable in attributes from short-term Treasury bills (meaning very little difference in interest rate or liquidity), then banks may act quite passively in their holding of these. If there is such slack, then the path of the monetary base as determined by the automatic mechanisms or rules exerts less discipline in the short or medium term on the overall monetary system and the economy.

Lessons for monetary reformers from gold standard

Friedman and more generally the monetarists did not consider this problem – how to design an ideal monetary base which would be a powerful pivot to the whole system. Their recommendation that the central bank should target a monetary aggregate including bank deposits – piloting a given monetary base aggregate (which, in fact, considerably changed its essential characteristics through time) such as to achieve the target – has never been implemented except remotely and was surely not the high road to monetary stability. (In the German and Swiss monetarist episodes of the 1970s the central banks targeted monetary base directly). The monetarists did not investigate in their published works the special properties of the high-powered money pivot under the gold standard and how its success was in delivering stability was not due to the genius of a designer but to the innate appeal of the yellow metal.

High-powered money (otherwise described as monetary base) under the gold standard included mainly gold coin and gold certificates. There were also bank holdings of deposits at the central bank or if this did not exist (the situation in the US) at city banks or the clearing house, respectively. Banknotes also circulated alongside gold coin and top quality ones could form part of what we would describe conceptually as the monetary base or high-powered money. The properties of high-powered money were highly distinct from those of wider monetary aggregates. For households, gold coins were the ultimate in safety, liquidity and suitability for effecting payments. They also provided a safe haven protection in the event of war or other catastrophes where the convertibility of the national money into gold could be suspended. And for banks, there were no close substitutes for high-powered money in terms of ability to meet instant payment needs – whether to satisfy bank customers requesting conversion of their deposits into cash or transferring their deposits to customers with other banks (so as to settle transactions for goods or assets). Assets which could be virtually immediately turned into high-powered money (cash) at trivial cost were scarce, and there was no central bank bestowing liquidity on selected paper (by making this eligible for instant discounting at the central bank window).

Yes, the central bank could make emergency loans to banks in a situation of liquidity crunch so long as they were still solvent but such loans were made at penalty rates so as to discourage this procedure, reinforcing thereby a solid demand for high-powered money. There were no payment cards to be used widely at zero cost (attributable to the fact that card companies exert market power with respect to retailers so as to limit the practice of charging extra when these are used relative to the price for cash settlement – see p. 140). And banks could not count on fluctuations in demand for cash being within small bounds as is now the case when deposits are insured and big banks can expect to obtain finance from government in emergency. Moreover, they had every incentive to manage their holdings of high-powered money efficiently as this paid no interest whereas money market rates were always positive. And the costs of running short on high-powered money could be very high.

Fractional reserve banking did introduce some potential instability into the demand for high-powered money as this could shoot up during a period of overall liquidity crisis when banks faced sudden demand for conversion of deposits into coin or cash. Yet such possibilities meant that banks held large amounts of reserves relative to their deposit base without even being ordered to do so in many cases. Yes, in the US, there were reserve requirements imposed by state or federal laws which added to the demand for free reserves (in so far as banks realized they would face penalty if they ran down their reserves below legal limit when these were suddenly required to meet payment needs). In Great Britain, the "leader of the orchestra" in the gold standard world, there were not reserve requirements set by law.

Sometimes violent fluctuations of short-term interest rates occurred as to bring about balance of supply and demand in the reserve market. A spike in rates would create incentive for banks to economise on reserve holdings and for customers to economise on cash (as against leaving deposits with their bank).

The supply of high-powered money was determined by a simple rule embedded in the automatic workings of the gold standard. The above ground supply of gold, the main component of high-powered money for those countries in aggregate on the gold standard, would increase over time in line with the amount of newly mined supplies of the metal profitable at the official gold price. In practice, the stock of above ground gold grew by an amount each year which varied between 1% and 3%. When goods and services prices in general were below normal, there would be an incentive to increase gold production and conversely. Advances in gold mining technology or new discoveries of mines were also relevant to the path of supply.

100% reserve requirement proposals are illiberal and unnecessary for stability

There is a long history of accusations that fractional reserve banking is a potential source of financial and monetary stability. The runs on banks which might develop during various types of crisis can be deeply destabilizing to the economy, and the need to avoid these undermines the appliance of strict rules setting the growth of high-powered money. Such concerns have led on to the proposal for 100% reserve requirements as applied to banks whose business is to create and service transaction deposits – a proposal endorsed for example by Milton Friedman (in the tradition of Henry Simons).

Yet this is surely illiberal in essence. If some households would like to hold somewhat riskier deposits issued by fractional reserve banks which come with a warning notice that "in emergency the bank might suspend their use as payments and convert into three month notes (which will be reconverted back into demand deposits as soon as conditions allow)", and they are happy with the extra interest rate they get on these, then why not? There would be no Big Brother in the background ready to provide full liquidity in any crisis at no penalty cost to anyone.

Some fractional reserve banks might seek to bolster the quality of their deposits by promising that they will keep to a high equity cushion and eschew bond finance. Indeed, as Myerson (2014) points out, early in the 20th century banks typically had equity capital worth about 25% of their total assets. In 2008, many large banks in Europe and America could finance their assets with only 3% less of equity backing. And some may promise that they will "in normal circumstances" hold a high reserve cover ratio. So there would be all types of deposits for all men and this would be underpinned by a solid aggregate demand for high-powered money in the ways required. There would be no deposit insurance and no "too big to fail".

Can there be a powerful non-golden pivot to monetary system?

If we pull out the golden rug from underneath this system as just described, can we still construct a secure pivot to the monetary system and accomplish the goal of monetary stability accordingly? The challenge is to replace by constitutional monetary law what occurred under autopilot as fired by the convertibility of money into gold at a fixed price. And note that gold convertibility in itself limited the power of governments to run deficits or engage in financial largesse such as is necessary for a powerful lender of last resort, comprehensive deposit insurance and government backstops for "too big to fail" financial institutions – all of which have been analysed here (see p. 137) as corrupting base money in its role of pivot.

We could argue counterfactually that if somehow these corrupting functions had existed under the gold standard, then monetary stability would not have been achieved there. Even high-powered money consisting mainly of gold would have been too fragile a pivot under such circumstances, lacking the huge stable demand which would secure its position. In fact, there are some grounds for optimism about the possible achievement of monetary stability without gold, even though its absence imposes handicaps. These include the facts that first, gold coin – the chief component of high-powered money under a full gold standard – is a less close substitute for alternative assets included in wider definitions of money than are the banknotes or reserves, which dominate high-powered money under a fiat system. Second, even constitution-embedded rules determining a fixed expansion of high-powered money expansion subject to very limited flexibility (based on where prices are now relative to the fixed anchor) can be broken with less impunity (in terms of possible political or legal consequence) than breaking with gold.

The agenda of monetary reform which US conservatives could present in the pursuance of and defence of the free society would form part of a full programme of economic and institutional reforms, which could help to bring victory at the ballot box. The overriding aim of monetary reform would be to create the conditions for enduring monetary stability. This means a fixed anchor to the prices of goods and services on average over the very long run (where these prices are measured without making any so-called hedonic adjustments to take account of improvements in the quality of consumer goods or services) and the elimination of monetary diseases whether goods and services inflation or asset price inflation. No goods and services inflation is consistent with periods of rising prices as required for the efficient operation of the invisible hands in sustaining economic equilibrium over time, but these will tend to be balance by periods of falling prices for the same reason.

In line with the aim of fostering a high and stable demand for high-powered money (monetary base), the government should withdraw from guaranteeing the payments transfer function or providing backstops to financial institutions whilst zealously promoting financial sector competition by using anti-monopoly powers These reforms would be popular in themselves as part of a free market agenda in addition to their monetary significance. The anti-trust law enforcement would be vigorous for example against credit card companies who abuse their market power such as to force retailers to accept their cards at no extra fee compared to cash payments (an abuse which incidentally undermines demand for high-powered money). Big denomination notes should be introduced such as to satisfy potential transactions and store of value demand for this medium of exchange (and bolster the monetary base as pivot). US dollar banknote denominations should include at least $500 and $1000 benchmarks. (After all, a one ounce gold eagle, worth around $1200 at end-2014, was part of the medium of exchange in the US under the gold standard). Reserves at the central bank would pay no interest. Those institutions marketing any form of payments function to their clients would have to meet demanding disclosure requirements so that the public and rating agencies could assign reasonable estimate to the risks of any impairment or suspension.

There would be no official regulations regarding composition of assets or liabilities for the balance sheets of banks, even those which market deposits coupled with a payments function (where funds can be withdrawn or transferred at any time on demand). Yet there could be a watchdog which polices mandatory disclosure requirements (so that a bank could not fraudulently or by mistake market deposits as being of a given high quality when in fact they were cutting their declared equity backing or increasing the riskiness of their assets or cutting their level of free reserves).

The monetary authority responsible for the creation of high-powered money in all its various forms (fiat banknotes, reserves at the central bank) would be subject to a fixed rule of x% expansion. X where this is set in line with estimated growth of demand in real terms. Boosts or subtractions from this rate of expansion would be made according to how far prices of goods or services on average are below or above the very long-run constant path to which the fixed anchor applies. The monetary authority would desist from any rate fixing in short-term money market or attempts to manipulate expectations regarding long-term interest rates. These would be determined freely without official intervention in any form. The aim would be to include all of this in an amendment to the US constitution.

Why high-powered money must pay no interest

The insistence here that the monetary reform programme should stipulate reserves pay no interest is in in sharp contrast to the recommendation of present-day conservative monetary reformers such as Cochrane (2014). As already mentioned, Friedman was in favour of interest payments on reserves at a market rate (although he preferred a gradual deflation such as the going real interest rate was earned on cash, meaning that households did not falsely seek to economize on their holdings of this when its production cost is in fact zero, see p. 112)

Here is a quote from the Cochrane argument:

> The Fed's plan to maintain a large balance sheet and pay interest on bank reserves, begun under former Chairman Ben Bernanke and

continued under current Chair Janet Yellen, is highly desirable for a number of reasons – the most important of which is financial stability. Short version: Banks holding lots of reserves don't go under.

This policy is new and controversial. However many arguments against it are based on fallacies. People forget that when the Fed creates a dollar of reserves, it buys a dollar of Treasuries or government-guaranteed mortgage-backed securities. Reserves that pay interest are not inflationary. Period. Now that banks have trillions more reserves than they need to satisfy regulations or service their deposits, banks don't care if they hold another dollar of interest-paying reserves or another dollar of Treasuries. They are perfect substitutes at the margin. Exchanging red M&Ms for green M&Ms does not help your diet. Commenters have seen the astonishing rise in reserves – from \$50billion in 2007 to \$2.7 trillion today (early 2015)– and warned of hyperinflation to come. This is simply wrong as long as reserves pay market interest.

In this book, the view has already been expressed that quantitative easing (QE) in the form of creating massive reserves which pay interest at or above the market rate of interest is not in itself inevitably inflationary (see p. 9). That is where agreement with Professor Cochrane ends!

If in various ways the QE policy causes short, medium, or long-term interest rates to be driven below the neutral level, monetary disease forms, whether in the form of asset price inflation or goods and services inflation or both. The expansion of the Fed balance sheet may incite irrational expectations that cause such an outcome (especially if asset expansion is concentrated on long-maturity government debt). (see p. 17). Moreover, the growth of the balance sheet might occur in a way which adds to government distortions of the economy (whether subsidizing the mortgage sector or to lowering the cost of finance to federally funded programmes).

It is true that in a monetary system where the monetary base has been designed successfully as a powerful pivot, there would likely be more of it relative to economic size than in the recent past. And where the main components of monetary base are liabilities issued by the central bank, this means essentially a larger central bank balance sheet.

Is it possible to constrain the extent to which a large balance sheet favours big government?

The accumulation of gold coin on the asset side of the balance sheet is promising in this respect. And if indeed the process of monetary reform increases the demand for dollars and reduces the private demand for gold, the flow of metal into the central bank (Federal Reserve) would not entail any resource cost in the form of additional new mining activity.

Alternatively, the central bank could accumulate loans to the government on the asset side of its balance. Matching liability expansion (in the form of non-interest bearing reserves) would be the source of seigniorage income (the government effectively financing itself at the zero rate on reserves). In principle, the federal government should match that seigniorage income with a reduction in taxes. Hence, in the long run, the government debt outside the central bank would grow faster (but from a lower level) than under alternative regimes where monetary base is much smaller. In effect, the income which the government gets from providing a large fiat monetary base to the public and so allowing a well-pivoted monetary system to take shape is refunded via lower taxes. The problem here (for the monetary reformers) is that political commitments to return seigniorage to citizens through lower taxes may not be fulfilled even if enshrined constitutionally, meaning that in fact the monetary revolution would contribute to higher spending by the government.

The pivotal role of the monetary base depends crucially on non-payment of interest on reserves (or banknotes) at least in the normal circumstances of market short-term rates of interest being significantly positive. Under that situation, high-powered money is the proverbial hot potato which banks and the non-bank public seek to economize on holding, and if they find themselves with excess amount, they try to get rid of it as quickly as possible. That is where the power behind high-powered money comes from! Money market rates shift in line with efforts of households and banks to continually readjust their holdings of high-powered money as its supply becomes more or less plentiful in aggregate. Specifically, it is the interest elasticity in the demand for non-interest bearing reserves which means that money market rate fluctuations can reconcile a fairly rigid path for the supply of high-powered money with considerable short-term shifts (including white noise) in demand.

As illustration, if demand for high-powered money (as designed by the monetary reformers in non-interest bearing form) is tending to outstrip supply, then money market rates rise. The increased opportunity cost to holding (non-interest bearing) high-powered money would cause the public to switch (at the margin) holdings of cash into bank deposits and (within the universe of bank deposits) from bank deposits against which reserve holdings are large (the safest form of deposits) to less reserve intensive deposits (the interest rate gap between the two widens as the level of interest rates rises). One illustration of such a shift could be from current accounts (sight deposits) to fixed-term deposits. Banks themselves could not shift much independently of their customers (making transfers from reserve intensive to less intensive liabilities) except to the extent they could tighten up on sloppy practices which meant they were holding more reserves than what they needed to meet the given risk grading by the independent agencies and to minimize high costs of temporary cash shortages.

If reserves were to pay interest at the market rate (as Cochrane would like), then all such flexibility is lost. The only way in which the central bank could guide the supply of high-powered money growth along its chosen path would be to fix short-term rates and hope for the best. Hope would be fulfilled if the central bank had estimated the right intersection between supply and demand for high-powered money consistent with the chosen path. If this turned out not to be the case, then the central bank would adjust the interest rate in the market for reserves (day-to-day money). But such a discretionary regime for rate changes could easily turn out to be the thin end of a wedge to a wide manipulation of interest rates and interest rate expectations.

Money rates stuck at zero are abnormal

Under a stable money regime with a powerful non-interest bearing high-powered money pivot as described, one should not expect that money market rates would be stuck at zero for long periods of time. Were the central bank to generate such an expansive path for high-powered money that this was indeed the situation, then high-powered money would lose its power. As money market interest rates come close to zero, there is barely any opportunity cost to holding high-powered money, and so efforts of households and banks to adjust their portfolios wither in significance.

If these zero rates are far below say the neutral level for medium-term rates and this situation is not just temporary, then market rates at these medium-maturities would sag well below neutral (but they would likely remain substantially positive reflecting well above zero forward rates in the term structure). This would promote monetary disease whether in the form of goods and services inflation or asset price inflation. (The extent of the disease should be small under normal circumstances if overall monetary order remains firm). Some holders of high-powered money (in the context of substantially positive neutral level for medium-term rates) might decide to accelerate their purchases of goods and services rather than suffer zero rates of interest on their short-term liquidity especially if these higher medium-term rates indicated to many that prices would likely rise in the future. Businesses might act similarly.

Long periods of high-powered money glut would be symptomatic of a badly designed monetary system. At such times, the pivot of the monetary system becomes less sharply pointed.

The distinction between high-powered money and other short-term bill markets becomes blurred. The glut of high-powered money can exert a stimulatory influence via pinning short-term rates at zero if the neutral level of market rates especially for medium-maturities is substantially positive. But the long history of discretionary monetary policy shows that such attempts to fine tune the business cycle end in failure.

Alternatively, in the case where the neutral level of rates both for short and longer term rates is abnormally low, then high-powered money loses all sources of conventional power. Non-conventional sources can emerge under conditions of high-powered money glut – including the interplay of strong irrational forces in the market-place – but these are full of longer term danger. The conventional power source eventually becomes restored without interventions via a process of price fluctuations through time (falling below the long-run constant path during the period of recession matched with expectations of recovery further ahead, meaning the real interest rates become negative and remain so even as nominal market interest rates start to climb).

Gluts in the supply of high-powered money did not occur under the gold standard as falls in interest rates induced large enough changes (increases) in the amounts (whether in the form of gold, banknotes or reserves) that the public and banks wanted to hold at still positive (albeit far below peak) rates of interest. Walter Bagehot observed in 1873 that "John Bull can stand many things, but he cannot stand two per cent". As Alex Pollock points out (2014), Bagehot meant that "a low rate of interest, long protracted, gives rise to hazardous gambling in speculative undertakings. That is a 19th century way of saying low rates would produce asset price inflation". Bagehot did not identify why John Bull never had to suffer rates below 2%, but if he had spelt it out, he would have explained the highly distinct nature of the high-powered money aggregate (no interest paid on it, large metallic content, not any close substitutes in terms of high liquidity, no lender of last resort except at high penalty, no deposit insurance, no too big to fail). Without short-term interest rates making that last dip toward zero in recession, a larger role would be played by the self-recovery force of prices dropping below the constant long-run flat trend and expectations building of a subsequent recovery (hence, negative real rates).

The frequency or extent to which the Bank of England had to act in that way was diminished by the high interest elasticity of demand for high-powered money. Small falls of interest rates below normal level would bring big shifts of demand toward cash and away from sight deposits or from term deposits into sight deposits and banks would increase the amount of reserves they held above the normal level. We should expect the same elasticity under the monetary system as outlined in this manifesto. And so, in the hypothetical situation discussed above (in the monetary reform plan) of banks with different advertised levels of reserve backing (some 100%), we would see considerable shifts in response to small changes in interest rates, which might in fact mean that rates falling to zero would be a very rare occurrence. As we shall see below under the gold standard, short-term rates never fell below 2% in London precisely because the interest elasticity of demand for high-powered money was so large in a system of large amounts outstanding relative to economic size and where this was such a distinct asset. The zero rate bound problem is in many respects a creation of too big to fail and deposit insurance.

How to sell the monetary reform manifesto and tread gently on gold?

Having outlined the manifesto for monetary reform, is it feasible to recap its main selling points in terms of a popular conservative message and to confront in strong rhetoric the criticisms which would be raised by its opponents. The message is that the monetary stability achieved by virtue of the reform would mean greater prosperity for all, less inequality (no more crony capitalism between the Fed and Wall Street), no more monetary favours to big government and stable prices in the long-run and an environment where individuals can accumulate savings for their future without having to ride the wild waves in financial markets as generated by monetary chaos. The US dollar would dominate the global economy as an unrivalled hard currency.

The conservative revolutionaries drawing up the manifesto for monetary reform would have to carefully consider their position on a "return to the gold standard". In principle, they could advocate that the US dollar again become convertible into gold and gold coin at a fixed price. Then the gold price against other major currencies (for example, the gold price in yen or euros) would be determined by fluctuations of the dollar in terms of these. It would be entirely unpredictable how much gold the US Treasury (or its agents) would buy or sell cumulatively over the early years of the US gold standard – that would depend largely on the price set and the extent of international confidence in US monetary reform and the new dollar which emerges with this. In practice, the US authorities could not allow the path of monetary base to be subject to such huge uncertainty, and there would have to be a strict set of rules outlined here for expansion of this (monetary base). At inception, much of the base would be in non-metallic form. If there were such terrific inflows of gold into dollars that all non-gold elements in the base (largely government and quasi-government paper) had to be sold toward meeting the rule, then the Treasury would have to issue additional bonds (beyond those liquidated by the Federal Reserve) for the purpose of buying the surplus metal.

The case for the "US return to gold" would be first that a metallic content to high-powered money would help produce a broad stable demand for this aggregate, essential to the well-functioning of the monetary stability framework described here. In addition, it could strengthen political support for monetary reform.

The case against would include the potential cost (to the US taxpayer) of huge sterilization operations (to mop up a glut of high-powered money created in a process of massive dumping of gold for the new hard dollar) and the windfall gains which might be distributed around the world at the cost of the US taxpayer. And the opponents of a return of the US to gold could assert that demand for monetary base in the ersatz gold system could indeed be broad and stable as outlined in the regime described here. This features a fixed anchor to prices in the very long run, no lender of last resort, no too big to fail banks, large denomination banknotes (the counterpart to gold bars in the monetary base which would satisfy hoarding demand) and tackling of credit card company monopoly-type abuses.

How would the US monetary reformers respond to criticisms?

A top criticism would be the apparent omission of "full employment" as an aim and more broadly this is a return to the harsh environment of the gold standard world where governments did nothing to even out wild swings in the business cycle and ameliorate corresponding swings in employment and wages. The appropriate riposte is that the modern "compassionate central bankers and their political masters" have harmed rather than promoted the prosperity enjoyed by their fellow citizens. The biggest downturns in employment and aggregate incomes have occurred in the late stages of asset price inflation disease created repeatedly by the monetary policy do-gooders who worry about high unemployment but whose interventions often reduce employment. And when the disease ultimately exits, there remains a long-run hangover of diminished risk appetites and obsolescent capital (human and physical) built during the wave of mal-investment which weighs on future economic prosperity including employment opportunities.

The well-meaning Keynesian central bankers of the 1960s thought they were generating economic prosperity, high employment and the accompanying conditions which would finance the Great Society. When the Great Crashes of 1969 and 1973 and the Great Recession of 1973–74 occurred, they made no apology for their role in these disasters but persevered with what they regarded as creative new policies to help the unemployed get back to work. Although these efforts met with some initial apparent success, they ended with a second Great Recession in 1980–82. Skip forward to the QE policies from 2009 onwards. Reports circulated that Professor Bernanke and subsequently Professor Yellen had great concern for the unemployed and under-employed and that was why they were working so hard on creative new monetary policies.

They were never held to account for their prior conduct of policy or policy recommendations during the expansion phases, which subsequently generated the busts and caused so much human suffering. Perhaps Senator Bunning came nearest to expressing those sentiments when he spoke to the Senate in late 2009 and begged lawmakers there not to approve Bernanke's reappointment as Fed Chair. The senator pointed out that he alone had opposed Bernanke's appointment four year earlier on the grounds that he would continue to amplify the interventions of Greenspan which had caused such violent waves of asset price inflation and deflation. Bunning did not use those precise terms, but he told Bernanke "you are the moral hazard"! Unfortunately, the senator veered off track when he faulted Bernanke for not following the Taylor Rule. As we have seen here, this rule is a neo-Keynesian interventionist machinery in neo-classical lamb's clothing, and the Republicans, even five years later, were mistakenly following the lead of this ex-Bush official.

Four years later, when the Senate was considering Yellen's appointment, there was no one in Bunning's mode to hurl the obvious question at the aspiring Fed Chief. Why at that crucial FOMC meeting of July 2–3, 1996, when the Greenspan Fed was deliberating whether to pursue the aim of price stability as conventionally understood – taking advantage of the IT-related boom in productivity to at last firmly anchor prices in a long-run perspective – why had she taken the lead in arguing that instead the aim of policy should be permanent inflation at 2% p.a.? (The committee meeting led by Greenspan unanimously agreed with her at the end of a tortuous and unenlightened debate amidst much hilarity, which seemed strange regarding such a weighty matter, see FOMC transcript). Did she regret all the misery which the resulting cycles of asset price inflation and deflation had caused since then or did she even understand cause and effect in this matter? Instead, the senators had to listen to protestations of how the new nominee felt for working families and for those unable to find work and how she would continue QE policies and other intervention policies toward improving conditions in the labour market!

A follow-up point likely to be raised by the critics of monetary reform as outlined here could be who would defend us from the perpetual threat of deadly deflation? The news here is that under the monetary order, there would be no deadly deflation danger. Yes, there would be transitory downward swings of prices as in a business recessions twinned with expectations of subsequent rebound of prices. That is how the capitalist system generates recovery from recession and adjusts over time to temporary bulges in savings relative to investment opportunity.

The attempt by central bankers and their political masters to suppress this inter-temporal price adjustment which is crucial to economies finding an equilibrium path over time end up generating asset price inflations and hold back the cyclical recovery. This has been the experience of Fed QE.

Without QE, yes, many prices and some wages would have fallen through the Great Recession and even beyond. But expectations of subsequent price recovery would have meant real interest rates were negative and more so than ever achieved under the QE experiment. Moreover, real disposable incomes would not have been squeezed by the sky-high prices of commodities including oil which were the direct result of asset price inflation disease in the early years attacking those markets (oil, emerging market debt and equities, see p. 19). More generally, there would have been a much more vigorous rebound of business spending than what took place in an environment where everyone and their dog were deeply suspicious of the high prices in the equity market and in some other asset markets which had been brought about by QE, fearing in consequence a subsequence crash and recession. Yes, there was strong stimulus in some areas (for example commodity –including oil – extraction industries, exports to emerging markets experiencing asset price inflation, auto sales gaining from a private equity driven boom in sub-prime auto loans, aircraft sales financed on ultra-cheap terms by leasing companies empowered by the private equity bubble). But all of this was likely to end up as another example of mal-invest-ment under conditions of monetary disequilibrium.

A further possible criticism is that monetary policy is too important to be handed over to a largely automatic system of rules. Just as we would not like to be operated on by robots without humans in control, so it is with money. And it is certainly the case that in the monetary system set up in accordance with the manifesto, there would be no monetary maestros in the styles of Benjamin Strong, William Chesney Martin, Arthur Burns, Paul Volcker, Alan Greenspan and Ben Bernanke. The whole world would not be straining to interpret the latest word change in a convoluted communique from Janet Yellen about how she and her colleagues view the condition of the US labour market. Instead, there would be a largely anonymous group of technicians in the monetary authority applying the rules regarding the issuance of high-powered money, and alongside these, there would be guardians who policed the standards of transparency in the financial system (so that the public could be sure that the monetary products they were buying are indeed authentic as regards reserve ratios and equity cushions).

Even so, what would happen in a panic, and indeed, panics did some-times occur in the era of the gold standard? A first point is that a panic – in the sense of a rush by the public to withdraw cash from the banks and more broadly a huge increase in the demand for liquidity – would be of a lower order of seriousness in the system constructed in accordance with the manifesto than what has been encountered historically. Deposits of the 100% reserve backed variety or backed by high equity cushions would not experience runs. Yes, transaction deposits of lower quality could experience runs, but by construction, the issuers of these would suspend their instant convertibility into cash (as indeed occurred in runs on US banks prior to the creation of the Federal Reserve). Moreover, panics are a feature of late stage asset price inflation disease. As this disease would be much milder in so far as it occurred at all, so would the danger of panic be less.

Yes, there were panics under the gold standard, as for example in 1907. These had origins sometimes in an earlier override or corrup-tion of the automatic mechanisms expanding the monetary base which had resulted in the spread of asset price inflation disease. For example, Rothbard (2002) blames the 1905–07 boom and bust on the US Treasury for accumulating surplus deposits within the banking system meaning that high-powered money had grown in excess of what would have been warranted by gold supplies (which themselves were boosted at this time by the technological revolution – the cyanide process – in gold mining). Alternatively, in gold standard history, there had been episodes of financial innovation which resulted in the marketing of new types of transaction deposits, which meant a decline in the demand for high-powered money relative to long-run trend (fractional banking was one such innovation). Yes, under the monetary system, according to the manifesto here equivalent such errors could occur and asset price inflation diseases break out. But their scale should be of a lower cumulative order than in the 100-year experience of the Federal Reserve.

Then there is the strand of criticism that similar monetary orders to the one presented in the manifesto have been tried before and failed. Didn't the Wall Street Crash and Great Depression occur under the international gold standard and it was only the repudiation of that standard which allowed recovery to take place? And the monetary order in the manifesto could be described as an ersatz gold standard in some respects (especially if much of the world were to join the dollar standard). And didn't the monetarist experiments in Germany, Switzerland and the US, in the 1970s and early 1980s, which share some features with the ideal system in the manifesto, also fail? The first question has already been answered here (see p. 58) to the effect that the gold standard was not recreated after World War I, contrary to Bernanke-ite and other historical folklore, and that the competitive currency devaluations which did occur cumulatively set back global economic recovery. We turn instead to the monetarist experiments.

The lessons of monetarist failure

In the US, there was no monetarist experiment of any consequence. Yes, Paul Volcker during 1980–82, pursued a policy guided by bearing down on the growth of high-powered money and abandoned official fixing of short-term rates. But the monetarist language which accompanied this policy was a smokescreen for a deliberate decision to hike those rates to such a high level that otherwise would have provoked even stronger political backlash. Volcker never intended to usher in a monetarist regime and indeed at the earliest opportunity repudiated the targets for high-powered money growth. The serious monetary experiments were in Germany and Switzerland. In the UK, the Thatcher government, despite much talk, never proceeded down the road of monetarism in any real sense, siding early on with the establishment officials who warned that there was no evidence to support the case for targeting monetary base let alone reconstructing the monetary system so as to strengthen its monetary pivot. (This case was never explicitly formulated even by Thatcher's personal economic advisers, whether Milton Friedman or Karl Brunner).

In Germany, the traditionally high level of reserve requirements provided a good starting point for the application of monetary base control by the Bundesbank in response to the threat of importing high inflation from the US. Starting in 1973, the Bundesbank made the target for high-powered money growth – formulated so as to be consistent with its projections for trend economic growth and chosen inflation path – the centrepiece of its policymaking. The Bundesbank did not abandon the fixing of short-term rates, but it made clear that changes to these would be made frequently so as to steer monetary base in line with target. Correspondingly, there was no attempt to influence market expectations as to the path for short-term rates. High reserve requirement meant that there was a fairly stable relationship between monetary base and nominal economic growth. There was no question of targeting a given low inflation rate over short or medium periods of time – nor was there any fixed anchor to prices over the very long run. There was a modest and variable rate of inflation throughout the say 10–15 year monetarist experiment. It is not clear that the Bundesbankers had any clear recognition of asset price inflation disease, although they did argue that their monetary orthodoxy made Germany less prone than the US or UK to financial instability in its various forms.

As the Bundesbank monetary experiment continued, it lost some of its distinctiveness. The Bundesbankers switched from targeting monetary base to the broad money supply. The bankers became ever more vocal in their criticisms of high reserve requirements and complained about how this put them at a competitive disadvantage to banks in foreign centres that were not subject to these. The requirements began to be whittled down, and the monetary base became potentially more volatile relative to wider economic aggregates. They never confronted the issue that the secure pivoting of the monetary system depended on high reserves being voluntarily held – as would be the case if there was no deposit insurance or other forms of support (including lender of last resort at low or zero penalty rates). Successive chancellors made increasingly blatant political appointments to the head of the Bundesbank. And this institution became subservient to the wider political aims of first German Monetary Union and then European Monetary Union.

In sum, the Bundesbank monetarist experiment which fascinated contemporaries produced a superior monetary outcome in Germany compared to other medium-size or large countries where monetary policy was directed still by central bankers and finance ministers of Keynesian persuasion guided only by their own discretion rather than rules. Although it had positive results, the experiment fell far short of representing the kind of stable monetary order as outlined in the manifesto here. Perhaps the most important and long-lasting lesson from this experience was that a hard money regime can enjoy huge popularity. At the pinnacle of the hard DM's fame, the Bundesbank and the DM were the most popular institutions in Germany. Today, the Federal Reserve is less popular than the Internal Revenue Service even though it has sought desperately to give priority to employment and suchlike objectives over sound money.

The Swiss monetarist experiment also holds lessons for today's monetary reformers. This was a purer form of monetarism than the German in the sense that the Swiss National Bank (SNB) did abandon completely the pegging of short-term rates, applying strictly instead a target for increasing the supply of reserves. But as a small open economy subject to large exchange rate swings, this target was ruthlessly over-ridden in the late 1970s when the franc rose to the sky as the global safe haven against inflation storms in the US. The experiment resumed in the 1980s but then went off the rails when a new more efficient form of interbank clearing was introduced which sharply reduced the demand by the banks for reserves. The SNB, slow to alter the target growth rate of the supply of the reserves, presided over a virulent episode of asset price inflation which infected the Swiss real estate market, eventually ending in the proverbial crash and recession. The monetarist experiment became discredited and ended with the SNB embracing the increasingly popular inflation targeting regimes.

The Swiss experience confirmed in even more stark form than the German how important an omission it was for the reformers not to secure the pivot of their system by creating the conditions in which there would be a large and stable voluntary demand for high-powered money (not dependent on artificially high reserve requirements or on particular states of technology as regarding the payments transfer function). And there was also the specifically Swiss lesson that it is very difficult if not impossible for a small country to lead the way in monetary reform when all the big countries especially the global monetary hegemon is enveloped in instability.

Now is never a good time to introduce monetary reform!

Finally we should consider the criticism that now is not a good time to introduce monetary reform. The transition from monetary disorder to order usually goes along with temporary economic hardship. That is not always the case. One exception is the ending of hyperinflation. The launch of the Rentenmark and then the Dawes Plan in Germany in 1923–24 ended almost miraculously the hyperinflation whilst quickly ushering in the economic miracle times of the mid-1920s.

In the midst of powerful asset price inflation, the election of a government committed to putting into effect anything approaching the monetary manifesto detailed above could bring a sharp fall in asset prices. At least that would be the scare that opposing politicians could use in the election campaigning and this scare might also have a dominant impact toward caution within the party favouring reform. Many would-be reformers might agree that it would be better to start monetary reform in the aftermath of evident monetary failure when the panic and recession stages of the last asset price inflation disease are causing much popular discontent, and the public is yearning for a better way forward in the future than at a time when many are enjoying the speculative thrall of present highs in asset markets, especially perhaps in residential real estate markets.

This approach to timing might be mistaken. After or during the crisis, the central bankers are joining the crowd in finding the obvious scapegoats. The Bernankes of this world can talk about holding their noses in Wall Street and whip up furor about everyone other than themselves. And their political masters can ridicule the reformers by revisiting the Keynesian folklore of the Great Depression and the alleged unnecessary hardness of the "deflationists". It is during better economic times when there is still much to complain about that monetary reform might stand a better chance of successful introduction. There are many who are discontented during the asset price inflations – the young who are priced out of the first home market and who as renters encounter space shortages caused by speculative hoarding or the still many unemployed or part-time workers whose human capital was destroyed in the course of previous asset price inflations and busts.

If the reformers can get their message across, they may indeed convince investors that the future will be so much more prosperous under monetary stability that equity prices would rise above their present levels which are inflated relative to the bleak prospects of continuing instability. Perhaps a wave of firmly based economic optimism based on their reform agenda would indeed bring greater prosperity for all without any immediate hardship except for those unfortunates who had lost their wits during the QE-induced income famine and associated asset price inflation fever such as to chase phantom long-run profits in a range of carry trades including the purchases of high-yield credits.

6
Japanese Tales in the Mythology of Fed Quantitative Easing

The power of narratives is strong in the teaching of monetary economics as in many other areas of learning. We should realize that many of these powerful stories which the teacher uses to demonstrate difficult hypotheses derive from folklore rather than fact. In particular, neo-Keynesian economists, including the architects of the Obama Great Monetary Experiment (Fed QE), have justified their prescriptions on stories of what went wrong during the Great Depression in the US or during the "lost decade" and beyond in Japan. In this chapter, we take aim at their Japan narrative and seek to replace it with one which yields quite different lessons from those which they have taught.

Japan's deflation myth as told by QE architects

The Japan story related by the neo-Keynesians (see Posen 1998) tells of a lost decade – the 1990s – following the Great Bubble of the late 1980s – which in fact extended into two decades. The cause of this lost decade, according to the storytellers, was a protracted deflation whose approach the Bank of Japan (BoJ) failed to foresee. By the time the BoJ started to seriously ease policy, it was too late. Deflation meant in the circumstances of Japan that the monetary system fell into the "zero rate trap". In the sclerotic post-bubble economy, the level of the neutral rate of interest was very low, most likely well below zero for short and even medium maturities. And so, market short-term rates could not fall to the neutral level (given the zero rate boundary) or to below neutral as would have been essential to monetary policy becoming stimulatory. Falling prices and the fact that households could make real returns just by holding cash eroded the appetite of Japanese investors for risky investments, adding further to the sclerosis of the economy.

This narrative is factually incorrect. The CPI in Japan at the peak of the cycle in 2007 was virtually at the same level as at the trough of the post-bubble recession in 1993 and up a few percentage points from the 1989 business cycle peak. Prices fell persistently through 2008–12 in part explained by cyclical factors (the Great Recession and the Global Financial Panic) and in part by the relentless climb of the yen powered by the Obama Great Monetary Experiment (GME). The Japanese yen gained a hedge premium as the one international money not on the global 2% inflation standard as set by the Federal Reserve and issued by a central bank whose chief (Masaaki Shirikawa) did not fit in with the now dominant mantra of "fighting deflation" from the global central bankers' club.

In broad terms, we can say that Japan alone amongst the nations of the world in the years from 1990 to the "Abe coup" at the BoJ (early 2013) has enjoyed stable prices from a long-run perspective as understood in the gold standard world. That is a plus of the Japanese monetary experience, not a minus. Yet that anchor has been founded on fluke of circumstance (price expectations adjusting to a series of yen shocks in particular and then a depression of the neutral level of interest rates by the progress of economic sclerosis) rather than there being a powerful pivot to the monetary system in the form of a strong and stable demand for high-powered money together with tight limits set by "constitutional rules" to its growth in supply.

Partly in consequence of the fluke nature of the price outcome, but also partly due to economic rigidities and frictions which have contributed to that fluke, Japan has not enjoyed the full benefit that the invisible hand can bring through adjusting prices down and up through time so as to steer the economy close to an equilibrium path. Yes, prices have fallen during recessions (except the first recession of 1991–92) or during periods of especially rapid terms of trade improvement or productivity growth. They have risen during cyclical booms or at times of big increases in the price of oil. That is how it should be in a well-functioning market economy under conditions of monetary stability (see p. 109). But these swings have been anaemic compared to what would have happened under a powerfully pivoted framework of monetary stability with fully flexible market adjustments as was the case under the gold standard.

If we refer to price indices in Japan which adjust fully to take account of quality improvements (so-called hedonic adjustment) – such as the private consumption deflator – then we find these fell slightly (albeit that some distortions in measurement caused this fall to be exaggerated – see BoJ research 2003) over the period 1992 to 2008. It was also true that if price indices had been adjusted in this way during the age of the gold standard, they would have been trending down very slightly, rather than the observed flatness from a very long-run prospective for non-adjusted price data. Yet this did not preclude economic prosperity. Indeed, as we argued in an earlier chapter (see p. 112), a long-run fixed anchor to prices strengthens the power of the invisible hands via inter-temporal swings in prices (up or down) to steer the economy efficiently.

Did Japan really suffer a lost decade?

As to the lost decade which features in the QE architect narrative, this is more apparent than real when we turn to the data. The only period during which the Japanese economy underperformed other advanced economies (as measured by the growth of GDP per capita) was from 1992–97. In fact, recent work from the Bank for International Settlements (see BIS 2015) suggests that Japan seriously outperformed the US during the first decade of the 21st century when proper adjustment is made for demographic influences. In particular, real GDP per working age population grew cumulatively by 20% in Japan from 2000–12, compared to 11% in the US. For the period 2000–07, the comparative statistics were 15% and 8%, respectively.

During the actual lost half decade of 1992–97, the year-on-year rise of the Japanese CPI only fell to zero from a significantly positive level during the course of 1994 and did not remain below zero except fleetingly until the recession of 1997–98 in the midst of a severe banking crisis. So there is no one-to-one fit statistically between deflation and the lost half decade. Rather, the issue is the "good deflation", which did not take place in the early 1990s, and the good price recovery, which thereby failed to occur in the mid-1990s. And the fact that the Japanese economy performed on average in line with its peers from 1997 onwards (according to the GDP per capita criterion) and strikingly better than the US in the 2000s on the demographically adjusted measure above would still be consistent with Japan suffering from various malaises – some monetary in nature, though, not falling under the heading of deflation.

If the lost decade (1991–97) was not due to deflation or to the BoJ's failure to prevent deflation, what was the cause? A first point to make is that even under an ideal regime of monetary stability with the invisible hand there would have been economic hardship given the extent of the bubble economy which preceded this. (Just for the record, though, in the world of counterfactual history we would say that the bubble would not have occurred in the first place under conditions of monetary stability). The source of Japan's bubble economy in the late 1980s was ultimately the Volcker Federal Reserve pursuing a disequilibrium monetary policy related to the aim of depreciating the dollar during the mid-1980s US growth recession and in the context of great pressure from the Reagan Administration ahead of the mid-term elections of November 1986 (see p. 97).

The new dose of US monetary disequilibrium drove the yen to the sky, to which the Japanese authorities responded by themselves pursuing a policy of monetary disequilibrium with the aim of stimulating domestic demand and hopefully moderating the rise of the yen. The extent of the disequilibrium was not obvious to central bankers pursuing implicitly an inflation target as Japanese inflation in fact fell to near zero at first under the influence of the super strong yen and the strong rise in productivity which accompanied the capital spending boom. Once, however, irrational exuberance faded and the Japanese stock market plunged from its bubble highs (in early 1990), investors and business people back in sober mood started to realize the full extent of the mal-investment and overinvestment which had occurred.

The process is not easy for an economy to find its way back to an equilibrium path with such an overhang of overinvestment and mal-investment. Equity risk appetites shrink drastically in response to the shock of huge losses. Given so much surplus capacity, the scope for profitable investment may be severely curtailed. And yet private savings are likely rising as debt burdened consumers and businesses cut back spending.

Ideally, interest rates would fall to very low levels in line with depressed neutral levels, the authorities would guard and even strengthen a legal and tax framework which encouraged entrepreneurship – the finding of new investment opportunities which could absorb surplus labour and savings. A prompt fall of many prices and wages together with expectations of subsequent cyclical recovery of these on average would mean that interest rates in real terms could become very negative, even though nominal rates could not fall below zero.

In a global context, if indeed the bubble and bust has been more severe in this particular economy than elsewhere, the national currency would fall in line with the emergence of larger savings surplus, a matching capital export surplus and very low interest rates. That would provide some stimulus to the export sector. Wages would fall also such as to generate higher profit margins which in turn would help accelerate the recovery of employment and capital spending. A further force toward higher profits would come from the shutting down of mal-investment now economically obsolescent. Indeed, the wiping out of such past investment means that the effective stock of capital becomes scarce relative to the overall supply of labour – encouraging some fall in real wages and increase in profits. This might all occur in the form of a severe short-lived recession followed by a remarkably strong economic upturn.

Hardly any of this happened in Japan – and so the lost decade (1991–7) was even more of a lost decade than it had to be. It is true that there was no sharp recession following the crash. And too big to fail banks rolled over loans to zombie borrowers, thus, slowing down any process of economically obsolescent capital being shut down allowing profit margins to rise in various industrial sectors. Japanese labour markets back in the early 1990s were dominated by lifetime employment practices and little flexibility (that changed considerably through the next two decades), and wage rates were slow to fall, if at all, meaning that the wage share of national income bulged. Prices continued to rise to a small extent even during 1991 and 1992 (although the official data may well be overstating prices for this period when there was much unofficial discounting).

How to explain the feebleness of self-recovery forces in Japan 1991–95?

The BoJ resisted and "succeeded" in slowing a market-driven fall of interest rates through 1991–92 as it continued to monitor lagging inflation data and failed to realize the extent of the real estate slump developing. Moreover, Governor Mieno was a fan of a strong yen and saw this as a natural counterpart to a bulging trade surplus, rather than viewing the latter as evidence of a growing savings surplus which should mean higher capital exports and lower interest rates. The governor may have been sensitive to concerns that a lower yen in consequence of cutting rates aggressively could have been a red rag to a bull – the bull here being the currency warriors in Washington. In fact, the US from 1991–95 was waging a full-scale currency war first under the Bush and then under the Clinton Administration. The Greenspan Fed was in general playing its part in the overall campaign except for the brief period of monetary tightening through 1994 (see p. 99).

In Washington, no one countenanced the view that Japan's rising trade surplus was natural (as the counterpart to a rising surplus after the bursting of a bubble economy). Instead, mercantilist vision blinded all. Washington pressed for fiscal stimulus in Japan rather than monetary stimulus in the belief that this would mean a stronger than otherwise yen and lower trade surplus. There were many in the Japanese government willing to play along with that theme given the votes which they hoped to win in their constituencies for aggressively stepped up pork-barrel spending.

If there was any good news about the invisible hand guiding a recovery of the Japanese economy, it was in the surge of foreign investment which got under way into the Tokyo equity market. It is hard to know whether this got equity risk premiums back to normal levels, from the likely high levels in the aftermath of the crash, or the abnormally low levels (when earnings prospects were viewed in sober fashion rather than with rose-coloured spectacles) during the bubble periods. And the continuing bad news in this respect was the partial disconnect in Japan between the equity market and the business capital spending process.

Measurement of equity risk premiums is any case more of an art than a science once we look beyond the often cited crude measures (most particular current earnings yields less the real yield on say 10-year government bonds). Earnings projections beyond one year are highly relevant to valuations yet there are no objective metrics for these. The still prevalent interlocking shareholdings at that time in Japan meant that one would expect price-earnings (P/E) ratios to be higher than in other countries where these did not feature. On the other hand, these interlocking shareholdings coupled with the "main bank" role in corporate groupings severely impeded the growth of a market in corporate control (in which hostile takeovers feature largely). The lack of such a market allowed inefficient corporate managers to remain in control who lacked any vision for spotting and seizing investment opportunity. The fact that the ratio of companies equity market capitalization to book value in Japan was low (and remains low) by international comparison would be consistent with a scarcity of intra-marginal firms making high rates of profit – and the expectation that this would continue to be the case would tend to weigh on earnings prospects compared to say the US market.

Empirically, there are no clear statements to be made here. But the inefficiencies mentioned – in particular, the lack of discipline from a market in corporate control on lacklustre managers pursuing shareholder unfriendly practices with little possibility of these being swept aside in a takeover – could weigh down average expectations of earnings growth from equity investment. This may not mean a lower level of investment in the economy as a whole if much inefficient capital spending is taking place which could not be justified according to the normal criteria of finance theory (positive net present value using the equity cost of capital). But it would mean a disappointing level of national income relative to the amount of labour and capital employed.

It is plausible that the Japanese experience of loss in the bust weighed generally on tolerance for risk even outside the equity market and may have thereby reinforced so-called home bias (aversion to assuming currency risk). And the huge spikes and volatility of the yen provoked by intermittent US currency warfare might have added at certain times to the reluctance of Japanese to cross the currency frontier to earn higher yields abroad, whether in equity or bond markets. That reluctance in principle would hold back capital exports and facilitate the execution in Japan of investment projects with low rates of return (by international comparison), including much wasteful public sector spending. On the other hand, there were also times of irrational exuberance in the yen carry trade when these influences (downward on capital exports and upward on domestic investment projects) would not be present and might even be in reverse. The overall importance of the yen carry trade gained in significance once the Bank of Japan embarked on growing monetary experimentation, first the zero-interest rate policy (ZIRP) launched in January 1999 and later quantitative easing (see below).

In general, the mobilization of household savings into Japanese government bonds (JGB) rather than higher-yielding domestic and foreign equity – the corollary of sick equity risk appetites – meant lower national income than otherwise over the long run. The growing proportion of Japanese equities owned abroad (and the underpinning thereby of Tokyo equity prices) may have diminished the extent to which domestic investment suffered over the long run. Even so, this meant that a growing proportion of corporate profits accrued ultimately to foreigners rather than to Japanese investors (including pension funds).

The Japanese government's methods of mobilizing household savings evolved. The banks, in particular, were given regulatory forbearance in accumulating huge portfolios of government debt, notwithstanding considerable potential interest rate risk involved. In the calculation of their required equity backing, government bond holdings were treated as zero weight. Now it is true that in a competitive open banking system banks would have ignored government guidelines, and the markets would have constrained their holdings of JGBS (in that these would mean higher risks for little return). But in the context of too big to fail mega banks that formed in Japan in the aftermath of the great bubble and especially through the banking stress of the mid-1990s that is not what happened. Huge support for government debt from the banks was the unspoken condition of their enjoying backstop government insurance in its various forms. Government sector pension funds allocated high proportions of their portfolios to JGBs. Government protected regional banks, credit unions, and postal savings also piled in.

Plagues of irrational exuberance since 1990 and their impact on Japan

Since the great bubble of the late 1980s, the Japanese equity and real estate markets have not recorded speculative temperatures anywhere near those same highs even though there have been three subsequent Fed-induced global plagues of irrational exuberance – the IT/telecommunications "bubble" of the late 1990s; the global credit bubble of the mid-2000s (featuring sub-prime mortgages in US, weak sovereign debt and Spanish mortgages and East European debts amongst other asset classes in Europe, and private equity in Europe and the US; and the QE-driven asset price inflation of the early and mid-2010s. Yes, Tokyo equities enjoyed good "bull runs" at these times (in 1998–2000, 2005–07 and 2012–15), but their valuations did not cut loose from the normal map (rising far into the sky) as in the late 1980s. The focus of irrational exuberance in these asset price inflation diseases was the so-called yen carry trade, in which vast short positions in the Japanese currency were built up by global asset managers. Japanese investors themselves became influence by the yen carry trade booms, building up vast quantities of higher-yielding foreign currency bonds at such times, in such favourite currencies as the Australian dollar, Brazilian cruzeiro and even Turkish lira. Yet the cumulative returns overall from these bond investments were on average well below those on equity (including direct investment whether in Japan or internationally).

Even though the Fed was the ultimate source of these asset price inflation episodes, monetary disequilibrium in Japan played an important role in how the disease spread there. We can illustrate this in turn. First, take the great Greenspan plague of the mid and late 1990s. The Japanese equity market was infected by the asset price inflation virus emanating from the Greenspan Fed in the mid and late 1990s, but only in its very last phase. As the Fed persevered in its inflation targeting policies despite the economic miracle of the IT revolution which was pumping up productivity growth, thereby depressing interest rates below neutral, irrational exuberance grew in new economy equities globally – and Japan with its prominent IT sector was widely seen as a key component of the global new economy. As the NASDAQ bubble formed, so did speculative temperatures reach high levels in the Tokyo equity market through 1999 and 2000. The slowness of the BoJ to tighten monetary conditions in the aftermath of the 1997 banking panic and recession (in Japan) had fuelled a huge carry trade in the yen during (short yen, long US dollars). The carry traders though encountered rude setbacks first during the short-lived global liquidity crisis of Autumn 1998 (sparked by the LTCM and Russian credit events) and then into late 1999 and 2000 as the BoJ prepared to tighten monetary policy and foreign capital poured into Japanese stocks.

Over investment and mal-investment characterized the brief Japanese economic boom of 1999–2000 concentrated in the IT and related tele-communications sector. The BoJ had been slow to raise interest rates from zero (the level to which they had fallen during the banking crisis and recession of 1997) eventually doing this in Autumn 2000 (see Momma and Kobayakawa, 2014) when we now know asset price infla-tion was already turning to asset price deflation and the global economy approaching a recession. Under a regime of monetary stability, Japanese interest rates would have risen sooner. It is dubious how much if at all this would have insulated the Tokyo equity market from the asset price inflation disease unleashed by the Fed as global investors, joined by local investors, chased Japanese new economy equities higher, interpreting capital gains as confirmation of the high optimistic speculative hypoth-eses about the new economy and with those gains being amplified by the situation of US interest rates being below neutral.

The BoJ, all the same, had done the opposite of insulating Japan from the Greenspan virus of asset price inflation. With the economy still apparently weak in early 1999, having passed through the 1997–98 recession (stemming in part from Asian crisis of 1997, then the emerging market crisis of the following year featuring the Russian default, and also related to the Japan banking crisis of 1997 and the increase of the sales tax in that year), the BoJ embarked on its zero interest rate policy (ZIRP). The BoJ justified this by the need to counter the "possibility of mounting deflationary pressure and prevent further deterioration in economic conditions". The zero interest rate policy, launched in February 1999, had involved steering overnight money rates to virtually zero (just fractionally above) whilst preventing any volatility in those rates. This was accomplished without creating a large amount of excess reserves. In a classic testimony to the futility of such fine-tuning, this policy was launched just when the US economy and global economy was re-accelerating from some softness surrounding the above-mentioned crises, and the asset price inflation virus was in a new powerful stage!

Bank of Japan pioneers quantitative easing in the early 2000s

During the recession of 2001–02, the BoJ pioneered a quantitative easing (QE) monetary policy, a first experiment of its form on the global scene in modern times (in Chapter 7 we discuss the form of QE under the Roosevelt Administration in the mid-1930s). The operating target of monetary policy changed from the overnight call rate to the outstanding balance of current accounts held by financial institutions at the BoJ. The initial aim was for a current account balance of around 5 trillion and the BoJ raised the target step-by-step; at its maximum (during this first QE experiment) the balance of current accounts reached around 30–35 trillion yen. For reference, 30–35 trillion yen was about five times as much as the amount of required reserves and constituted about 7 per of nominal GDP (compared to 25–30% for Fed QE in 2014).

The launch of QE and its intensification coincided with considerable anxiety in Japan about the climb of the Japanese yen in the context of exceptional US monetary ease and from early 2003 Fed's extraordinary emphasis on "fighting the danger of deflation" (see below). A key difference from the later Obama GME and the subsequent Abe monetary experiment in Japan was that the BoJ did not engage in a programme of massive purchases of government bonds. The BoJ introduced the so-called banknote principle whereby JGB purchases conducted for facilitating money market operations were subject to the limitation that the outstanding amount of JGB holdings (on the central bank's balance sheet) should be limited within the outstanding amount of banknotes in circulation. The BoJ made clear that such purchases were executed for the purpose of conducting monetary policy and not for financing fiscal deficits.

The QE policy as rolled out also included an element of "forward guidance". The BoJ announced that the new procedures for money market operations would continue in place until the "core CPI registered stably at zero per cent or an increase year-on-year". The intention was to remove the public's perception that the central bank had a deflationary bias after the BoJ had discontinued the zero rate policy early (as above). The idea was to leave little room for a flexible interpretation of the commitment. This forward guidance was amplified in October 2003 when the BoJ made clear that QE would continue until the change in the CPI would register at zero or above for a few months, and there would be a recognizable tendency to this effect. Moreover, many policy board members would have to forecast that the change in the core CPI would stay above zero during the forecast period in the BoJ's outlook report.

Opinion amongst the public and in the markets was that this monetary experiment would be fairly short-lived with a total exit at its end. And so the features of long-term interest rate manipulation and generation of considerable uncertainty about long-run inflation which were elements in Fed QE and later Abe QE did not enter into this first version of QE in Japan. And Japan at this point had certainly not joined the global 2% inflation standard which the Federal Reserve had launched by stealth in 1996 (see p. 148) and which the euro-zone joined fully in Spring 2003 (see Brown, 2013) having been an informal member since its founding (1999).

Indeed, in March 2006, in light of steady recovery in the Japanese economy and prices rising, the BoJ resolved to end QE. The yen had fallen considerably since the highs at the time of QE's initial phase amidst a growing global carry trade in the Japanese currency and a strong momentum of capital outflow from Japan. The neutral level of interest rates was now plausibly above market rates across all maturities. Broader money and credit growth was accelerating. Accordingly, the BoJ announced that it would change the operating target for monetary operations from the current account balance back to the uncollateralized overnight call rate. It also decided that initially it would guide the overnight rate toward remaining effectively at zero%. The BoJ proceed to run down the excess reserves – with the intention of regaining control over the overnight money rate, positioning to raise this from zero at a later point. Given that the main asset accumulated to offset the growth in reserves had been T-bills, this operation could occur quickly without disrupting the bond markets (other than via expectation effects).

Boom in the yen carry trade during the mid-2000s

By February 2007, the overnight rate reached 0.5% and was maintained at that level until the BoJ reversed its policy in response to the Lehman shock (Autumn 2008). That was a painfully slow pace of adjustment upward, especially in view of the continuing strong depreciation of the yen during 2006–07 (against the background of a rise in US and European interest rates) as the speculative temperature in the yen carry trade reached new heights.

The Japan QE experiment of the first half of the 2000s coincided with "monetary innovation" by the Greenspan Fed and by the ECB. In Spring 2003, the Greenspan Fed (which Professor Bernanke had joined as governor the previous autumn) had embarked on its "breathing inflation back into the economy" policy, concerned by the danger of deflation in the continuing aftermath of the IT bust and a recession made more difficult by the September 2001 attack on New York and the uncertainties related to the US and Allied interventions in Iraq launched at the start of 2003. The novelty of the US policy was the stated aim of "fighting deflation" (in tune with the IMF and G-7 campaign against the danger of deflation) and related to that the use of forward guidance regarding the short-term interest rate peg (that the rise of this would be glacial). Medium and long-term interest rates correspondingly lagged well below neutral levels and the Greenspan-Bernanke 2000s asset price inflation disease emerged.

The ECB's policy and monetary framework changes announced in Spring 2003 (strict inflation targeting with a lower limit to inflation of 2% p.a.) meant that the disease spread into Europe in rampant form. The highest speculative fevers were recorded in sub-prime US mortgage debt, leveraged loans related to private equity, the US residential real estate market, Spanish, UK, French and various Southern European real estate markets, financial equities – most of all in Europe and last but not least in the yen carry trade. This is where BoJ policies of monetary disequilibrium – the QE experiment and the related "battle against deflation" – played a role.

It was strange how the BoJ became convinced by Keynesian opinion in Washington that there was indeed a "deflation problem" in Japan even though at this point there was no intention of joining the 2% inflation standard. The institution might have instead welcomed the fact that Japan had achieved long-run price stability such as had not been experienced since the gold standard world and designed a comprehensive framework of monetary stability that could have solidified those gains. And it could have emphatically pointed out that the road to superior economic performance depended on a drawing up and implementing a range of economic reform not by following monetary fashion set in Washington which so often before had proved to be deadly wrong. There were voices of opposition outside the BoJ, for example, from Professor Eisuke Sakakibara (one-time "Mr. Yen" when a leading Ministry of Finance official) warning about how the anti-deflationary policy was exposing the Japanese economy to financial instability centred on the yen carry trade and that the periods of falling prices were in fact consistent with a fixed anchor to prices over the long run. They called for radical reform especially in the government sector of the economy. But this did not materialize.

The attraction of the yen in the carry trade was its low or zero interest rate (depending on the maturity of the borrowing) compared to substantially higher (nominal) interest rates in euros, pounds and dollars. And of course, yen borrowing was matched against some of the accumulations of high-yield dollar or euro debts, including asset-backed mortgage paper and leveraged loans. That was a game played by hedge funds. As the game increased in scope, more downward pressure occurred on the yen, and the trend became the friend, firing up irrational expectations with respect to further profits to be made. Japanese investors and banks in general were not at the front of the global crowd buying high-yield credit products such as sub-prime US debt. Perhaps they were still weighed down in caution due to their giant bubble experience back in the late 1990s, which had culminated in the banking crises of 1997. But they did get fascinated by the speculative stories in Europe about the new age of financial integration opened up by the launch of EMU. Japanese savings poured into euro-denominated bond and money markets. And this flow reached great strength as the ECB in 2006–07 started to raise interest rates "boldly" just as the global asset price inflation disease was on the point of mutating into its next phase of steep speculative fall.

The super-high euro and the super-low yen in 2006–08 was a big feature of global markets at this time. The extreme cheapness of the yen (as measured in real effective exchange rate terms and relative to the average level of the previous 30 years) spurred overinvestment and malinvestment in Japan's export sector. This subsequently showed up when global asset price inflation entered its deadly end phase of plummeting speculative temperatures.

A counterfactual history to consider for Japan is what would have happened during the course of the great global asset inflation of the mid-2000s (the Bernanke-Greenspan asset price inflation disease) if the BoJ had been less focused on near-term prospects for prices and instead operated policy within a framework of monetary stability (in which transitory falls in prices, like transitory rises, are benign). Higher interest rates in Japan during these years would surely have curtailed the carry trade. Yes, they would have meant a more expensive yen, but relative to a level which became fantastically cheap. In real effective exchange rate terms, the yen in 2007 reach a level some 5% or more low than a decade earlier in the depths of the Japan banking crisis and the South East Asian crisis.

From carry trade bust to Shirakawa's hard yen

The transition of the Bernanke-Greenspan asset price inflation virus in the global economy to its next phase of steep speculative temperature drop during 2008 started a sharp turnaround in the yen upward as carry traders sought to liquidate their positions – at first in the trades vis-à-vis sub-prime dollar credits and asset-backed paper whether in the US or Europe. As the high risk sovereign debt market bubble and related bank debt bubble started to burst in Europe (the eruption of the Greek crisis in early 2010 was a wake-up call), the rush for the exit (made possible by massive rescue operations of the EU back-stopped by German taxpayers) resulted in huge upward pressure on the yen and downward pressure on the euro.

A further factor driving the yen up at this time was the perception that Japan alone amongst the big economies was not ready to pursue aggressive non-conventional monetary policy, unlike the US which by now (into 2010) was embarked on the first of several rounds of QE, the essence of the Obama GME. The DPJ government which had come into power in August 2009 (defeating the LDP government) was perceived as favouring "a hard yen" (and was advised by Sakakibara – see above). The BoJ Governor Masaaki Shirakawa was perceived in global currency markets as an orthodox University of Chicago economist who was out of tune with the global central bankers' club. He had become head of the BoJ in 2008 in a political situation where the LDP had already lost control of the Upper House of the Diet and their preferred candidate for the top post could not win approval there.

Shirakawa seemed to suggest that there was nothing wrong with temporary episodes of deflation and that Japan's economic problems lay elsewhere. And in any case, although the BoJ in principle had been aiming for a long-run average inflation rate of 1% p.a. ever since the early 2000s, it had never acted as this was a top priority even during its QE episode. It had made clear that financial stability concerns could mean that it would override aiming for 1% inflation even in the medium term.

Hence, in the context of the Obama GME launched in phases from 2009 onwards, the yen gained attraction as a safe haven currency. This was the one large money where the central bank was not in line with aggressive inflation targeting. Yes, the BoJ under Governor Shirakawa gradually started to bend its policies with obvious reluctance in the direction of current monetary fashion in the US, but a spine of resistance was evident.

In October 2010, the BoJ embarked on its "comprehensive monetary easing" programme. This involved holding the short-term policy rate at virtually zero (fractionally above), forward guidance (keeping zero rate until price stability was attained – meaning presumably 1% p.a. in the long run and an asset purchase programme (expanding the BoJ's balance sheet) limited, however, to government bonds of less than 2 years' maturity and not breaking the rule that total bonds held should not exceed the amounts of banknotes outstanding).

In global markets, all of this did not take away seriously from the image of the Shirakawa BoJ being the last bastion of monetary orthodoxy. And the DPJ government in Tokyo (which had succeeded the LDP government in 2009) was viewed as having some inclination toward such orthodoxy. Indeed, it was the DPJ's objection to a senior finance ministry official put forward by the then LDP government getting the top job at the BoJ in 2008 (the DPJ already had control then of the Upper House where the appointment had to be approved) that led to the appointment of Shirakawa. The LDP nominators were hardly keen.

True, the Bundesbank may still have been exerting some restraint on the extent to which the ECB would pursue non-conventional monetary policies, but that restraint became more and more dubious through a succession of EMU crises during these years. Again and again, German Chancellor Merkel had failed to back the Bundesbank in its opposition to ECB interventions ostensibly to "save EMU". A succession of existential crises and the ruptures of the Maastricht Constitution with respect to EMU eroded any residual safe haven aspect of the euro. Many investors also recollected that during the 2008–09 panics the yen jumped against all currencies as the carry trade imploded (meaning that short positions in the yen were closed). Hence, there was the perception that the yen could in fact be a "bad news good" (an asset which performs well in price when the news is bad). That perception was rooted in part on the experience of the yen carry trade boom and bust. The next time around (as viewed from the perspective say of 2010–11), there may not be a carry trade boom in this form. (In fact, as we shall see below, a large yen carry trade did emerge later in this cycle see p. 177).

Even so, Japan's huge international net creditor position implied that were the next global financial crisis to be accompanied by any tendency toward net repatriation of capital as often occurred at such times, the yen would be a gainer in some degree. And Japanese banks unlike say European banks did not have huge exposures to potential asset classes where temperature might fall sharply (in the case of Europe, this exposure was to Italian and Spanish government bond markets in particular), although there could be some questions about Chinese and emerging market related credits. (And during the crises in European banking in the years 2009–12, Japanese banks had been prominent in buying international loan assets from hard-pressed euro-banks). All in all, during

2010–12, the yen gained in international appeal, reflected in its strong appreciation. The triple natural disaster of Spring 2011 (earthquake, tsunami, nuclear accident) did not change that perception as in the immediate aftermath the yen actually gained ground on speculation that Japanese companies (including insurers) might be repatriating foreign capital.

Triple disasters and Obama's Great Monetary Experiment bring Japan political earthquake

Yet that triple disaster was one factor behind a political earthquake in Japan which would ultimately undermine the yen's brief episode as a lone currency star. The other factor was the upward spiral of the yen driven by Obama GME, which in its early years drove the dollar down (except against the euro when it was suppressed by those existential crises in EMU). The sky-high yen spread gloom in the powerful export corporations (and their workforces). Popular disgruntlement with how the DPJ government had responded to the disaster together with concern at the new setback to Japanese prosperity made the electoral scene ripe for economic populism. And the LDP leader, Shinzo Abe, had the right banner with his promises of ending deflation and promoting" low infla-tion", increased government spending and higher wages for the so-called salary-men (leaning on the corporate leaders in the export sector to pass on benefits of yen devaluation to their life-time employees). Yes, he spoke also of structural reform, but there was understandable scepti-cism about how substantial this would be. Ending deflation was widely understood correctly as code for yen devaluation (code required so as not to inflame those politicians in Washington always concerned about foreign manipulation of exchange rates as a tool of unfair trade)

Alongside this was a nationalist message which resonated with voters growingly concerned with China's increased military threat and apparent economic weight. The military threat and Japanese economic stagnation made a story which could influence Washington favour-ably toward a policy of yen devaluation – one which it would normally oppose. In fact, in this case, given that the policy was presented in the guise of fighting deflation – an objective shared with the designers of the Obama GME – US opposition would have been incoherent. Washington seemed to welcome the "bold counter-deflationary policy" in Japan on the basis that countering economic weakness there would be good for all even if he yen weakened and indeed undershot its likely long-run trajectory. In late 2014 IMF Chief Lagarde praised the "courage of PM

Abe" in launching an intensified further round of QE towards "fighting deflation". Alongside, the Obama Administration made no objection either to the Abe government's legislating a powerful official secrets act which many critics in Japan saw as a serious affront to political liberalism. Washington had long been pressing Tokyo to tighten up on security leaks, which included US sensitive information, but this legislation went far beyond that specific purpose.

Abe had made clear during the election campaign of late 2012 (he became PM at the end of that year) that he would introduce a powerful version of the US GME into Japan. This version would include the virtual dismissal of the present leadership at the BoJ and its replacement by a head ready to design and implement the quasi-money printing programme enthusiastically and loyally; there would also be a massive commitment to purchase long-maturity government bonds, blowing apart all previous restraints to this, with the intention of bringing down long-term interest rates to well below 1% p.a.

Even if the BoJ were to purchase each year for several years bonds equal to 10–15% of GDP against the background of a government deficit running at 5–7% of GDP and a gross government debt to GDP ratio of 230% that would leave a huge stock of debt in the market, so price fixing might be difficult. The Japanese corporate sector (including private equity), global speculators and foreign borrowers might become huge payers of long-term fixed-rate yen under various strategies implemented in the swap markets or non-government bond markets. They would take advantage of what they could see as an extraordinary opportunity. Regional banks in Japan which had survived on the basis of "playing the yield curve" in JGBs might respond eventually to its flattening by closing down and liquidating their portfolios of bonds en masse.

Yet the architects of Japan's monetary experiment could hope that the strengthening of irrational forces which QE seemed to cause based on recent US experience together with the extent of the bond buying mobilization programme (see above), and various institutional restraints on the corporate sector tapping capital markets would achieve the desired manipulation (of long-term rates). How could the Obama Administration object, especially as the architect of its monetary experiment had written and spoken extensively about how the central bank should manipulate long-term interest rates in accordance with a 2% inflation standard?

The Abe programme of introducing a high-powered version of the Obama GME in Japan so as to reverse the climb of the yen, which had occurred during the period in which Tokyo continued along the track of orthodoxy despite Washington's lurch into monetary disequilibrium, followed a familiar script in Japanese history. Many times since the 1960s the Federal Reserve had embarked deliberately on the path of monetary experiment (Keynesianism in the 1960s, Nixon price wage controls and Burns election-winning mega monetary stimulus in the early 1970s, the Volcker dollar devaluation 1985–88, Greenspan-Bernanke fight against deflation and breathing in inflation 2003–06). Each time a consequence had been a big depreciation of the US dollar, usually most of all against the yen. Eventually, Tokyo had always responded by deciding that the littlest of all evil choices was to copy US monetary disequilibrium in Japan, bringing a respite for the yen and the export sector.

The medium-term consequences of this choice had always been to load on the Japanese economy all the same mal-effects, usually magnified, that the US economy itself eventually suffered. That storyline ran through the huge fiscal and monetary expansion in Japan during the early 1970s culminating in high inflation and eventually Great Recession; it fitted with the emergence of the bubble economy in the late 1980s – a particularly virulent strain of the asset price inflation originating in the Volcker Fed. And it fitted with yen carry trade bubble together with the overinvestment and mal-investment in Japan's export sector during the mid-2000s.

The stable money free market alternative to Abe economics

There was a grand alternative monetary route which Japan could have taken in the face of the Obama GME. The government and BoJ would have explained to the public that acute US monetary instability was imposing a burden on the Japanese economy and the outlook was challenging. In order to secure long-run economic prosperity in Japan, the best way forward would be to stick to and reinforce the principles of monetary stability whilst accepting that there should be considerable flexibility downward (but subsequently upward) in wages and prices (in yen terms) especially in the traded goods and services sector. A programme of sweeping economic deregulation was now essential to meeting the challenges.

The programme would include such elements as promoting an efficient market in corporate control, aggressive alleviation of impediments (such as zoning) to new construction, removal of obstacles to entry whilst tackling restrictive practices in the retail and wider service sector, removing hurdles to start-ups and venture capitalism and finally ending financial repression and the related mobilization of Japanese private savings to finance the deficit. The latter could have included some priva-tization of pension provision, meaning much greater scope for house-holds to choose how to allocate funds for their retirement. A supply side package would have included large cuts in marginal tax rate and in the mainstream corporate tax rate – balanced in turn by greater cuts in government spending. Corporate tax reform could have featured leap-frogging the rest of the world by removing distortions which favoured leverage and using the tax saving from this to lower the overall corporate tax rate. In turn, the stimulus this would have given to equity issuance and de-leverage would have promoted the amount of equity issuance overall and the expansion of equity would have facilitated hostile takeo-vers and more generally an efficient market in corporate control (the first objective listed above).

This latter would have stimulated greater efficiency in the process of corporate managers seeking and discovering investment opportunity; managers who hoarded retained earnings without matching investment opportunity to the benefit of shareholders would have found them-selves subject to hostile takeover. With the scope for profit opportunity improving (and much more possibility of the intra-marginal well-man-aged entrepreneurial corporations commanding premium valuations and getting extraordinary rate of returns), the culture of investment in Japan would have swung toward equity risk-taking, promoting prosperity.

There would have been deregulation in the financial sector such as the scrapping of too big to fail protection in the banking industry, a phased ending of deposit insurance and dismantling of the postal saving system. Anti-trust law and its enforcement would have been strength-ened in both the financial and non-financial sectors (which would help the strong yen show up as reduced prices for consumers).

Yes, these would have been hard times for the export sector. But the big declines in import prices and more generally a dip in many prices and wages below the level of the long-run fixed anchor would have caused spending to be brought forward. And this would have been a great time for Japanese businesses and households to invest abroad. For example, households could more easily have afforded foreign homes. Small and medium-size businesses could have afforded (within their total possible yen capital budgets) to have made foreign acquisitions. Much of this investment activity would have spurred related economic activity in Japan even though there would also have been some negative substitution effects (with production being moved abroad). And there would have been increased economic activity in Japan in import related fields (especially in distribution).

The converse of negative risk premium for foreign investors in the yen (attributable to its safe haven property) would have been a positive premium for Japanese investors daring to cross the currency frontier into foreign assets. They could have looked forward in general to some tendency for the yen to depreciate from present lofty levels meaning that the expected return on foreign assets would be heightened from their perspective. That would have been a useful boost at a time when the global plague of market irrationality with its origins in Fed QE had driven many prices in global markets to a level where future long-run returns could be thin.

The growth of the yen as a global money would have benefited Tokyo as an international financial centre which in turn would have created new investment opportunity in Japan's economy. This was the period when the European alternative to the dollar had failed. Yes, further back, the Deutsche mark had starred as Europe's hard money alternative to the unstable and inflation prone US dollar. The advocates of EMU had claimed that the new currency would be even more impressive than the DM as a competitor of the US dollar. By the second decade of the 21st century it was obvious that this could not be the case. Flaws in the design and concept of monetary union and a lack of political will in Berlin had culminated in any superior record of Europe than the US for monetary stability being extinguished. The ECB Chief was a full member of the global central banker's club, suffering from the deflation phobia which gripped all its members and following the same principles of inflation targeting and interest rate manipulation.

The euro's failure was Tokyo's chance to market the international appeal of its monetary orthodoxy. Foreign inflows into JGB as a highly liquid asset in this chosen money would have one of the main counterparts to huge Japanese capital outflows into foreign markets. Incidentally, these inflows would have provided scope for a steady and non-crisis driven improvement in the public finances without resort to the money printing press at the cost of huge potential future instability (as has occurred under Abe economics).

Abe smashes the hard yen and Japan's defences against Fed plague

All of this was not to be. Shinzo Abe won a populist campaign in late 2012 of which the economic policy content was fighting deflation, "breathing in" low inflation and boosting government spending so as to achieve prosperity. Yes, there was a lot of talk about the third arrow of economic reform – but had not every prime minister of the last 30 years promised this? There were no indications from his entourage of ministers that he would have more success against entrenched interests. Much of the emphasis of the Abe programme was on raising the price of Tokyo equities and the associated wealth effect bolstering consumer and investment spending.

Why would the Japanese equity market rise? Well, in the export sector where large cap Japanese stocks were disproportionately represented there would be profit surges related to devaluation of the yen. For international Japanese companies, there would be translation gains on their foreign investments. If that was all, it would not be so much – and many would-be investors could imagine that these gains might be very fleeting and quite modest in dollar terms though large in terms of yen if that currency fell far.

Abe economics was launched (in early 2013), soon after the Obama Fed had started its QE infinity programme. The asset price inflation virus in the global economy had become yet more powerful in consequence. Many yield starved global investors were even more than before prone to infection by the global plague of market irrationality. Here was a half-plausible story to chase – that Abe was going to bring about economic renaissance in Japan.

Even so, global investors were cautious to get entangled in the yen given the evident danger that the high-powered version of monetary experimentation in Japan could in some scenarios bring about currency collapse. Moreover, in several mainstream scenarios, Abe economics could mean a big fall of the yen, especially were Japanese investors to respond to the monetary uncertainty and manipulated long-term rates (at negative real levels) by stepping up the proportion of foreign assets in their portfolios. And so, the funds that came into the Tokyo equity market were largely joined with short positions in yen. Some aggressive international investors took much larger short positions in yen than were necessary to match their holdings of Japanese equity.

More broadly, that old "canary in the mine" indicating the presence of virulent asset price inflation having infected the Japanese universe was again singing loudly. The canary is the yen carry trade. With long-term yen interest rates pinned down at close to zero and inflation expectations inflamed by monetary uncertainty, the Japanese currency finance (in fixed-rate form) became a favourite funding vehicle for speculative build-ups whether in junk bonds (dollar or euro denomination predominantly), US equities, European periphery debt and so on. It was to face growing challenge in this role, though, as interest rates on the euro fell below zero and the ECB in early 2015 embarked on its own aggressive version of QE.

A new fillip to the yen carry trade came from the BoJ's surprise announcement in late Autumn 2014 of its stepped up QE programme (with government debt purchases amounting to over 15% of GDP for the next year) in response to the decline of GDP in the aftermath of the sales tax hike (in April 2014). (In practice, it was unclear whether the sales tax increase had induced a fall in spending or whether in fact the much heralded hike had led to intensified spending in the year before – in which case the small apparent successes for Abe economics at that stage were illusory. It was no surprise that the Abe government and its BoJ chief should have eschewed the latter explanation and preferred to announce that they were fighting a new recession whose cause was the sales tax increase.

On that basis, Prime Minister Abe called an snap election (two years earlier than the legal time-limit for the lower house of the Diet and giving the opposition less than three weeks from the announcement date to campaign – an affront to the normal standards of a democratic process), taking advantage of disarray in the political opposition and declaring that the next sales tax increase previously scheduled for 2015 would be delayed until 2017. The result of the election (December 2014) was not in doubt – the German financial newspaper Handelsblatt described it as a victory for Keynes and a defeat for Japanese democracy.

Could this intense QE experiment in Japan lift inflation there on to a steady 2% path – consistent with full adherence to the global 2% inflation standard? Or was the most likely scenario that the monetary experiment would fail – either by inducing much higher inflation, even hyperinflation or not bringing more than a transitory lift of inflation from zero?

In principle, driving Japan toward a steady state of 2% p.a. inflation would require the creation of a stable monetary pivot – say a reformed monetary base aggregate growing at a steady rate through time in a deregulated financial environment as discussed earlier in this book (see p. 135). Even if this was done, there are serious questions about the sustainability or optimality of such a system (see p. 53). And in any case, how do we get from here (prices stable or slightly falling) to there?

The sustained breathing in of steady state inflation into Japan (or any other economy) would need market interest rates to be below neutral during this process. In the context of the zero rate bound, lack of investment opportunity domestically, and considerable exchange risk aversion, that inequality may be hard to achieve especially at short or even medium maturities. In the long maturities, it may be possible, especially if there is "successful" manipulation down of long-term interest rates. But such inequality at long maturities is much more effective at generating asset price inflation than goods and services inflation (see p. 23).

Even with dampened investment opportunity and persistently high exchange risk aversion, it is possible that the neutral interest rate at short or medium maturities could rise if the public raise their expectations of inflation in line with government rhetoric or with actual experience of higher prices in the traded goods sector (due to currency devaluation). Persistent currency devaluation achieved by new and bigger QE shocks could induce the Japanese public to shift away from the yen. Their increased demand for foreign monies and more generally foreign assets would mean a rise in the neutral level of interest rates in Japan. This would bring scope for the BoJ thereby to create a gap between market rates and neutral (with market below neutral).

In principle, the Abe programme could be "successful" in terms of its objective of breathing in some inflation, especially if some other upward pressures on the neutral rate (across different maturities) were emerging. These pressures could come also from an expansion of investment opportunity in Japan, less aversion to foreign exchange risk, falling savings (perhaps related to demographics, perhaps to underlying budget deterioration).

How durable that success would be is very much open to question and in any case inflation which emerges might be far from the steady state of 2% p.a. (highly volatile and with potential to spike). The global asset price inflation disease with its original source in Fed QE (to which the below neutral long-term rates in Japan would make a contribution) could move at any point into its next dangerous phase, meaning recession in the global economy (including Japan). And long-term interest rates could suddenly spike at any point if and when the collective irrationality driven by monetary disequilibrium and broader market manipulation were to snap. Successive currency devaluations in Japan could at some point trigger a massive flight out of the yen and the birth of a hyperinflation psychology in which foreign currency (the US dollar) became the effective currency in Japan.

All this monetary experimentation has had a powerful negative side-effect – the creation of huge monetary uncertainty. We have seen already in this volume (see p. 23) that asset price inflation, which is fully anticipated and recognized, may be worse than no stimulus in that households and businesses worry greatly about the possible phase of asset price deflation and crisis at some uncertain point in the future. In the case of the Abe monetary experiment, businesses in the export sector may be somewhat unresponsive to the allure of high profit margins induced by the weak yen if they focus on the likelihood that global asset price deflation whenever it comes could mean a big reversal. In addition, the spectre of great possible monetary storms in the future – even hyperinflation and currency collapse – could not be helpful to the generation of economic renaissance in the present.

7

How Quantitative Easing by the Roosevelt Fed Ended in a Crash

No one had yet coined the term quantitative easing (QE). From 1934 to 1936, the Federal Reserve's balance sheet expanded by a similar percentage of GDP as from 2009 to 2013. Moreover, the monetary base at that time, including bank reserves at the Fed, was all non-interest bearing, unlike in recent years (under the Great Monetary Experiment (GME)) when reserves have paid interest at an above market rate (25bp vs. say 0–10bp for short-dated Treasury bills). Also, adding to the power of high-powered money in this early episode of QE (compared to under the GME) was the pro-cyclical fluctuation of prices.

Goods and services prices had fallen far during the years of steep recession (1930–33) – with some broad indices down by 30% or more cumulatively. In real terms, market interest rates became highly negative at zero or even moderately positive levels as expectations of continued economic upturn and price recovery strengthened. In consequence, the neutral level of interest rates (in nominal terms) climbed and a wide gap formed between market rates stuck at zero for short maturities (and up to 2–2.5% for long Treasuries) and the plausibly higher neutral level. Accordingly, broad money aggregates and bank credit rebounded vigorously through 1934–36 as banks found profitable lending opportunities at substantially positive loan rates.

So from the standpoint of early 1937, almost five years on from the first sighting of a stock market and economic cycle low in summer 1932 (in fact, the NBER dates the cyclical low point as March 1933 to take account of the double dip which occurred in early 1933 related to the seizing up of the financial system amidst widespread anticipation – correct – that Roosevelt, once inaugurated as president, would take the US off the gold standard) it could be claimed that QE had been much more successful than was the case in Spring 2014 within the GME (five years on from the Spring 2009 lows). In the first episode, this was one of the strongest economic recoveries ever from Great Recession. In the second, it was the weakest. Even so, the first episode ended very badly. Only a little further on from that early 1937 vantage point, one of the biggest stock market crashes in Wall Street history was to take place (a 40% fall from August to November) and the economy was to plunge into severe recession (with the cyclical downturn as defined by the National Bureau of Economic Research (NBER) lasting from May 1937 to June 1938). What are the lessons from that first episode of QE for the present second episode? That is the subject matter of the present chapter.

No architect designed Roosevelt QE

The direct source of monetary base expansion under the Roosevelt Federal Reserve was massive inflows of gold into the US from January 1934 when the Administration refixed the dollar price of the yellow metal (at $35 per ounce, up from $21 when the gold standard was suspended in March 1933). These inflows reflected capital flight from Europe, especially the gold bloc countries (including prominently France, Switzerland, Belgium and Holland), triggered at first by concerns that their currencies would break with the truncated gold standard. When this finally occurred in Summer 1936, massive dishoarding of gold in Europe followed with an important part of the proceeds heading for the US stock market by then widely seen as in a bull market sustained by strong economic recovery.

The Fed essentially created high-powered money (reserves) as the counterpart to these inflows (the Treasury Department issuing gold certificates against the gold which went into Fort Knox and the Federal Reserve issuing deposits against the gold certificates – the Treasury using those deposits to pay for the metal acquired at the official price). The top officials in the Federal Reserve and US Treasury fully realized that these unsterilized purchases of gold were potentially an important form of monetary stimulus. Yet the conduct of monetary policy was essentially passive. There was no architect in the Fed who had explicitly designed a monetary experiment drawing on academic research which he or she had authored. And as against QE in modern times, this did not involve mega- purchases of government debt, although as we shall see, the Fed and the White House did see themselves as having considerable potential influence on the price of US Treasuries (see p. 192) Given the huge amount of excess reserves produced, the money market remained stuck at virtually zero.

There are folklores and historical tales for this first episode of Fed QE, but unlike the Great Boom and Bust which preceded it (the mid-1920s up until 1933) there is no Austrian School version which has found its way into the widely read literature. The tales are about how a powerful economic recovery developed through 1935–36 and why this came to a sudden end in a cyclical downturn more severe than the first phase (Summer 1929 to mid-1930) of the Great Depression. The storytellers describe how one of the most severe stock market crashes occurred almost like a bolt out of a blue sky. In fact, as we shall see, the sky had darkened for some considerable time, although many investors wearing rose-coloured spectacles and believing strongly in the power of the "new economic policy" had not perceived this.

Monetarist, Keynesian, and anti-new deal tales of 1937–38 recession

According to the presently dominant history tale – monetarist – the source of the early dramatic end to the business cycle recovery was a grave blunder in policy by the Federal Reserve which tightened policy from late 1936 onwards out of misguided concern about inflation (see Friedman, 1963 and Meltzer, 2003). By implication, the monetarists praise the rapid monetary base expansion together with dollar devaluation as responsible for a powerful stimulus during 1933–36.

There is also a Keynesian explanation for the crash and recession, telling the story of Roosevelt's tax increases and general fiscal tightening in early 1937 (see Kindleberger, 2013). The Keynesians praise the fiscal loosening and other new deal measures bolstering "aggregate demand" as responsible for the fast pace of expansion preceding this.

We can also find a tale of the anti-new dealers, who see all the government interventions in the economy – cartelization, exhorting big business to raise wages, financial sector regulations – as undermining profit opportunities and the forces of creative capitalism. These interventions were responsible for the eventual failure of the recovery, though there is no strong time line here (Amity Shlaes, 2008). These anti-new dealers cross over in terms of membership with both the monetarists and soon to be described Austrians.

Finally, we have a very embryonic tale which fits with the Austrian School (Brown, 2014). According to this tale, irrational exuberance developed in the US equity market and some other asset markets through 1934–36 (especially 1936) under the influence of what would be described today as QE plus currency devaluation. Then in early 1937, the deadly end phase of asset price inflation arrived, with speculative temperatures starting to drop, plummeting ultimately in late summer and autumn. The transition of the asset price inflation disease from its mid-phase (in this case booming US stocks) to end phase coincided early on with the Federal Reserve's fairly token efforts to tighten monetary policy. It is implausible, though, that these were the most important factor in bringing on the end stage of the disease.

As to the strength of the economic expansion through 1934–36, an Austrian School narrative would emphasize the self-recovery mechanisms which proved strong enough to offset the drags from government intervention. One of those self-recovery mechanisms was a pro-cyclical behaviour of prices (down sharply during the depression, expected to rise during the recovery, hence, powerfully negative real rates). There was no such narrative to tell during and after the Great Recession of 2008–09. And the potential wealth effects of asset price inflation were not so widely neutralized (as in the second decade of the 21st century) by a realization amongst businesses and households that the end stage of this disease would likely be deadly. Asset price inflation disease as described in this book was as yet a largely unrecognized phenomenon, albeit that the origins of diagnosis were already to be found in Austrian School economic writings.

One reason why an Austrian tale has been absent in the established literature about the Crash of 1937 and the Roosevelt Recession has been the partly archaic nature of asset price inflation as described in these older Austrian texts available to contemporary observers (see p. 12). According to these, asset price inflation is a distortion in the relative price of capital goods and consumer goods brought about by monetary disequilibrium which is responsible for overinvestment during the boom.

Asset price inflation concept evolves beyond Austrian origins

This Austrian theory of the business cycle fits well in the particular with the 1920s boom followed by bust. But it is hard to place directly into the mid-1930s as that crash and recession occurred without evident overinvestment. Indeed, capital spending had not gained any remarkable strength during the expansion of 1934–37, explained in part by the extent of overinvestment in the preceding boom but also by the government interventions which curtailed present and prospective profits and burdened entrepreneurship. Even so, one Austrian School economist has tried to argue the case for possible overinvestment in 1936 amidst a bounce in productivity (see Catalan, 2010).

As described earlier in this volume, the modern concept of asset price inflation has evolved considerably from its early 20th century origins. The key element is a strengthening of irrational forces in the financial market-place as driven by monetary disequilibrium. The virus of asset price inflation causes distorted probabilistic vision – in particular a tendency to underweight the probability of dangerous scenarios becoming reality and overweight a small number of positive scenarios (in which returns would be high).. This distortion is greatest in asset markets where there are enticing speculative stories. One can describe several channels from monetary disequilibrium to this distorted vision (desperation for yield in a world with persistent inflation albeit at a low rate unbroken by periods of falling prices, positive feedback loops).

Asset price inflation is usually but not always accompanied by that other and much better known economic disease of monetary origin – goods inflation. But the emergence of the latter in statistically recognizable form is sometimes hidden by powerful downward real forces on wages or prices. The start of monetary inflation in the goods markets can be hard to determine in the context of some residual tendency of prices to recover from cyclical lows reached during the preceding recession. Contemporaries may be convinced that they are witnessing just such a cyclical recovery of prices and so be late in diagnosing monetary inflation.

Asset price inflations would come to an end even without actual central bank intervention. Indeed, the intervention often makes the end more violent, but it would have happened anyhow. Two potential ways in which asset price inflations end are first, growing expectations that present "stimulus" policies characterized by huge monetary disequilibrium will start to be reversed, and second, the speculative stories which have been exciting "irrational exuberance" become so misaligned with any likely reality that the rose-coloured spectacles splinter.

How can we fit these ideas about the asset price inflation virus in particular, to the experience of the mid-1930s?

Plague of market irrationality slower to form in 1930s than in 2010s

In 1934–35, it is possible that the asset price inflation disease was barely present. This is different from the QE experience of 2009–14 when speculative temperatures spiked very early in markets related to commodities (especially oil, iron ore, copper, mining equities) and emerging markets (especially China). The initial speculative stories in that later episode largely stemmed from China and blended with "limit oil" and perpetual outperformance of the emerging market economies relative to the decadent and crisis blown (over-leveraged) advanced economies.

In both episodes, short-term rates were abnormally low (at near zero, compared to a minimum rate of around 2% during the era of the gold standard – see p. 144 – albeit, allowing for considerable day-to-day fluctuations). Long-term risk-free interest rates (as on 10-year US Treasuries) at around 2.5% in 1934–35 may have been barely positive in real terms or actually negative allowing for the cyclical rebound in prices from depression lows which most likely lay ahead. Yet the neutral level of long-term interest rates in real terms was also plausibly low at this point given the extent of risk aversion and low profitability. As symptoms of asset price inflation disease eventually began to appear in 1936 (including high speculative temperatures in US equities and commodities), a very strong economic rebound was also evident to all. Short-term interest rates remained stuck at zero and long-term interest rates remained stable at low nominal levels and even fell somewhat – despite the likelihood by then that the neutral level had climbed. By contrast, when the first symptoms of asset price inflation emerged in the later episode, during 2010–12, the pace of US economic recovery was the weakest following any great recession. But there was strong economic expansion across the emerging market economies, including China and Brazil and a range of commodity producing economies (including Brazil) where the mining industry is prominent.

Globally and also in the US, production and prices turned sharply upward in the second half of 1936. In the US, commercial lending was picking up well. Keynesian historians argue that consumer spending got a lift in late 1936 from the payment of a bonus to the veterans of World War 1, which the Roosevelt Administration approved ahead of the Congressional and presidential elections of that November. Contemporary commentators described an upsurge in automobile production and residential construction. Wage rates were picking up – in part driven by cyclical factors and in part by growing unionization. In fact, by mid-1937, nominal GNP had risen above the 1929 level (construction still 40% below previous peak and population 10% higher over the decade). In the four quarters of 1936, GNP had increased by 9%. By the end of 1936, the total return on US equities since 1929 was positive. In 1936, the US equity market and commodity markets boomed and this continued into early 1937 amidst new buying from Europe. The US stock market roughly doubled from Summer 1935 to late 1936.

In the later QE episode of the 2010s, the rise of the stock market was less concentrated in time.

Where was the evidence of asset price inflation in all of this? Diagnosis of asset price inflation is always difficult. That is one reason why Milton Friedman most likely shied away from the concept – hard to reconcile with his agenda of positive economics. The diagnosis of this disease depends on much clinical judgement rather than empirical testing. How would a clinician have proceeded to judgement in say late 1936 or in the first half of 1937?

Symptoms of irrational exuberance in 1936–37

In particular, were contemporary investors tending to look at the future through rose-coloured spectacles, putting unrealistically low probability weights if any on various bad scenarios, and roused by positive feedback loops from rising asset prices to put exaggerated probability weights on good scenarios and their related speculative hypothesis? Were they putting too little weight on actual bad news stories and possible future bad scenarios? Holders of Treasury bills and money (in the form of banknotes and deposits with safe banks) had made good real returns during the period of falling prices (1930–32), but they might be justifiably anxious about potential large negative real returns over the long run as the Roosevelt Administration could revert to vast further monetary experimentation. Such malaise featuring also virtually zero money market rates is a powerful stimulant to asset price inflation, albeit dependent on the emergence of speculative stories.

One good speculative story was that the Roosevelt monetary experiment seemed to have brought strong economic recovery at last. In rational sober mood, investors would have remained deeply sceptical of that story, putting much more emphasis on competing hypotheses (including in particular the pro-cyclical behaviour of prices as strengthening the invisible hand). Monetary instability, though, undermines rationality and sobriety. A bad news story was the break up of the European gold boc in Summer 1936, and so the dollar hadrisen sharply against the European tradable currencies (the mark by this pint was not tradable) including Sterling. he cheap dollar had been one source of stimulus to the US economy through 1934–36. Moreover, the rise of the dollar could mean a waning of inflation fears (stoked up by the Roosevelt gold and money policies) and interest rates in real terms could thereby become less negative (in short maturity markets) and more positive in long-term markets even though nominal rates remained unchanged.

In US domestic politics, the Congressional and presidential elections of November 1936 loomed. In the event, this brought a landslide victory for President Roosevelt and the Democrats. Right up until election night, however, many of the opinion polls (crude in this era) were predicting a defeat. In the course of the election campaign, there was much populist attack on big business and Wall Street by the Democrats. And key elements of the New Deal – in particular pro-union legislation – which had been stalled by court rulings might well be implemented were Roosevelt and the Democrats to obtain victory. Roosevelt's promises of high taxes on retained corporate profits were surely likely to diminish further the propensity of business to spend – and as we have seen capital spending was a weak feature of this cyclical recovery.

In looking at economic prospects going forward into 1937 and beyond, there were various grounds for concern. Some of the economic strength recorded in late 1936 could be due to one-off factors – for example, the automobile producers trying to beat a threatened strike early in 1937, veterans spending their bonus. The modest business spending outlook militated against big further labour market improvement or sustained real income gains. And crucially the possibility of a world war within the next few years had become highly significant. Robbins (2007), in his contemporary history of the Great Depression and its aftermath, notes how the danger of war had an important negative influence on business confidence at this time. In March 1936, German military forces had entered the Rhineland, violating the terms of the Treaty of Versailles and the Locarno Treaty. Imperial Japan, having seized Manchuria in 1931 and installed a puppet regime there (Manchukuo) had begun to push from south of the Great Wall into northern China and into the coastal provinces.

Price-earnings ratios even in early 1937 (after the powerful stock market rise of 1936) were about average. But that does not prove the absence of asset price inflation disease, though, in our times Fed Chief Yellen has made such a claim. (Subsequently as P/E ratios rose to well above normal range, Yellen sounded some warning notes). It could be that earnings of the corporate sector were for a variety of reasons above sober projections of long-run trend and that the future was more troubled (by various dark scenarios) than usual – both of which considerations would have meant P/E ratios should have been well above historic norms.

Carry trade activity, often a symptom of asset price inflation, is not evident in 1936. Its absence could be explained by the extent of evident exchange risk (given the violent fluctuations of currencies in these times) and the recent experience of default on the mega carry trade activities of the previous great asset price inflation (in the mid and late 1920s), especially as regarding German credits. It is true that in the second QE episode of the 2010s carry trades became resurgent despite the experience of these going bad in the asset price inflations of the previous two decades (examples included the Mexico bust of 1995, the Asian crisis of 1997, and the yen carry trade of the 2000s), but there had been no spectacular losses on the scale of Germany in the 1920s and much bail-out activity.

Roosevelt Administration's concerns about excessive speculation

How far were the various authorities within the Roosevelt Administration including the Federal Reserve concerned by late 1936 about excessive speculation and what role did any action by them play in the transition of asset price inflation to deflation during 1937? Friedman and Schwartz (1963) write, for example, the desire within the Fed and elsewhere to tighten policy in early 1937 was highly understandable. Economic expansion had been proceeding albeit irregularly for four years and steadily for two. Wholesale prices had risen nearly 50% since March 1933. Stock market prices had roughly doubled since mid-1935. New York Fed President Harrison (who had succeeded Benjamin Strong in that role in 1928) and others in the Federal Reserve System felt strongly that in the past the system had always been late in reacting.

In early 1937 President Roosevelt expressed concern that speculation was becoming excessive and commodity prices were being bid up to heights which could not be sustained. The Bank for International Settlements (founded May 1930 to administer the payment of German reparations under the Young Plan) in writing about this period a year later (in their report published May 1938) commented "rubber prices reached 13d in April (1937) as against a fair price of 9d; the market price of copper reached £80 vs. a reasonable price for profit (in Rhodesia) of £35. These examples could be multiplied many times".

There was talk in the marketplace of the US cutting the price of gold, and this speculation became one source of transitory downward pressure on equity prices and commodities (through early Spring 1937). Then Roosevelt stated in a speech early April 1937 that the US had no plans to cut the gold price. But markets did not believe him. And in early May (1937), the BIS in its annual report made a Delphic statement about lowering the gold price. By June, though, this speculation about the US cutting the price of gold had died down given the fall in the equity market and commodities during the spring. Equity prices rebounded in early summer, though, not back to their previous highpoint of late winter 1937.

The Dow Jones stock market index, which had ended 1936 at around 170, had peaked at 194 in mid-March. Then it had fallen to around 165 by late May. During early summer, there was a small rebound to around 185 in late July, a brief plateau until mid-August, then the plunge (to 113 in mid-November).

Back in January (1937), when concern about excess speculation and inflation was perhaps at its peak in Washington, the Federal Reserve had decided to raise reserve requirements in two stages (February and April) toward reducing further excess reserves (having taken a preliminary step in this direction the previous August). Friedman and Schwartz are particularly critical of this step: "what rendered the action unfortunate in retrospect was that the system failed to weigh the delayed effects of the rise in reserve requirements in August 1936, and employed too blunt an instrument too vigorously; this was followed by a failure to recognize promptly that the action had misfired and that a reversal of policy was called for. All those blunders were in considerable measure a consequence of the mistaken interpretation of excess reserves and their significance".

Flawed monetarist criticism of Fed actions in early 1937

In appraising this criticism, we should take account of the total monetary picture in early 1937. At the end of 1936, Roosevelt had ordered the Treasury to sterilize the further inflow of gold, and in the next half year gold purchases were fully funded by Treasury bond issuance. This order stemmed from concern already mentioned about excess speculation and possible emerging inflation pressures. Hence, these were no longer a source of monetary base expansion. Excess reserves, however, had bulged in consequence of non-sterilized purchases during a period of peak gold inflows in preceding months.

Hence, the growth in supply of high-powered money slowed sharply from the beginning of 1937 whilst the legal floor to the demand for high-powered money (based on reserve requirements) increased suddenly in two stages. Neither amounted to a significant tightening of monetary conditions in the first half of the year. Yet both policy steps together might have influenced expectations about the monetary outlook further ahead, though that is not self-evident.

In particular, the slowdown in high-powered money growth following a bulge in the previous half year was surely little more than a change of rhythm within a still rapidly increasing profile. And as regards the actual demand for high-powered money, it is unclear that a hike in the legal minimum amount of reserves, far below the actual amount of reserves held, had any overall significance. Why would a hike in the legal minimum mean that banks would want to hold a higher than other-wise level when they already had a huge cushion to meet the normal swings in holdings of reserves brought about by payment fluctuations? Moreover, the introduction of deposit insurance and non-penal rates for borrowing reserves at the Fed (both elements of New Deal finan-cial system reforms) surely meant that the amount of excess reserves required for ironing out such fluctuations was much smaller than had been the case historically.

It is plausible that bank managements regarded most of the excess reserves on their balance sheets simply as investments at a time when near substitutes (short maturity Treasury bills for example) were also yielding zero rate of return. When market rates are at zero, then the non-interest bearing nature of reserves did not mean that banks would be under any incentive to economize on holding these. Yes, if the neutral level of short and medium-term rates were above the current market level of near zero, then banks should find growing opportunity to convert excess reserves and other similar assets into business loans and earn good margins on these. That occurred during 1935–36. It is plausible, though, that by early Spring 1937, such opportunities were shrinking in line with the asset price inflation disease already transi-tioning into its late stage of falling speculative temperatures and overall business conditions cooling (see below).

In fact, short-term money rates only blipped slightly higher (maximum 40bp in terms of Treasury bill rates) for a few weeks as the increased reserve requirements came into effect in early Spring 1937 and then sunk back to zero (see Calomiris, Mason and Wheelock, 2011). This would be consistent with the of increase in legal floor to reserve demand not boosting overall demand for high-powered money and with the decrease in growth of supply (of high-powered money) not causing any overall shortage at prevailing zero rates of interest – all of which is in contradiction of Friedman and Schwartz's assertion as quoted above. Under the circumstances described, putting up reserve requirements would not alter bank plans or strategies for lending, and it would not set up any competition for short-term funds. If asset price inflation had continued for some considerable more time in its phase of high specula-tive temperatures, then, yes, money market rates would have started to rise as business loan demand and related opportunity for banks to earn good margins remained buoyant. That was not to be the case.

A monetary policy announcement shock in 1937?

An alternative monetary hypothesis for the recession and crash – different from the Friedman and Schwarz view – is that there was an announcement effect as described above (an immediate fall in perceived danger of future inflation). The real yield on bonds suddenly jumped. That could in principle set of a stock market crash (see Eggertson and Pugsley, 2006).

The vulnerability of the stock market or any asset market to a fairly modest increase in real rates as described would be most if these were already infected by asset price inflation to a serious degree. Then the modest increase could be the catalyst to a return to prevailing rationality. That possibility has not been discussed in the literature to date, but it would fit in with the hypothesis here in which the crash and recession of 1937–38 are explained as outcomes of an episode of severe asset price inflation as generated by monetary disequilibrium. "Fitting in with", though, does not mean that one should put a high weight on this one explanatory factor to the exclusion of other possible catalysts (including geo-political events, domestic political events, and disappointing business or economic data) to the transition of the asset price inflation disease into its deadly end phase featuring steep falls in speculative temperature and ultimately severe recession.

Perhaps we can detect some such shift (down) of inflation expectations at the time of the outbreak of speculation on a cut in the gold price and the setback to the stock market in early spring. But that did not persist. The confiscation of private gold holdings, the failure of the Supreme Court to uphold the gold clause and the power of "monetary radicals" within the administration would surely have left many investors concerned about continuing monetary instability in the future including inflation, even if there were now a temporary remission. The possibility of world war erupting within the next few years was not trivial by this point, and this would bring a bout of high inflation.

It is plausible that the successive rise in reserve requirements and the slowdown in high-powered money creation through the first half of 1937 had an influence on asset prices via its impact on long-term interest rates. The swings here were quite modest though. In late 1936 short and long-term interest rates were at the lowest levels experience to that time (around 2.4% at 10-year maturities).

The bond market broke on March 12, 1937 (with the stock market peaking simultaneously) coinciding with a continuing uncertainty about Federal Reserve policy, with the 10-year rate climbing to 2.52%.

That was enough to bring a crisis meeting between Treasury Secretary Morgenthau and Fed Chairman Eccles (see Meltzer, 2003). The latter claimed the rise had nothing to do with Fed policy, attributing it instead to British rearmament, the demand for war materials, and concerns about the federal budget deficit. On March 27, 10-year yields spiked further to 2.72%.

By then, Meltzer (2003) relates that Eccles had come into agreement with Morgenthau about the desirability of action to support bond prices though New York Fed President Harrison continued to argue that the rise (in yields) had to do with inflation concerns (especially regarding rearmament). At the April 6 policy meeting, Morgenthau told Eccles that he wanted a "big broad stroke". The 10-year yield was above 2.8%. Eccles, Morgenthau and Roosevelt met to discuss the issue. The upshot was that purchases of bonds by the Federal Reserve began for the first time since 1933. Yields fell promptly, and that was the peak for this cycle.

US economy slows in advance of the 1937 Crash

Business in the economy went sideways from March to August 1937 (albeit with the benefit of hindsight the NBER date the peak of the cycle as May, with the recession starting then). Kindleberger (2013) analyses the path of the economy as follows. "The spurt of activity in late 1936 had been dominated by inventory accumulation, especially in the automobile sector where there was fear of strikes. It was the same in steel and textiles. Long-term investment had not risen to great heights. Also the fiscal situation was tightening. In early Autumn 1937 Roosevelt had still be arguing for bringing the budget into balance by 1937".

In sum, it is difficult or implausible to attribute the flattening of the economy in the first half of 1937 to the increase in reserve requirements or the rise in bond yields which occurred in early spring. In fact, more negative for business confidence at that time could have been the Supreme Court judgement in May in favour of the New Deal's union legislation (Wagner Act) and the tax hikes on corporate profits in the wake of Roosevelt's election victory.

The plunge of the equity markets from late summer – together with a similar downswing in business confidence – is a credible factor in the sudden and severe economic downturn which started around the same time and featured a crumbling in business investment. Why did the stock market and business confidence fall so sharply and deeply when the evidence to hand at the beginning of the plunge suggested only a "levelling out of economic activity"?

Here, we should consider the starting conditions of irrational exuberance which had built up during 1936. Equity and commodity markets in early 1937 were gripped by speculative fever with its origin in the Roosevelt monetary policy (which had gone much further in the direction of disequilibrium during 1936 as short-term rates remained pinned at zero whilst the neutral level of rates across the maturity spectrum surely rose). As we have seen, in such circumstances, investors were slanting downward the probability of bad scenarios ahead. The outside world was getting uglier in many respects. The US economy was slowing. Geopolitical tensions were increasing. And the sustainability of indefinite low bond yields had come into question.

We can debate the weight of each factor which caused ultimately the rose-coloured spectacles worn by the irrational exuberant investors to splinter – evidence of flat business conditions, the Japanese full-scale military actions which started against China in early summer and leading on to the Battle of Peking, the May judgement of the Supreme Court and the continuing devaluation of the French franc, amongst others. But they all come together ultimately to have that powerful effect.

The lesson of 1937 for today

What is the lesson of the 1937 history as reinterpreted here for the present? The Obama Fed has been determined not to repeat the mistake of the Roosevelt Fed as diagnosed by Friedman and Schwartz. This means no premature abandonment of QE or rise in interest rates. Rather, the Fed should delay any normalization of policy stance until the economic expansion is much more advanced than it was in early 1937. According to the narrative in this chapter, that is the wrong lesson to have drawn and by acting on it the Obama Fed will bring about most likely a bad result. The founding fault of Fed QE, whether as practised in 1934–36 or 2009–14, is that it creates a virus of asset price inflation. That virus does not have a good ending – unless an economic miracle intervenes. Did the Federal Reserve's policy actions in early 1937 make the outcome worse than it otherwise would have been? That is far from obvious. First of all, the overall shift in monetary stance does not appear to have been considerable. Second, the steep decline in speculative temperatures which occurred from late Summer 1937 had much more to do with the splintering of rose-coloured spectacles under the impact of outside events which would have occurred with or without the monetary adjustment in question. Asset price inflations burn themselves out sooner or later. In 1937, that was sooner rather than later. The speculative stories which had featured in the terrific rise of equity and commodity markets during 1936 became tired through early and mid-1937, including crucially the hypothesis that economic renaissance had at last blossomed.

At the time of writing, we do not know for sure the form which the late stages of the asset price inflation originating with Obama Fed QE will take or whether indeed the late stage has already begun as suggested by the steep speculative temperature falls in commodities (especially oil and iron ore), commodity currencies and emerging market assets. Already, it is clear that the experimenters could not avoid unleashing waves of commentary and speculation about their exit plan – when and by how much policy would eventually normalize. That may not be crucial to the course of the disease, any more than it was in early 1937. Yet no two episodes of the disease are identical. And in this plague of irrational exuberance monetary normalization might yet play a larger role.

Now is never a good time to normalize monetary policy in the sense that this might be the trigger to steep speculative temperature falls. Indeed, beyond a certain point in the asset price inflation disease, a harsh end phase is already built in so it may be best for the central bank to sit back as spectator rather than accelerate and deepen the eventual crisis, hoping all the time for the late arrival of economic miracle which would allow it to proceed with normalization. Had that point already been reached in Autumn 1936 or in Spring 2015? In real time, it is hard to say so, although criticism based on looking through the rear-view mirror could yet turn out to be powerful.

A *Wall Street Journal* lead article (see WSJ, 18/3/2015), headed "The Patience of Janet" took the side of those critics who argued that 1937 was a bogeyman and that the Fed should not hesitate further to start "policy normalization". The un-named editorial authors wrote: "We are beginning to hear the same pleadings now from Washington and Wall Street for the Fed not to raise rates as a decade ago when the Fed stayed at 1% for a year despite 4% GDP growth. Raise rates and stocks might fall. Or we might return to recession as in 1937 – the most overworked analogy in economics".

The *Wall Street Journal* editors in question may turn out to be right about the Fed still having the scope to start normalizing policy in Spring 2015 without making the end stage of the asset price inflation disease which its QE policies had created even worse. Indeed, normalization then might according to its advocates lessen the acuteness of the disease's present phase (bringing, for example, some modest fall in speculative temperatures in equity and credit markets) meaning a less severe end phase. But the editors were surely wrong in terming 1937 as the most overworked analogy in economics.

Legendary trader Stanley Druckenmiller together with Christian Broda (2015) followed up with an attack in the same newspaper on the 1937 "mythology". They state that "the differences between the current policy conjuncture and these historical analogues are striking". Yes, there are differences. But if the stock market had a living mind, then the primordial force operating within its subconscious would be 1937. Yes, you can do a Google search and find any number of recent false alerts. But a faulty fire alarm doesn't mean there's no such thing as a future fire. The real and important question is: How can we design a better alarm system?

"The danger of 1937" can be described in generic terms. Since its very inception, the Federal Reserve has repeatedly experimented with monetary stimulus as a tool to quicken expansion in the aftermath of serious recessions. And so the the Fed has in effect been the source of asset price inflation early on in the recovery. By providing "vigorous" monetary stimulus – meaning lower interest rates and faster monetary growth than what would have occurred under a system of rules designed for monetary stability – speculative temperatures across a range of asset markets spiked. In turn, the presence of asset price inflation disease has made Fed policymaking especially hazardous. Policy normalization runs the danger of triggering a transition of asset price inflation into its deadly end stage. This is no overworked analogy but a serious ongoing issue as regards the US and global monetary environment.

The pattern can be traced all the way back to the Fed's stimulus to lift the US economy out of the 1920–21 recession (see Chapter 3). That stimulus involved what was at the time an unconventional policy tool – a powerful expansion of the monetary base beyond what was consistent with gold flows. In the early 1960s, the Fed applied non-conventional tools in the aftermath of the last "Eisenhower recession" designed to take advantage of the Keynesian perceived trade-off between unemployment and inflation. The stock market roared. Later, in the early 1990s, the Greenspan Fed experimented with abnormally low rates for longer in the aftermath of the end 1980s bust. And in the early 2000s, its experimentation deepened under the influence of the new governor from Princeton (Ben Bernanke) and amidst concerns about deflation following the NASDAQ crash and related recession led by the telecommunications sector.

Yet the 1934–36 and 2009–15 episodes stand out amidst all these periods of stimulus experiment on account of their extreme nature.

Not far behind is 2003–05 – a period of intense monetary stimulus in the early recovery phase accompanied by asset price inflation culminating it its particular version of 1937 (the 2008 market crash and subsequent recession). There is another distinguishing feature of these three episodes – the failure of even a partial economic miracle to arrive. What do we mean by this?

In statistical terms, an economic miracle is the emergence of productivity surge together with buoyant business spending. Instead, in the three periods mentioned, capital spending by business remained cautious. In the other episodes, economic miracles allowed the Federal Reserve in principle to normalize monetary conditions and cure the asset price inflation disease already present due to its earlier stimulus without precipitating an early market crisis and recession. For example, in the mid-1920s, there had been the flourishing of the 2nd industrial revolution and détente in Europe. In the mid-1990s, there was the IT-related productivity surge. Even so, Fed reluctance to allow monetary conditions to normalize fully – meaning that interest rates in the marketplace sagged below the neutral level consistent with near or full miracle economic conditions – caused asset price inflation disease to return in these two examples, culminating in the bubble-and-burst of 1929 and 1990.

Yes, it may well have been better if the Obama Fed had never embarked on its Great Monetary Experiment or second best if it had aborted it early. But a point might come where the GME has been running for so long that it would be better to let it come to an end endogenously as asset price inflation disease enters its final phase rather than unduly hurrying that transition. Alternatively, there may still be a late cure possible which would mitigate that final phase. That is a judgement call in which there are no grounds for confidence that the Federal Reserve will make the right choice.

8
A Guide to Surviving the Plague of Market Irrationality

The global plague of market irrationality with its origins in Fed quantitative easing (QE) has made some people very rich. The permanence of those riches, though, depends in many instances on the right answer to a follow-up question. When should the (so far) fortunate investor exit various infected markets, and even take short positions there, before the asset price inflation disease moves on to its final deadly phase in which speculative temperatures plummet, whether in non-synchronized fashion or all at once as in a financial panic?

The plague also has impoverished and continues to impoverish many people – for example, the elderly living from the income on traditionally safe investments such as money market funds; young people looking for residential accommodation in metropolitan centres where real estate speculation has become endemic driven by stories of the incessant search for safe haven by wealthy foreigners; and households of feeble means which spend a large part of their incomes on fuel and food, both whose prices skyrocketed during the early phase of the asset price inflation when this infected commodity markets.

Fed QE rescued some people who would otherwise have suffered greatly (in terms of their financial well-being) from the end phase of the asset price inflation disease which attacked the global economy during the 2000s with its origin in the Greenspan/Bernanke Fed and its policy of "breathing in inflation" from 2003 to 2006. The massive expansion of the Federal Reserve's balance sheet in the years after the 2008 panic featuring the accumulation of mortgage backed securities and long-maturity Treasury debt on the asset side helped to limit the downward correction of real estate prices from levels reached in the previous "bubble" and indeed to promote a strong rebound in some cases.

In the absence of QE, losses in real estate would have been greater and more drawn out, inflicting great pain on landowners and lenders. The barons (unlimited partners) and other stakeholders (limited partners) in the private equity business who had amassed huge leveraged stakes in the mid-2000s were saved from a near death experience in 2008 by the launch of the Great Monetary Experiment. This rapidly spread a new disease of asset price inflation. Speculative temperatures in the markets for junk bonds issued by private equity-owned businesses-soared to unprecedented levels and their underlying equity investments rebounded in value. This was truly bonanza time for private equity.

The owners of mineral wealth – and businesses involved in its extraction – enjoyed a fantastic bonanza in the early 2010s, thanks largely to Fed QE. Rental income from mineral rights is a notorious source of crony capitalism which has flourished under the Great Monetary Experiment. In the global financial industry, riches have been amassed by a range of participants – whether talented labour with the required expertise, entrepreneurs or equity owners. A chief activity has been the selling of products and services to yield hungry investors. Private equity and high-yield bonds provide the pot of gold at the bottom of the rainbow for some financial firms often in the form of vast fees from mergers and acquisitions.

Hibernation is not possible

For those on the "outside track" – not the private equity barons or the mineral wealth owners or the landlord class, for example – Fed QE and the plague which it created was nothing to celebrate. Rather, it was a source of misery, at least psychological. Wealth preservation and growth would require "active management".

Whereas under conditions of monetary stability and accompanying market efficiency, it is possible for the disciplined investor to set a passive strategy which would be very adequate for his or her aims – for example, a given percentage of the total portfolio in well diversified groups of equity alongside fixed-rate bonds, money and real estate and deciding on a long-run currency composition – this is not possible in a global plague of market irrationality. There, the investor worries about a big eventual crisis – when asset price inflation moves on to its dangerous stage – and realizes that price signals are so distorted and irrational forces so strong, that passive investment would be lazy and dangerous.

Efficient market theorists might tell the investor that it is futile to try to diagnose the various stages of asset price inflation and time market entries and exits accordingly – better to just sit tight and make sure simply that one is not exposed to personal bankruptcy risk as plagues come and go. Intuitively, many investors know that this is not the best strategy and they can recognize examples of better strategies in the past which did not just turn on luck.

In principle, the investor under plague conditions could decide to hibernate until these are over. But where is hibernation possible in practice? Converting wealth into gold in the safe box is not hibernation. Swings in the price of the yellow metal could be large. Yes, as we shall see, gold has a role in surviving the plague, but not in a strategy of hibernation. Holding large denomination banknotes (500 euros or 1000 Swiss francs) or short-maturity high-quality bonds might be a form of hibernation, but this could be very expensive in terms of opportunities foregone. Most investors are likely to conclude that they cannot afford to hibernate.

Yet in deciding to actively invest in the market place when large chunks of this can have become infected by asset price inflation disease is a treacherous undertaking where the investor must keep his or her wits and not become trapped by the many siren calls. One of these is "that there is nowhere else to go". Who has not heard these tired phrases from the equity or credit paper sales persons who tell us that with cash yielding zero or less there is no alternative, but to pile one's wealth into these assets even at inflated prices. Well, there is an alternative of course. The investor can sell when the prices are inflated even though he or she might well suffer opportunity loss if they rise still further. But over the period of the plague as a whole, including its unpredictable end phase, the investor could salvage a good return as against the large loss which might materialize from being enticed by the siren and perhaps expecting to perfectly time the exit when asset prices are at their peak.

Like Balzac said of the successful author – he or she should observe the crowd carefully from the window but not go out to join it – so it is with the rational investor during a plague of market irrationality. In aggregate, much of the crowd's wealth will perish in the plague. The active investor can avoid that outcome only by luck (loaded against him or her) or by skill or some combination of the two. And skill in diagnosing and predicting the course of the monetary disease is surely a key ingredient of success.

Note Dr Shiller's categories of mental disorder but don't ask for a prescription!

Professor Robert Shiller, the pioneer of research into irrational exuberance, never recognizes this as a feature of the monetary disease which

Austrian School economists describe as asset price inflation. He analyses it instead as a psychological disorder of idiosyncratic origin. In consequence, he cannot venture a strong view on how investors should survive the plague.

For example, in a *Wall Street Journal* feature on Shiller's current thinking (in early Autumn 2014 during a mini-sell off in the equity market), Jason Zweig (2014) writes "his central message that emerges from the course of three conversations over the past few weeks is a deep humility in the face of irreducible uncertainty. Many analysts have warned lately that Professor. Shiller's long-term stock-pricing indicator is dangerously high by historical standards. Professor Shiller agrees that the indicator might be high relative to history but how do we know that history hasn't changed?"

A key aspect of not joining the crowd in the Balzacian sense above lies in the monetary dimension unrecognized by Shiller. The investor should retain a deep scepticism of the monetary officials and not become influenced by all those sycophantic interviews in the financial TV programmes or sharing in the frenzy of the Fed watchers (or ECB or BoJ watchers). Yet the investor has to know the state of general credulity about the monetary experimenters and carefully assess whether this is increasing or diminishing. For example, at some stages in the plague, there is hero worship of its authors – whether Alan Greenspan, Ben Bernanke or Janet Yellen.

The investor should follow the rise and fall of new speculative stories both in the monetary dimension and more widely. At their peak, these entice a broad spectrum of yield hungry investors. Hopefully, the investor should have some diagnostic ability with respect to both the rising and falling stages. And the investor should apply knowledge of the asset price inflation disease historically to detect possible patterns and the approach of its next phase – most importantly, when widespread falls of speculative temperature loom.

The investor should be aware of the particular forms of irrationality which become virulent during asset price inflation disease. These flaws in mental processes are the same as set out by Shiller (2000). In particular, we have referred in this volume to the positive feedback loops from price gains aggravated by long-term rates below neutral to putting increased likelihood on some half-plausible speculative hypothesis becoming the truth. And the investor should be on the lookout for various forms of extrapolative illogicality, especially in the carry trades which flourish under this disease.

A succession of high profits can bring in crowds of trend followers who somehow speculate that the crowds will get bigger and bigger (a form of Ponzi scheme in that the late-comers are likely to lose heavily). There is no Ponzi – it is a disorganized spontaneous Ponzi scheme. There may be, however, financial firms doing very well out of facilitating and even front-running the speculative flows.

Real estate mania and its toll on human happiness

Extrapolative illogicality is particularly prominent in residential real estate markets, where a form of hibernation demand emerges during asset price inflation plagues. Individuals who regard themselves as non-expert in financial markets and have a sense of the magnified dangers to their long-run financial well-being come to think that at least a home is a home. If they have salvaged a place or several places to live, hopefully desirable, then at least they can enjoy some tranquillity, especially if they have not over-mortgaged themselves in the process.

As an owner occupier, the individual is the recipient of a notional flow of rental income which is spent on an equivalent consumption item – rent for this particular area of residential space. If rents rise sharply, the individual loses as a consumer but gains as an investor – and conversely. This negative correlation between notional consumption and income flows enhances the appeal of residential real estate though the individual should be careful not to categorize as normal consumption what he or she has only undertaken in grossly expanded form in response to plague conditions. In normal times, would the wealthy individual be consuming residential space up to the whole of his ordinary income or even more (including notional rents) and brandishing keys to each dwelling on a ring tied to his waist?

Who hasn't encountered the stress within families about real estate which can occur during episodes of asset price inflation? The parents who wish to help their children secure a place to live (rather than incur the costs and uncertainties of renting) and in effect become the source of gift to the lucky individual from whom they are making the purchase. In aggregate, this mistaken kindness to children becomes an element in the asset price inflation disease. Thoughtful generosity to one's child would have meant gifting money on condition that it is not spent on real estate recording high speculative temperature. And within a marriage or partnership, adults who should know better than joining the band-wagon of investors counting on ever rising real estate values and thereby effectively negative rents (for owner occupiers so long as it lasts), find that domestic peace depends on defying their better judgement. An element of panic lurks in the background sometimes. If prices were to continue spiralling upward and rents were to rise alongside (perhaps due to a shortage of space as owner occupiers hoarded increasing amounts beyond what they would consume in the absence of hyped up expectations of capital gains), perhaps these individuals really would not be able to continue living where they have become accustomed to as renters, drawing on all the special conveniences which they value. The danger of "nomadic existence" might be particularly frightening to one or other partner.

The ratio of turnover volume in say a year to stock of the asset outstanding is typically low in residential real estate. The small flows might be related to stories which catch the imagination. We here about the Chinese buyers flocking into Sydney or San Francisco or the Taiwanese buyers in Tokyo or Russian oligarchs buying one out of ten high-priced homes in London or the world's wealthy taking their grey funds from offshore centres and securing them instead in metropolitan centres where the authorities do not have zealous registration procedures which might yield information to tax authorities. Yet even if such flows were to persist for some time, how much would they amount to in terms of outstanding stocks?

In any case, all these Chinese stories depend on asset price inflation continuing to keep speculative temperatures high in the market for Chinese credit products. If global demand for the latter were to weaken sharply and the flight of capital out of China to remain powerful or even gain strength, then the Chinese currency could collapse meaning a big decrease in the purchasing power of Chinese investors in foreign real estate markets or anywhere else. At the time of writing (April 2015), Beijing was having some considerable success in its policy of pumping up Chinese stock prices with the aim of "stimulating" the economy. It remains unclear, though, whether this would trigger any strengthening of capital inflows into China. Indeed, the reverse could be true if global investors became scared of the bust to follow the bubble. In the short run, though, the equity market bubble in China could feed speculation on an early economic rebound there and that could be broadly positive for capital inflows.

Decision making in asset price inflations without prosperity

We should distinguish investment decision making in real estate or any other markets infected by asset price inflation in an economic environment which lacks any sparkle (for example, the years 2010–15 or

1935–37) from a situation where that disease accompanies an economic miracle or mini-miracle (such as in the mid-1920s or mid to late 1990s). The first type of decision making is more difficult, simply for the reason that the second type occurs in the context of a rising economic sea where it is possible for all to climb, and the cost of the disease to most individuals is opportunity foregone rather than loss of prosperity and wealth.

For example, well before the asset price inflation disease formed, investors were making high returns on US equities during the industrial revolution of the 1920s or in the IT revolution of the 1990s. Monetary disequilibrium generated by the Fed in each case did eventually become the source of an asset price inflation disease. Investment became especially hazardous in a climate where irrational forces gained considerable force. But that was not the starting position.

By contrast in "the most unloved equity bull market of 2009–15" there was no story of economic miracle. In fact, throughout productivity growth and business capital spending were in general lacklustre. There was a continuous chorus of complaint about excess regulation, declining median real incomes and how the newest technological changes could be enriching a few but spreading poverty to many more.

Yes, there were passing episodes of excitement about economic stories. For example, in the first phase of asset price inflation as generated by Fed QE, much of the excitement was about emerging market economies, how these were poised to outperform the now decadent West and gain from the great new opportunities of access to information technology in a global village. Alongside, there were the stories of the Chinese century and limit oil. As energy prices spiralled upward, the speculative hypothesis gained weight that shale oil and gas would transform the US economic outlook. Canada with its vast tar sand resources became the lucky country. And the old country to enjoy that label, Australia, now found itself in an all-time mining bonanza driven by an iron ore price which had reached the sky under the influence of the real estate bubble and construction boom in China. In fact, underneath many of these stories was massive credit and real estate/construction bubble across the emerging market world and a colossal speculative hoarding of commodities in China all stemming ultimately from Fed QE (see Chapter 2).

In broad terms, we can distinguish bull equity markets built largely out of monetary disequilibrium and with little real substance at any point from those where there is a grabbing economic story of enduring prosperity accompanying it. There were powerful advances in US and German economic prosperity during the mid-1920s (the two largest economies at that point) and globally in the mid and late 1990s founded in both cases on strong productivity growth and technological revolution. The pity is that the monetary disequilibrium policies of the Benjamin Strong Fed in the first episode and the Alan Greenspan Fed in the second infected the prosperity with asset price inflation which ultimately culminated in market crash and recession.

Don't look to P/E ratios for timing the exit from an infected equity market

How can the investor recognize the time to bail out of the equity bull market infected by asset price inflation, whethergor not there was a real miracle at some point in its existence or not? Some analysts, Fed officials and regulators have suggested that it is enough to look at price-earnings (P/E) ratios and check whether these are within historic norms. But that begs many issues.

Certainly in the late phases of the 1920s bull market or the 1990s bull market P/E rates were well above normal range, though, that is what might have been expected if indeed the dominant expectation was for economic near miracle times to continue. Irving Fisher was of that opinion. A main justification for the opposing view was pessimism regarding the end-stage of the asset price inflation disease which had formed through the preceding years and infected a wide range of markets including crucially the German credit, real estate and equity markets (see p. 86). The asset price deflation phase when it came was to prove deadly. However, this was not a disease known to Irving Fisher though it was written about in some specific forms by contemporary Austrian School economists or others of similar views (see Hayek, 2008 and Robertson, 1940).

In other situations, the P/E ratio may be within normal range but earnings well above normal – or well above where they are likely to be when averaged across a range of plausible future scenarios. We have seen already (see Chapter 7) that in early 1937 P/E ratios in the US equity market may have been about normal but there were considerable dangers – higher than usual – of earnings falls further ahead related to monetary, economic and geopolitical issues. Five years or more into the equity bull market of the years 2010 onwards, the big question in assessing P/Es is how far E has been directly catapulted well above normal level by the particular process of the asset price inflation disease this time. A further question is how far expectations of near-term growth in earnings per share could have been distorted upward by financial engineering.

Specifically, the concern is that the corporate sector has engaged in many forms of financial activity and engineering which could bolster apparent actual earnings and exaggerate recent underlying earnings per share growth – for example, issuing long-maturity debt at thin credit margins to buy higher yielding debt in the present liquid markets, substituting zero rate (or near rate) floating rate debt for higher current cost fixed-rate debt, playing various forms of carry trade in currencies (moving funds into high-yield currencies). Paying cash back to shareholders in the form of equity buy-backs rather than extra dividend might generate a quickened pace of earnings per share growth and enlarged capital gains. turn, these could feed irrational extrapolative expectations about underlying profits performance going forward. top, the general fall of interest rates to low levels means that corporate profits have increased significantly relative to overall business earnings (before interest deduction), and yet this could not be counted on to continue as rates eventually normalize. If indeed a new age of stable prices is dawning and rates would remain lower than in the past, then there would be less hidden income on its way in the form of erosion of the real value of outstanding corporate debt (from the viewpoint of stock holders) by inflation.

Then there are the apparent increases in earnings which could occur through hidden forms of additional leverage now possible (whether explicit debt issuance or taking on ultra-cheap leasing commitments now possible in that companies providing these had access to the high-temperature speculative markets in high-yield credit). Also, there are the high business profits in some sectors which stemmed directly from the booming market in high-yield credit (for example booming auto sales, aircraft sales boosted by cheap leasing made possible by the private equity boom, and financial sales froth in Wall Street). Finally, there are those distortions to market metrics which resulted from the record high equity buy-backs. In fact, these amounted to the same in fundamental terms as higher cash dividends, but they had differing implications for the widely monitored crude earnings per share measures.

There may be grounds for suspecting that earnings would fall in the future related to the passage of the asset price inflation disease into its late and sometimes devastating stages. Already in late 2014 and early 2015, it could be seen that speculative temperatures were falling in various markets which had been at the forefront of the disease – Chinese real estate, other emerging market bonds and currencies, commodities (especially oil and gas). The loss of profitability for many US multinationals could be exacerbated if this next phase of the asset price inflation disease would bring a stronger US dollar (the first phase had gone along with dollar depreciation).

In diseased conditions, the economy is the financial market

Is it possible that an expert view on the outlook for the US or global economy would help the investor to determine when to hibernate, preserving his or her gains made so far until the plague of asset price inflation is over? Yet under these diseased conditions, the economy is the financial market and the financial market is the economy. The amount of interdependence between the financial markets and economy is especially high. And much economic activity is fuelled by the heat from speculative temperature rises. So when these speculative temperatures fall for any reason (and this may well be unrelated primarily to the latest turn of the macroeconomic data), there is a strong impact on the forces determining the path of the cycle.

In the asset price inflation generated by Fed QE, several subsectors of economic activity were stimulated by the high temperatures especially where the frothy markets in high-yield credit made it possible to obtain overall remarkably cheap finance at extraordinarily high leverage ratios. Hence, even though we have argued that in general business spending in the advanced economies was restrained by monetary uncertainty, these important subsectors were an exception.

For example, US automobile sales were revved up by a boom in sub-prime auto-credits, which in turn was driven by the bubble-like demand for high-yield paper especially related to private equity transactions. Many of the sub-prime auto finance companies were owned by private equity institutions. Aircraft sales gained from the extremely keen leasing terms which the airlines, especially in Asia, could obtain thanks to the boom in investor demand for high-yield credit paper (with many of the providers owned by private equity groups which according to usual practice had injected high leverage into these) . The shale gas and wider energy and extraction industries booms had drawn strength from the ease of newcomers issuing high-yield credit at fine terms and in large quantities (even though in principle given the huge uncertainties related to future price of oil a low leverage ratio would have been more in tune with market rationality). And large segments of the machine tool and wider manufacturing sectors had gained from the boom during 2010–13 in the emerging market economies where corporate leverage had climbed far as fed by the QE virus. If for any reason the temperature fell in the high-yield credit markets, there would be a cool wind through the global economy.

In broad terms, experience of the asset price inflation disease in previous cycles suggests the easy money is made in the early stages. Navigating the intermediary stages when temperatures may already be set to fall in some asset markets (although still rising in others) and when the risk of a sudden transition to the end phase can happen at any time is more hazardous. That does not mean the investor should decide to hibernate at that point, although some might do so, especially if sitting on good cumulative returns to date. After all, as King Solomon observed in Ecclesiastes, "there is a time to make war and a time to make peace, a time to make love and a time not to..." He did not say explicitly that there is a time to make money and there is a time to remain on the side lines. But he may well have done!

What drove great bull markets in the past?

Let's go back one stage to clarify what we mean by a bull market. If markets are efficient, then the term "bull market" would make little sense. Sustained periods of above normal rates of return could not be reasonably anticipated in advance even though they might be identified in retrospect. Yet the term persists so hard in the language of the marketplace that it would be irresponsible for any serious commentator to dismiss the concept (of bull market) in its entirety.

Perhaps the best way to describe a bull market in accordance with popular understanding is one where a run of high returns is occurring under the influence of a speculative hypothesis or story which has been gaining ground, helped very likely by positive feedback loops (price gains making the story more credible) as well as by the arrival of new supportive evidence for the original hypothesis. Trend followers and other market technicians who spot these processes at work decide to get on the bandwagon even though they may have little conviction about the underlying story. None of this means that market efficiency is totally in suspense.

Throughout the bull episode, there is the possibility that further evidence may contradict the lead hypothesis and trigger a big price fall. Or idiosyncratic factors could cause the trend followers who are betting on a continuation of this market pattern to take profits and similarly cause a sharp reversal in the market. Some of the trend followers realize this fully, but they may be operating within an institutional reporting system and individual reward scheme where it makes sense to bet on a continuation of moderately large gains albeit at the risk of a sudden large reversal (loss). Outsiders, though, not subject to such perverse incentives, should be able to spot strategies to take advantage of this and which collectively neutralize their market impact.

We can cite the great US equity bull markets in the past century– the booms of 1923–29, 1961–66, 1982–87, 1995–2000 – to demonstrate these characteristics. In the 1920s, the story was rapid productivity growth driven by the 2nd industrial revolution (mass assembly line, electrification) together with German reconstruction (after the war and hyper-inflation). In the 1960s, we had the European and Japanese economic miracles coupled with the new age promises of Keynesian economics in the US. In the 1980s, there was the swing of the political pendulum in the US to low taxes and to deregulation (Reaganomics) and a related boom in business capital spending. And in the 1990s, the story was the IT revolution and the related boom in productivity.

Alongside each of these episodes was a growing US monetary disequilibrium which created a virus of asset price inflation (in the mid-1980s this was the Volcker Fed pursuing dollar devaluation, see p. 97). The virus attacks the forces of market rationality and fosters the metamorphosis of the bull market into a bubble which subsequently bursts.

There have also been other US bull markets in equity without any overriding story of productivity surge and accompanying economic miracle. These have included the bull markets of 1935–37, 2003–07 and 2010–15. Instead in these markets, there have been many themes within individually popular sectors of the market. And there has been a big monetary story – the Fed conducting a big experiment meaning that "this time should be different". All these stories, monetary and non-monetary, have attracted a following enlarged in various ways by the monetary disequlibrium.as described in this volume. .

And so in 2003–06, there was the fight against deflation and the claimed successes for monetary frameworks of inflation targeting at the ECB and Federal Reserve. The central bankers trumpeted the age of moderation and the success of inflation targeting. With rates manipulated well below neutral, hungry investors were inclined to follow the story and positive feedback loops made this more credible. Frothy credit markets and booming carry trades fostered by the disequilibrium monetary policy in turn produced spectacular profits.

The yen carry trade in these years recorded high speculative temperatures as hedge funds and many other types of investors chased what seemed like a continuous source of profit. The stories chased in the carry trade were mainly versions of the hypothesis that Japan's huge savings surplus should find its way into higher return opportunities in the outside world. And a string of positive returns on the trade and continuing decline of the yen whetted the appetite for more of the same.

Financial sector equities most of all in the US and Europe "enjoyed" high speculative temperatures. European financial equities gained from optimism on financial integration in the new age of the euro. In the US, the credit boom related to sub-prime mortgages and private equity was accompanied by the speculative hypothesis of great financial innovation and opportunity. This thrived on the disequilibrium monetary policy, producing big winners on Wall Street. Investors chased these stories in the credit and equity markets – including the one about the American dream and home ownership.

How to navigate the stories of the QE bull market?

Turning to the bull equity market of 2009 onwards, there was no overall theme of great economic prosperity in the advanced economies – in fact, it was the opposite. There was continuous disappointment about the pace of the economic expansion and about productivity growth and general living standards. If there was a dominant story behind the bull market, it took the form of "there is nowhere else to go in a world of zero interest rates".

Early on in the bull market, there was much optimism about the emerging markets as having become the long-run driver of global economic growth as they would converge with the advanced economies taking advantage of information technology to do so. On top, there were lots of individual sector stories – shale oil and gas in the US, the latest innovations whether in social media or elsewhere from Silicon Valley or the equivalent – and a story about US profits in particular. These seemed to rise and rise strongly despite the weak economic background.

How could this be? There were various explanations at hand – the boom in profits from the emerging markets (whilst this lasted), the collapse of interest payments on debts, the decline of credit risk premiums, the corporate sector reaping income from zai-tech (participation in carry trades, hidden rises in leverage, investments in high-yield credit) and the boom in energy sector profits stemming from shale oil and gas extraction as induced by the sky-high energy price (so long as it lasted). In parts of the financial sector, profits boomed reflecting that good times were back in mergers and acquisitions, private equity, carry trade and, of course, in the high-yield credit sales arena.

It could be that some of the apparent earnings growth in the non-financial sector was attributable to a non-detectable increase in leverage.

After all, corporations were issuing record amount of debt, taking advantage of low fixed rates and low credit spreads. In principle, much of this debt was matched by expanded liquidity, but was the matching one to one or were the huge equity buy-back programs in combination with the debt issuance meaning net equity withdrawal? And even if this were not happening, how real was the apparent liquidity in the corporate sector. Many corporations were building up their holdings of corporate bonds, whether in the advanced or emerging market economies. The liquidity of these interlocking bond holdings could dry up at some point.

The monetary experimentation brought its own stories. Some investors and commentators believed or semi-believed in the success of the experiment and that the US economic outperformance of Europe reflected the more aggressive stance of the Federal Reserve. As highlighted already in this volume, there was widespread scepticism and anxiety about the eventual outcome. There was the story about Abe-economics and how the achievement of 2% p.a. inflation in Japan (instead of price stability) would bring prosperity there. And there was the story about how the Merkel-Draghi coup within EMU had solved the debt crisis there and established a basis for economic renaissance. Alongside, there were all those stories about vast amounts of money or liquidity on the sidelines created by the monetary experiment waiting to come into equities at some point and already fuelling price rises there.

How could the individual investor who had decided to pursue an active strategy of wealth management through this extraordinary monetary experiment best navigate the rise and fall of these speculative stories – some small and some large? A first point to note is that stories do not just rise and fall independently of the facts. When these jar with the story, its power to convince or excite, even if spun by the most eloquent of tellers, diminishes. So in some degree, the investor trying to profit from a story does well to focus on the likely timing of the contrary evidence. That is of course simpler said than done.

Many investors in 2010–11 may have doubted the narrative that China and the emerging market world were in the dawn of a new age of economic supremacy and that a long super cycle of high commodity prices would accompany this. But when would the data begin to jar in a way which could not be ignored? After all, there was a long history of China scepticism and the sales propaganda of the big commodity firms buttressed by research inside these and in the equity research departments of big financial institutions was awesome. And when it comes to popular economic theories or popular central bankers the time lags between reality and story jarring can be particularly unpredictable.

When economic data amplifies the storytelling

In particular, at what point could markets lose any respect at all for those stories about the potential success of the monetary experiment led by the Fed, or the "doing whatever it takes" by Mario Draghi at the ECB, or the "war against deflation" conducted by Shinzo Abe's Bank of Japan? There was the counter example of Alan Greenspan's rapid fall from grace as the monetary maestro. But he had not been associated with any particular doctrine, other than skill in fine-tuning. Implicitly, he had espoused inflation targeting whilst denying this, but the doctrine did not collapse with his popularity.

In fact, a centrepiece of the Great Monetary Experiment was the "fight against deflation", meaning inflation should be targeted at 2% p.a. The financial media in large part (with some exceptions) supported the fight, sounding the alarm when inflation fell "too low", as occurred in Summer 2013, especially in Europe. Even those commentators who disliked the Great Monetary Experiment and warned that it would fail disastrously realized that in the historical folklore it might get the credit for the US economic expansion from 2009 onwards. After all, Keynesian economics resurfaces again and again as a politically popular doctrine despite its great failures in practice. An economics doctrine preaching quasi money printing, helicopter drops of banknotes and government spending is a powerful genie once out of the bottle.

Even so, the point comes when facts are facts. There are so many ghost towns that cannot be denied, there are the anecdotes of the trips from the airport to the city centre with all the cranes inactive (could it really be a long lunch hour), we have the actual announced bankruptcies and there is the revealed fraud. There is the plunge in the price of commodities as evidence of the global business cycle turning. And there is the economic data. The latter is very problematic as to its effect on market action. Sometimes, market sentiment toward a particular story is so strong that interpretations of the data which are consistent with that are given undue weight amidst the strengthened forces of irrationality unleashed by monetary disequilibrium.

We could cite the example of 2014 with the distortions of the big winter freeze of 2013–14. GDP dipped in the first quarter of 2014 by 1–2% p.a. Also, unsurprisingly, there followed two quarters of strong economic rebound. . The big story in the US equity market, though, at the time was how the US economy was taking off into a higher flight path in which capital spending would at last drive forward productivity. And there was the music of apparently at last modest rapidly employment growth, albeit that the sceptics warned that this was mostly part time and or low paid low productivity work. The cancellation of long-term unemployment insurance at end 2013 and the launch of Obama Care had also contributed to observed labour market "strength". At best the labour market upturn was indicative of the invisible hand at last gaining effectiveness against all the barriers in restoring balance to the labour market, albeit at a remarkably low clearing price in a large segment. The contemporaneously strong economic data in terms of latest rate of change was music to the ears of the equity market bull, however dubious. Indeed, in the fourth quarter of 2014, economic growth fell back to barely 2% p.a. growth, and this was followed by near zero growth in the first quarter of 2015.

For market participants of a historical bent, this was all reminiscent of the situation in Germany during 1929 – a particularly severe winter had camouflaged from contemporaries a serious recession which was already under way (the stock market bubble had peaked in 1927). A warning sign for the discerning had been the rise in the support for the Nazi party in various regional elections (see Brown, 2014). Wall Street had ignored the signs of German recession – or rather had been content not to look beyond the camouflage of the post-winter rebound – amidst the late speculative frenzy leading up to the October 1929 crash. That was a much more serious error potentially – given that Germany, the 2nd largest nation on earth then, had been at the centre of the global debt bubble of that era in which US loans had been the key element – than the one highlighted by Friedman and Schwarz (that the US economy had been declining since August 1929). After all, to miss a peak of a business cycle by two months is par for the course, but not a persistent longer recession in the number 1 debtor economy on which the US banking system was highly geared (as would be revealed in the 1931 crisis).

A search for "quiet spots" amidst the dance of irrational exuberance

What were the hedges for investors who had been dancing in the music of the 1920s asset price inflation? At least with hindsight, we could say that these should have included a long position in gold and a short position in Sterling – and dependent on timing a long position in US Treasury bonds. The payouts from those hedges came with a big lag, though, behind the Wall Street Crash of October 1929. Instead the payouts occurred from Summer 1931 onwards – consistent with the view that the German banking crisis starting in spring that year was indeed the start of the deadly end phase of the asset price inflation disease. The point here is not to examine particular hedging strategies back then but to explore the general proposition that the active investor amidst a crescendo of irrationality as produced by the asset price inflation disease should examine carefully how his or her wealth could be exposed to the onset of its severe phase.

Given the inherent uncertainties in diagnosis and prediction regarding the disease, there are attractions to finding speculative opportunities to chase whose outcomes are negatively correlated with those for the other main constituents in the portfolio. And we should not overlook the option of retiring from an active strategy once big profits have been made in the environment of strong irrational forces disturbing the economic and financial landscape as under the plague conditions of monetary disequilibrium as described. Many investors find it hard to face the prospect that they might in retrospect retire from active strategy too early and get encouraged by big returns to date to overestimate their skills and chances in continued active management. They might become enticed by those siren calls from the financial TV programmes and elsewhere that "there is nowhere else to go" (except for equities and real estate) in a period of interest income famine, failing to pin themselves to the mast and recognizing that jumbo profits from the recent past can be realized and amortized over the remaining life of the asset price inflation disease.

In the "unloved" US equity bull market of 2009 onwards, a widespread defensive strategy was to take a short position in Australian dollars against US dollars. This strategy had particular appeal in principle to those investors who were chasing yield in the US equity market, in various currency and credit carry trades and even in the long-maturity US fixed-rate bond market.

The starting hypothesis was that speculative temperatures early on in the Great Monetary Experiment had reached very high levels in the Australian dollar. The boom in China, and in particular the construction boom there, had fed vast demand for iron ore imports and the sky-high price of these had contributed to a once in a century mining boom in Australia. Alongside a super investment spending cycle in Australia (developing its mineral wealth – not just in iron, but also for example in LNG) – had meant that interest rates in the "lucky country" were high relative to in those struck by interest income famine. The carry trade into the Australian dollar had become vast, not just from the traditional source of Japan but also from Europe and North America. Central bank reserve managers joined the pack, following the sales line about the high-yield obtainable on triple-A Australian government debt at a time when even the US government had lost its triple-A credit rating. Finally, flight capital from China into Australian real estate became a big story, with wealthy Chinese said to prefer the clean air in Sydney, and Chinese developers and investors hoping to make gains in the Sydney real estate market at a time when their own market had begun to sour. In real effective exchange rate terms, the Australian dollar reached a peak in 2012 some 30–40% above its average level of the previous four decades.

The prospect of large speculative returns from going short in the Australian dollar depended on an array of considerations. First, it was plausible that at some point the plague of irrational exuberance which the Fed and related QE policies had generated would move into its end phase of asset price deflation and recession. This might happen in China, emerging markets and commodity markets well before the final stage was reached in US and European equity markets and high-yield credit markets. In any case, the mining boom was pre-programmed to come to an end by the mid-2010s (with many mega projects completed by then) and so even without a fall in the price of the minerals the real exchange rate and interest rate level in Australia should fall back. But how was the speculator to time his or her entry and exit points. This story could have justified a short position in the Australian dollar at 90 on the way up – all the way to the peak of near 1.10 (US$/A$) – and when to get out? The answer was that timing had to be an art involving much intuition and also readiness to cut short positions and re-enter at a later point. When the Australian dollar was sky-high at 1.08 that is when the short position should have been at its largest. And the active manager who reached his or her maximum short position at 1.00 rather than 1.08 could thank the courage which stemmed from this defensive strategy for taking long positions say in equities or high-yield bonds for a more extensive period of time than otherwise.

Rotating between Australian dollars and Japanese yen

Should the investor have maintained a big short position even beyond Autumn 2014 by which point the Australian dollar had indeed fallen to below 90 US cents and the iron ore price to 50% of its 2011 peak, anecdotal evidence was building of a Chinese real estate market downturn, oil and gas prices were tumbling and emerging markets in general were disappointing expectations? Exiting the short seemed hasty.

After all, the Chinese credit downturn had not yet evolved into a stage of foreign inflows of capital into that country (largely in the form of carry trade) slowing sharply, There had been no full-scale emerging market crisis – at most only some rumblings in the currency markets. The Sydney real estate market had become the latest area of the global capital market to be recording record high speculative temperatures. The US equity market and the global high-yield credit markets were still generally buoyant even though there had been a little recent consolidation period and amidst the plunge in the oil price there were some jitters (especially given the amount of high-yield paper which had been issued by companies in the shale oil and gas sector). And a short position in the Australian dollar had a further attraction. Should indeed long-term US interest rates jump as many pundits warned once the long-projected take off of the US economy were to occur, then that currency unit should decline as carry trades into it were unwound.

Even so, by Spring 2015, big gains had been made on short positions in Australian dollars with the currency by then at just above 0.75 US cents even though the US equity market was now near an all-time high. The plunge in iron ore prices (down from $180 peak in mid-2011 to around $50) and in oil prices had taken their toll amidst growing evidence of the Chinese economy having entered the late difficult stage of the asset price inflation disease amidst anecdotal evidence of distress in its real estate and construction sectors. It was not too early to consider extending the search for quiet spots in the dance for irrational exuberance – in the sense that when the music stopped, the assets parked there would jump in value. "Quiet", though, would be a misnomer as in the interim the asset there might fluctuate considerable in price. Also in the early months of 2015 there was the growing noise from the officially sponsored speculative frenzy in the Chinese equity market. One such "quiet spot" could be the Japanese yen which by Spring 2015 had fallen to a level in real effective exchange rate terms which was around the low points of its 45-year floating experience. Yes, there was good reason for the fall (see Chapter 6) – in particular the amplified GME being run by PM Abe and his hand-picked Bank of Japan Chief – yet there were grounds for imagining the possibility that overshoot territory had now been reached. As in previous global asset price inflations a huge short position in the yen had developed (the so-called yen carry trade). Any serious decline in speculative temperatures globally would cause this to be cut back. And Japan, as the largest international creditor nation, would experience net repatriation of funds.

An alternative "quiet spot" (from the viewpoint of Spring 2015) to a long position in the Japanese yen was a short position in the Canadian dollar (against the US dollar). Much of what has been written here about the attractions of a short position in Australian dollars as one defensive strategy under the QE plague could apply to the Canadian dollar – also a currency driven sky-high in the early stages of QE as commodity prices surged. Also, there was a mining boom in Canada, primarily in energy, albeit somewhat less gigantesque than the Australian. And there was the feature of a bubble in the residential real estate sector in which Chinese investors were one story.

The carry trade has also been a feature in Canadian dollars since the onset of Fed QE though less strong than for the Australian dollar in that short-term interest rates in Canada barely reached 1% p.a. whilst long-term rates were at around US levels (as against Australian which were considerably higher). This meant that a short position in Canadian dollars might well be less of a hedge a short position in Australian dollars against a rise of long-term US interest rates. On the other hand, the short position should perform well in the scenario of end-stage global asset price inflation disease culminating in US recession.

When to go short in both equities and bonds

We have been discussing the use of currency short positions to hedge possible steep falls in speculative temperature as the asset price inflation disease progresses toward or even through its late dangerous phase. There is a more aggressive strategy to consider – the assumption of short positions in say the US equity and long-term interest rate markets. The rationale for doing this would be a high level of conviction that the GME has lifted equity and long-maturity government bond prices to far above their sustainable long-run paths, and there is a high probability of steep speculative adjustment downward in the near term.

Taking short positions in the US stock market (or any other stock market) is daunting,, in that it is the opposite direction to a powerful carry trade out of cash or low yield paper and into income earning stocks. When earnings yields on the S&P 500 are at say 5–6% and long-run average historical returns to capital in the stock market at higher than that, the taking of a short position under present extraordinary monetary conditions means accumulating zero or even negative earning cash on the asset side of the individual's balance sheet matched by stocks on the liability side with high potential outgoings (dividends and capital gains). And taking short positions is technically expensive – either in terms of borrower fees or paying administrative costs to professional managers. Some investors use special exchange traded funds which track the inverse of the equity market times a factor of two or three (so-called ultra-short pro-shares), but these expose any strategy to considerable basis risk (in that the amount of the bet falls sharply when the market moves down which means that any re-bound takes place from a lower base unless the investor continually adjusts the position, adding to transaction costs). None of this means that short positions should be out of bound for the rational investor, but his or her speculative views must have exceptional robustness to justify the strategy.

The investor who takes short positions in both long-maturity Treasury bonds and equities realizes that the prospective returns will not be perfectly correlated, although that is usually an advantage in terms of achieving an optimal combination of risk and return. For example, a stock market crash would mean most probably big gains on the short equity position offset by some loss on the short bond position. On the other hand, there are less severe scenarios where long-term interest rates could rise along the way to the stock market falling sharply; indeed, when the stock market does crash long-term rates may be fall to a level higher than now. And if the investor is wrong and the economy strengthens considerably whilst the stock market remains elevated, gains on the short positions in long-term bonds could even outweigh losses on the stock shorts.

Finally, if an economic miracle were to emerge – meaning a sudden acceleration of productivity growth and business spending – then there could be a powerful fall in long-maturity bond prices. The gains in equity prices could be smaller than the losses or at any rate mitigate the overall size of net loss.

In sum, the aggressive bear speculator on the course of asset price inflation ahead could well decide to be short in both equities and long-maturity Treasuries. Even so, the investor in shorting long-term interest rates would be aware that during most of the GME so far that strategy had been a big loser. (Early summer 2015 brought big gains.) And he or she should also realize that in the event of the Federal Reserve intensifying its monetary experiment for any reason or taking longer than now expected to curtail the experiment long-term interest rates could fall and equity prices rise, meaning a double whammy of losses from the combined short positions. In a well-constructed portfolio, such losses might be diluted by gains on a long position in gold.

The QE graveyard for bear speculators on treasuries

Fed QE has been a graveyard for many bear speculators on the US T-bond market. Ever since the Great Monetary Experiment was launched, there have been popular predictions of ultimately rising inflation pressure and of long-term interest rates rising in anticipation of this. And even without emphasizing these inflation predictions, there were the early bouts of scepticism for example through 2011–12 about whether in fact the Fed could manipulate down long-term interest rates for any length of time. In fact, such scepticism was well grounded.

The fact that the Fed was potentially building up a long position in long-maturity US interest rates to say 20% of the total amount of such risk outstanding (including non-government paper and swap markets) did not justify the view that it could fix these at its chosen level (see Chapter 1). The huge stock of long-term rate long positions outside the Fed had to be held by willing investors making their calculations about future inflation risks and the likely path of the neutral real level. We should also consider potential opening up of short positions (including long-term fixed-rate borrowing by the private sector) in fixed-rate markets (also swap markets) by speculators who judged that prices were out of line with fundamentals. Yes, the term risk premium might be somewhat less than otherwise, but arguably this was never substantial to start with. As highlighted in this volume, Fed power to drag long-term rates well below neutral depends in part on projections about the path of the official peg for short-term rates and in part on an array of irrational forces. These are empowered in part by the mental flaw of "anchoring" (investor's views of interest rates far into the future are too much sensitive to where they are at present). Yet none of this amounts to a tight control of long-term rates, nor does it prevent "fundamental forces" from over-powering the irrational forces and the rate pegging antics.

All of this the long-term interest rate markets discovered during the "taper tantrums" of Summer and Autumn 2013 when the Obama Fed started to hint at the possibility that the expansion of its balance sheet could slow and then stop within the next 18 months. That was the "Emperor's New Clothes" moment for the Obama Fed and its bag of tricks designed to convince markets it had tighter control over long-term rates than in fact it did. Even so, after the tantrums were over, many bear speculators on long-term rates were wrong-footed by a continuous and substantial decline in long-term rates through much of 2014 bringing them back to a level at end-2014 just some 70bp (at 10-year maturities) above their previous low points of 2012 and early 2013. The new stories behind this decline (in long-term rates) included a moderation in inflation expectations and evidence of economic weakness in Europe and the emerging market world – especially China. In addition, there was the plunge in long-term rates in Japan and Europe – the former driven by an intensification of the Abe monetary experiment and the latter by speculation that ECB Chief Draghi was preparing a QE experiment for Europe. As the dollar rose and commodity prices fell, the upturn of inflation in the US seemed an even more distant prospect.

Why were all those forecasts of (goods and services) inflation, which appeared from the start of QE and which seemed to weigh against investment in long-maturity US T-bonds, so wrong?

The first point to consider is the powerful real forces bearing down on prices. The nature of modern day technological change has been to produce a few high-stake gainers in the labour markets (those with particular talents and who could command therefore large rents) whilst creating more losers. The latter include prominently white collar workers performing routine tasks who find themselves displaced when these are taken over by intelligent machines. These workers with their human capital eroded have to look for non-routine jobs in the low skill low productivity sectors of the labour market, driving down wages there and even stimulating firms to substitute labour for capital. Digitalization continues to encourage firms to move production (of goods and services) offshore to cheaper labour countries largely in the emerging market world.

Despite this downward pressure on prices and wages, the Obama Fed had some success in meeting its "inflation target" through 2010–13 largely due to the effect of its monetary experiment in depreciating the dollar and driving up commodity prices (one of the first markets to be infected by the Fed QE asset price inflation virus). As speculative temperatures started to fall in those first markets and the dollar appreciated (helped along by the fact that Europe and Japan had ultimately responded to dollar depreciation by introducing their own version of the monetary experiment), US inflation and inflation expectations started to fall back.

The second point to consider in the failure of inflation to take off as many had feared in the early years of the Obama Monetary Experiment was the ultimately constricting influence this had on investment opportunity. The spread of Fed QE asset price inflation first into the emerging market world and commodity markets, then throughout the high-yield corporate debt markets and private equity and into the equity markets inspired widespread caution about the longer-term outlook. How deadly would be the later stages of the asset price inflation disease and any likely accompanying recession? And so Fed QE indeed knitted ultimately a low long-term interest rate trap. The constricted investment opportunity meant that the neutral level of interest rates remained low in the advanced economies, and so even abnormally low long-term interest rates did not jump start wider monetary growth and drive goods and services prices upward.

QE goods and services inflation danger is long run in nature

None of the above means that we should be sanguine about the long-term outlook for goods and services inflation as a consequence of Fed QE. But long-term stretches much further into the future than was featured in many of the early warnings. In important respects, Fed QE did weaken the defences of the US against a future episode of goods and services inflation disease. The explosive growth of the US monetary base and its virtual removal from the pivot of the US monetary system means most likely that the prospect is remote of the US ever shifting to a rules guided monetary policy under which interest rates are determined without official intervention and away from the highly discretionary practices of the present and recent Federal Reserve which have such an intense record of failure... If there is a silver lining here, it would be the possibility that the GME experiment might bring a crisis of such proportions that the monetary revolution as described in Chapter 6 would take place sooner than otherwise.

If and when the neutral level of interest rates starts to climb (as could occur if eventually despite all the handicaps placed by government and most importantly by the Federal Reserve investment opportunity flourishes or more sinisterly if the government deficit balloons), there is a raised danger of the Fed manipulating rates below a rising neutral path and so getting far behind the curve (whereby market rates would be low relative to the raised neutral level). The political pressure on the Fed to make this mistake would be all the greater because of the raised proportion of the Federal Government's debt which is in floating rate form (when aggregating the Federal Reserve balance sheet into the general government accounts) on which the interest paid had been virtually zero during the length of the Great Monetary Experiment.

The foundations of gold's defensive properties

The finding of weakened defences of the US in the wake of Fed QE against a future goods and services inflation virus attack is one positive argument for investors holding gold in their portfolios. Yet the hyped up dangers of immediate or near-term goods and services inflation in the early years of the Obama Monetary Experiment had carried its price to levels at that time which proved to be unsustainable. That experience suggests the wisdom of at least rechecking the role of gold in wealth accumulation.

Although in today's world gold is not money in the sense of providing a unit of account or functioning as a usual means of payment, it is nonetheless money-like or near money. Very small volumes are of large value; the metal is available in standardised units, whether coins or kilo-bars or bigger weights, storage costs relative to value are tiny, transporting costs relative to value are very small.

The rate of increase in the supply of above ground gold lies within a narrow and low range – 1–3% p.a. as has been the experience during the past century. Looking at the future, this range could fall due to growing scarcity of new metal and the increased marginal costs of extraction (less easily mined resources replace exhausted easily mined sources). And there is no risk of counterfeit or even genuine imitation – modern alchemists have been no more successful than the ancient. By contrast, modern technology may be able to increase the supply of rare diamonds or produce such fine copies of master paintings that no one could tell the difference between the original and the fake.

That is in huge contrast to the lack of any knowledge about or constraint on fluctuations in the supply of fiat money, including the US dollar. The fact that the real demand for gold though is potentially less stable over short and even medium term periods than for fiat money steadied by its broad transactions use means that fluctuations in gold's exchange rate (against the paper monies) can be large.

The large swings over recent decades in the price of gold (versus dollars) indicates the volatility of demand for above ground stocks of gold including periods when many investors fail to adjust their holdings of the metal in prompt fashion to spikes or crashes in the price induced by powerful trading waves in the day-to-day markets). A key rationale at all times for gold having a place in portfolios is the extent to which its real value is erosion-proof over the very long-run compared to fiat money (even taking account of interest payments). The implications of that rationale for the specific amount to be held at any point shift over time. Unsurprisingly, during periods when there has been particularly large uncertainty about the real value of the dollar in the long run, whether under the Arthur Burns Fed or under the Obama Monetary Experiment, demand has spiked. By contrast, during eras of perceived relative monetary stability, economic miracle and global peace, demand has receded far as during the 1990s.

Very long-run views about gold's real value are highly sensitive to assumptions about the form of monetary regime. Were the US, for example, to implement a strict monetarist constitution based around the principles of monetary stability but not anchored on gold, then the gold price could fall very sharply. On the other hand, if a US monetary revolution were to bring a re-anchoring of the dollar to gold, most likely at a price at or above present levels (in 2015), then there would be no such loss. And there are scenarios of monetary disorder and high inflation and societal breakdown where the gold price in real terms could be far above today's levels.

The role of gold in wealth management

This wide range of outlook for gold is not in itself a basis for shunning the yellow metal, particularly if we carefully take its potential hedging properties into account. Yes, a monetarist revolution not based on gold could mean a big fall in the gold price. But at the same time, other assets, including US equities and bonds, might rise far under such circumstances. Part of gold's attractions is as a "bad news, good news" which introduces an extra dimension of diversification into the portfolio. Gold tends to perform well during epochs of high geopolitical risk alongside disappointing economic growth low productivity and related sickly equity performance. This was the case par excellence in the decade from 1968 to 1978. The reverse was true in the 1990s.

It is plausible that the demise of the Deutsche mark and the Great Monetary Experiment have bolstered the underlying demand for gold. In the 1970s, global investors could diversify against US monetary risks by holding Deutsche marks, the nearest currency to hard money in that it was issued by a doctrinaire monetarist central bank in a very different mould from the Arthur Burns Fed. In the modern day, with the ECB and Bank of Japan and Swiss National Bank all pursuing similar or larger experiments to the Fed, no such diversification is possible. The only real monetary diversification is into gold.

Other factors bolstering the demand for the yellow metal have included the US and EU led campaign against offshore money centres and bank secrecy. Investors wary of their wealth being reported in the growing network of intergovernmental information sharing made possible by the technological innovation of Big Data decide that gold in a vault outside the banking system plays a special defensive role. They must still find ways in which to convert this when required into means of payment without triggering a report. Likewise, governments wary of possible US asset freezes extending into the global banking system see related advantages to the yellow metal, although this depends on it being in safe location. And then there are the governments who might harbour the idea of shifting in the far distant future to a gold standard for their national money and keeping this possibility open by having huge reserves in gold.

A familiar critique of gold (by commentators who question the role of gold in wealth accumulation) is the lack of benchmark regarding fundamental value. After all, for equities we have the P/E ratio (albeit that there are many difficulties in the way of defining a normal range of this – see p. 187). For real estate, we have the so-called rental yield (again with many problems of appraisal). For currencies we have purchasing power parity values, although the range of exchange rate fluctuations in practice and theoretically justifiable around these is wide. And for bond markets, we have long-term projections of inflation and estimates as regards the natural rate of interest.

For gold, we have the marginal cost of production but this is highly imprecise and can shift considerably in response to significant changes in the growth of underlying real demand for the yellow metal. It is not a benchmark of valuation independent of investment demand. As illustration, in an era of great monetary instability, heightened demand and a much higher price for gold mean that it becomes economic to mine gold from areas of the earth's crust which were previously uneconomic. Some gold analysts look for benchmarks in long-run price history – for example, pointing out that the price today (late 2014) is somewhat more than twice in real terms what it was when the US went on to the gold standard after the Civil War. But how can the analyst justify that the real price has increased by this amount, rather than much more or much less?

One such justification is the huge monetary uncertainty under today's fiat regimes against which gold is a hedge. Yes, there has been a big cumulative increase in the amount of above ground gold supplies, but demand for the hedge has surely increased at least in line with aggregate personal wealth in real terms and plausibly by much more than that. Meanwhile, the marginal cost of extracting the yellow metal from the earth's surface increases as ever more geologically challenging sources of supply have to be tapped. Note that this justification would militate against a return to the gold standard. A rising real price of gold (in line with the marginal cost of extraction) in the context of growing demand for the yellow metal as monetary base could mean a tendency toward a perpetual significant decline in prices of goods and services inconsistent with the fixed anchor in the ideal monetary order as outlined in Chapter 5. On the other hand, advances in mining and financial payments technology may mean that there would be no such tendency (see below).

Another possible justification lies in the observation that today all gold "money" is in the form of high-powered money (coin and bars, not bank deposits or bonds whose maturing principal is convertible into gold money). The total stock of above ground gold in 2010 (whether in form of jewellery, bullion or coin) has been estimated at around 150,000 tons (around 20% in official reserves), which at current valuations (early 2015) is about 35% of US M2 (see Turk, 2012). There is no vast market alongside in paper claims effectively denominated in gold but not backed by the metal as was the case under the gold standard (where bank deposits or bills in the main gold monies could be held as an alternative to the physical metal, offering the attraction of interest income, albeit at the cost of exposing the holder to the risk, small most of the time, of sudden inconvertibility).

In effect today, ultimate demand for gold is almost totally focused on the metal, rather than being widely diffused amongst a range of convertible paper income-yielding alternatives as under the gold standard. On the other hand, overall demand for gold assets (whether metal or paper) is less usually under a fiat money system in that there is not substantial demand for transaction purposes or as a short-term store of value to meet probable outgoings in the short and medium term. Interest-earning opportunities on gold (under the fiat money systems) are very limited (for example, in gold lending operations). And under the gold standard, banks hold large reserves of gold coin and gold-backed notes against their deposit liabilities whilst individuals hold gold coins routinely for the purpose of effecting retail and larger transactions. Yes, central banks and treasuries in some nations today hold huge gold reserves, but in total across all countries, these reserves (valued at present prices) are considerably less than the gold backing which would be required to banknotes and bank deposits under an international gold coin standard (such as in the pre-1914 world).

Gold ETFs are sometimes described as paper gold, but they are not. Rather, they are warehouse receipts on gold metal, albeit with high charges for safekeeping (compared to holding in a safe box). The intensity of metal demand under the present fiat money system means that for a given overall demand for gold exposure, the metallic element is particularly high in today's world. The overall demand for gold exposure (as an investor) in all its forms (paper and metal) is less under the present fiat money system than under a hypothetical global gold coin stand. The demand for the metal though could be much larger though given the nature of the hedge demand against monetary uncertainty and the other forms of safe haven demand discussed here.

We should also take into account that under a global gold coin standard transactions-related demand (including by banks) taken together with growing geological challenge on the supply side could mean a real gold price today much higher than under the pre-1914 gold standard. That is not a sure counterfactual statement, though, as even in a modern day gold coin standard we might imagine that transaction demand gold would be less intensive (relative to economic activity) than in the pre-1914 system given the advent of electronic payments clearing and credit cards; and the amount of reserves which banks would willingly hold against deposits might well be lower (as a ratio) than back then given the technological progress in interbank-clearing arrangements. As we saw in Chapter 5, deposit insurance, too big to fail and lender of last resort functions have all tended to reduce banks demand for reserves – although under a gold standard, the scope for these would be much reduced compared to what has been possible under fiat money regimes. In general, demand for monetary base under a gold coin regime is considerably larger than under a fiat regime unless propped up by high legal reserve requirements, especially if there are no large denomination banknotes. Gold coin and bars have safe haven properties even under a gold standard – for example, against the breakdown of that standard or its suspension – which buoys their demand compared to fiat banknotes under say an ersatz gold standard based on strict constitutional rules regarding expansion of the monetary base.

Insights into gold mining technology suggest that the marginal cost of future supplies of the metal from under the ground will rise at a faster pace than what we have known in the past, given the geological fact that the easy-to-mine gold supplies are becoming exhausted. Such speculative hypotheses about mining technology and increasing costs related to more difficult to extract remaining supplies have been current in the marketplace over several decades. Investors anticipating thereby a slowdown in the growth of supply of yellow metal consistent with any given price path might be ready to pay that much more in the present relative to historic value.

Ignore the critics of the gold-diggers

Critics who moan about the waste of resources in digging gold up from the ground (mining) to put back in another whole (a warehouse or bank vault) are missing the essence of the yellow metal's investment role.

Most gold is already above the ground. The past cost of mining is a sunk cost. Yes, intense monetary uncertainty and other forms of insecurity might mean some production in coming years will be at very high marginal cost. Much of the $30–$100 bn p.a. of newly mined gold though at end-2014 prices comes from intra-marginal sources, where costs of production are much less than price. Moreover, a big element in those costs as recorded is in effect rent to the owners of the below-ground metal rather than current resource costs of extraction.

Yes, a world (such as the present) in which gold plays a significant role in the accumulation of wealth will go along with related mining and safekeeping costs. Yet it is odd that the defenders of various highly unstable fiat monetary regimes should focus on these costs and related waste. These are small compared to the sum of costs related to maintaining and sustaining the fiat monetary system (including the armies of central bankers and regulators and compliance officers) and the economic damage wrought by episodes of inflation (whether asset prices or goods prices) as generated by this system. The more stable the fiat money system, the less would be demand for protection in the form of gold, and there could be some economizing on mining costs and even storage (if less valuable, then more under the mattress and less in vaults!). If gold were again to form an explicit element of the US monetary order as described in Chapter 6, this might mean somewhat greater mining costs per annum – but surely that is a tiny cost to pay for a much better than present functioning monetary regime.

The investor deciding how much yellow metal to include in his or her wealth does not need to ponder such philosophical issues about the societal costs or not of gold's role. But much self-discipline is required to keep to the principles of how to appraise its possible functions in wealth preservation and growth whilst desisting from the periodic speculative crazes in either direction. And a serious consideration of gold also requires that the investor does not listen to those sirens singing the tune that geopolitical danger should usually be disregarded in portfolio decision making as its impact is so unpredictable.

There may be little predictable on a day-to-day basis. But we can say that eras of high geopolitical danger tend to be marked by disappointing if any growth in economic prosperity – not least because the danger holds back progress into the forest of investment opportunity. Peace (not phoney claims of peace in our time delivered by populist politicians) and prosperity are joined even though practical demonstration is sometimes hard. Geopolitical danger at a significant level means a lower cumulative profile over many years (taking account of possible future sharp dips) of earnings and returns and markets bring this about even though they may seem impassive to the day-to-day run of the latest news.

Learn from history, but do not expect a repeat performance

This book has contained many episodes from monetary history. The purpose has been to learn from past experience of the asset price inflation disease – otherwise described as a plague of market irrationality always with its original source in US monetary disorder. There should be no expectation that history of the plague will repeat itself. Each one is distinct, although we can hopefully improve our powers of diagnosis and prediction of the disease's path in each specific case by gaining knowledge from the laboratory of history.

Turning to the present plague of asset price inflation with its origin in Federal Reserve QE, some leading Federal Reserve critics have suggested that its end phase will be broadly similar in its timing and consequence to the history of 1936–37 (see Chapter 7). Other critics have suggested that the Yellen Fed is following a virtually identical path to the Greenspan-Bernanke path through 2004–06, making painfully slow adjustment of monetary policy back to normality, and that the course of the asset price inflation disease will be broadly similar to the experience of 2003–08 with early 2015 the equivalent of 2005. Some GME advocates have responded that the US economy is now positioned as in the early 1960s, with asset price inflation disease and its frequent twinned disease of goods inflation not even visible as yet. And it is possible that an economic miracle could arrive as in 1924 or 1996 and mean that the disease is cured without crisis, at least until much later following a further episode of flawed Federal Reserve monetary policies.

It is very likely that all these forecasts are wrong and the reality – the actual path of the disease – will be distinct though displaying some features we should recognize from the past. The asset price inflation of 1936–37 took place in a world which was much less globally integrated than today – in particular Germany, then the 2nd largest economy, was outside the market system. And a powerful pro-cyclical path of prices (down during the recession, up in the recovery) had contributed importantly to an underlying economic upturn. Indeed that pro-cyclical path of prices meant near zero market interest rates exerted a powerful stimulus effect in 1935–36. That episode unlike the present was no exception to the Zarnowitz rule that the bigger the recession, the stronger the subsequent recovery. And turning to the asset price inflation of the mid-2000s, there had been no Fed QE then – unlike had been the case in the 1930s or the 2010s. Plausibly asset price inflation emerged later than in the business cycle upturn starting in 2001 than in 2009. In the present cycle, a virulent form could be suspected in several global asset markets even whilst the economic upturn in the US, Europe or Japan is weak by historical standards.

In approaching the subject of wealth management with a deepened understanding of the asset price inflation disease, the individual will undoubtedly come across much buzz in the day-to-day journey through the marketplace, which seems like a troublesome distraction from the main theme. That will always be the case and in any strategy to survive the plagues of market irrationality the individual should listen to the buzz, however discordant, but not allow this to damage his or her capacity to make sober-rational judgements. Indeed, it is the buzz and the disagreements (about the relevance or diagnosis of asset price inflation disease) which provide scope for the individual who does not become distracted to survive and even profit from the plague.

Bibliography

Acemoglu, Daron, Johnson, Simon, Kwak, James and Mitton Todd, "The Value of Connections in Turbulent Times: Evidence from the United States" Working Paper, Berkeley Hass Business School, 2013

Aliber, Robert Z., *The New International Money Game*, Palgrave Macmillan, 2001

Bagus, Phillip, "Deflation: When Austrians become interventionists" *Quarterly Journal of Austrian Economics*, 6(4): 19–35 Winter 2003

Bank of Japan Research and Statistics Department, "Why is the rate of decline in the GDP deflator so large?" July 2003

Baruch, Bernard, *The Public Years* Pocket Books, New York, 1962

Bernanke, Ben, *The Federal Reserve and the Financial Crisis* Princeton University Press, Princeton, 2013

Bernanke, Ben and Frank, Robert, *Principles of Macroeconomics* (5th ed), McGraw Hill, New York, 2014

Bernanke, Ben "Why are interest rates so low?" Ben Bernanke's Blog, Brookings Institution, March 30, 2015

Bobitt, Philip, *The Shield of Achilles* Anchor, New York, 2002

Bordo, Michael D. and Haubrich, Joseph G., "Deep Recessions, Fast Recoveries and Financial Crises: Evidence from the American Record" Working Paper Federal Reserve of Cleveland, 2014

Borio, Claudio, Erdern, Magdalena, Filardo, Andrew and Hofmann, Boris, "The Costs of Deflations: A Historical Perspective" *Banks for International Settlements Quarterly Review*, 31–48 March 2015

Broda, Christian and Druckenmiller "The Fed's Faulty 1937 Excuse", Wall Street Journal, April 15, 2015

Brown, Brendan, *Euro Crash: How Asset Price inflation Destroys the Wealth of Nations*, Palgrave Macmillan, 2014

Brown, Brendan, "How Wilson and the Fed Extended the Great War" Mises Institute website, November 2014

Bullard, James, "Seven Faces of 'The Peril'" *Federal Reserve Bank of St. Louis Review*, September/October 2010: 339–52

Burns, Arthur, *Prosperity Without Inflation*, Fordham University Press, New York, 1957

Butkiewicz, James L. *Governor Eugene and the Great Contraction*, Emerald Group, Bingley, UK, 2007

Calomiris, Charles, Mason, Joseph and Wheelock, David, *Did Doubling Reserve Requirements Cause the Recession of 1937–1938: A Microeconomic Approach*" Working Paper No. 16688, National Bureau of Economic Research, January 2011

Catalan, Fingold, "Dangerous Lessons of 1937" *Mises Daily*, February 2, 2010

Cieslak, Anna, Morse, Adair and Vissing-Jorgensen, Annette, *Stock Returns over the FOMC Cycle*, Working Paper, National Bureau of Economic Research, June 2014

Cochrane, John, "The Danger of an All-Powerful Federal Reserve", *The Wall Street Journal*, August 26, 2013

Cochrane, John, "A Few Things the Fed Has Done Right", *The Wall Street Journal*, August 21, 2014

Davies, Gavyn, "The Very Long-Run Equity Bull Market", *Financial Times*, November 10, 2014

DeLong, Bradford J., "Should We Fear Deflation" *Brookings Paper* No.1 1999

Eggertson, Gauti B. and Pugsley, Benjamin, "The Mistake of 1937: A General Economic Analysis" *2006 Bank of Japan Monetary and Economic Studies*, Special Edition, December 2006

Ferguson, Naill, *High Financier: The Lives and Time of Siegmund Warburg*, Penguin, New York, 2010

Feroli, Michael, Kashyap, Anil, Schoenholtz, Kermit and Shin, Hyun Song, *Market Tantrums and Monetary Policy*, Conference Draft, University of Chicago Press, Chicago, February, 2014

Friedman, Milton, *A Program for Monetary Stability* Fordham University Press, New York, 1960

Friedman, Milton, *Capitalism and Freedom,* University of Chicago Press, Chicago, 1962

Friedman, Milton and Schwartz, Anna, *A Monetary History of the United States 1867–1960*, Princeton University Press, Princeton, 1963

Friedman, Milton, *The Optimum Quantity of Money*, Aldine Transaction, London, 2006

Gambacorta, Leonardo, Hofmann, Boris and Peersman, Gert, "The Effectiveness of Unconventional Monetary Policy at the Zero Lower Bound: A Cross-Country Analysis" *Journal of Money, Credit and Banking*, 46(4): 615–42, June, 2014

Grant, James, *The Forgotten Depression: 1921 – The Crash that Cured Itself*, Simon and Schuster

Haber, Stephen and Levine, Ross, "The Federal Reserve's Too Cozy Relations with Banks" *The Wall Street Journal*, November 9, 2014

Hayek, Friedrich von, "Prices and Production" Ludwig von Mises Institute, 2008

Hoover, Kevin D., "New Classical Macroeconomics" in David R. Henderson (ed.), *Concise Encyclopedia of Economics* (2nd ed), Indianapolis, 2008

Hūlsmann, Jörg Guido, "Deflation and Liberty" Ludwig von Mises Institute, 2008

Kindleberger, Charles, *The World in Depression, 1929–39*, University California Press, 2013

Krishnamurthy, Arvind and Vissing-Jorgenen, Annette, "The Effects of Quantitative Easing on Interest Rates" *Brookings Paper*, 2011

Lachman, Ludwig, *Capital, Expectations, and the Market Process*, Institute for Humane Studies, Mento Park, 1977

Laubach, Thomas and Williams, John, "Measuring the Natural Rate of Interest" Board of Governors of the Federal Reserve System, November, 2001

Mankiw, Greg, "Observations on Negative Interest Rates" Mankiw's Blog, April 19, 2009, available at: http://gregmankiw.blogspot.ca

Meltzer, Allan H., *A History of the Federal Reserve, Vol. 1: 1913–51*, University of Chicago Press, Chicago, 2003

Meltzer, Allan H., *A History of the Federal Reserve, Vol. 2, Book 1, 1951–69*, University of Chicago Press, Chicago, 2009a

Mises, *The Theory of Money and Credit,* Foundation for Economic Education, New York, 1971

Momma, Kazuo and Kobayakawa, Shuji, "Monetary Policy after the Great Recession: Japan's experience" Javier Valles (ed.), Working Paper of Funcas Foundation, June 2014

Myerson, Roger B., "Rethinking the Principles of Bank Regulation: A Review of Admati and Hellwig's *The Bankers' New Clothes*" *Journal of Economic Literature*, 52(1): 197–210 March 2014

Patinkin, Don, *Money Interest and Prices*, MIT Press, Boston (1989)

Pollock, Alex J., "Why Not Negative Interest Rates?" *The American*, May 21, 2009

Pollock, Alex J., "A Cheer or a Bronx cheer for the Fed" Library of Law and Liberty, September 2, 2014

Posen, Adam, *Restoring Japan's Economic Growth*, Institute for International Economics, Washington DC, 1998

Reinhart, Carmen M. and Rogoff, Kenneth S., *This Time is Different*, Princeton University Press, Princeton, 2011

Roberts, Priscilla, "Benjamin Strong, the Federal Reserve and the Limits to Interwar American Nationalism: Intellectual Profile of a Central Banker" *Federal Reserve Bank of Richmond Economic Quarterly*, 86(2): 61–98 Spring 2000

Robertson, D.H., *Essays in Monetary Theory*, P.S. King, 1940

Robbins, Lionel, *The Great*, Ludwig von Mises Institute, 2007

Rothbard, Murray N., *A History of Money and Banking in the US*, Ludwig von Mises Institute, 2002

Salerno, Joseph, "An Austrian Taxonomy of Deflation – With Applications to the US" *Quarterly Journal of Austrian Economics*, 6(4): 81–109, Winter 2003

Sechrest, Larry J., "Alan Greenspan: Rand, Republicans and Austrian Critics" Mises Centenary Symposium, "Part 2: Ayn Rand among the Austrians" *Journal of Ayn Rand Studies*, 6(2): 271–97, Spring 2005

Shiller, Robert, *Irrational Exuberance*, Broadway Books, 2000

Shlaes, Amity, *The Forgotten Man: A New History of the Great Depression*, Harper Perennial, 2008

Siems, Thomas, "The Long Slog: Economic Growth Following the Great Recession" *Dallas Fed*, 2(4): 1–4, November 29, 2013

Silber, William, *When Washington Shut Down Wall Street*, Princeton University Press, Princeton, NJ, 2007

Stein, Jeremy, "Overheating in Credit Markets: Origins, Measurement and Policy Response" speech at St. Louis Federal Reserve, February 7, 2013

Taylor, John B., "Economics One", Taylor's Blog, October 17, 2012, available at: http://economicsone.com/

Turk, James, "The Above Ground Gold Stock; Its Importance and Size" *Gold Market Foundation*, September 2012

Turner, Philip, "Is the Long-Term Interest Rate a Policy Victim, a Policy Variable or Policy Lodestar" Working Paper No. 367, Bank for International Settlements, 2014

(The) Wall Street Journal, "The Patience of Janet" editorial, March 18, 2015

White, William, "Is Monetary Policy a Science? The Interaction of Theory and Practice Over the Last 50 Years" Working Paper No. 155, Federal Reserve Bank of Dallas, September 2013

Zarnowitz, Victor, *Business Cycles: Theory, History, Indicators and Forecasting*, University of Chicago Press (Studies in Business Cycles, 27), Chicago, 1992

Zingales, Luigi, *A Capitalism For the People: Recapturing the Lost Genius of American Prosperity*, Basic Book, 2012

Zweig, Jason, "Robert Shiller on What to Watch in This Wild Market" *The Wall Street Journal*, October 10, 2014

Index